THE RIDDLE

OF

SHAKESPEARE'S SONNETS

THE RIDDLE OF Shakespeare's Sonnets

The text of the SONNETS,
with interpretive essays by EDWARD HUBLER,
NORTHROP FRYE, LESLIE A. FIEDLER,
STEPHEN SPENDER, and R. P. BLACKMUR,
and including the full text of
OSCAR WILDE'S
THE PORTRAIT OF MR W. H.

BASIC BOOKS, INC.
PUBLISHERS   NEW YORK

FIRST EDITION

All Rights Reserved

© 1962 by Basic Books Publishing Co., Inc.

Library of Congress Catalog Card Number 62-9372

Designed by VINCENT TORRE

PR
2848
·H78

CONTENTS

Shakespeare's Sonnets and the Commentators
    EDWARD HUBLER   1

How True a Twain   NORTHROP FRYE   23

Some Contexts of Shakespeare's Sonnets
    LESLIE A. FIEDLER   55

The Alike and the Other   STEPHEN SPENDER   91

A Poetics for Infatuation   R. P. BLACKMUR   129

The Portrait of Mr W. H.   OSCAR WILDE   163

The SONNETS   257

INDEX   337

INDEX OF FIRST LINES   343

EDWARD HUBLER

Shakespeare's Sonnets
and the Commentators

With the possible exception of *Hamlet*, no work of Shakespeare's has called forth more commentary and controversy than his sonnets, and on no other work has more nonsense been written. There is, indeed, ample reason for diversity of opinion. We do not know when the sonnets were written, to whom they were addressed, or if they are autobiographical at all. "In them," said Wordsworth, "Shakespeare unlocked his heart," and Browning replied, "If so, the less Shakespeare he!" The paucity of fact encourages speculation, and the reader who would begin a consideration of the sonnets had better begin with such facts as there are.

A few pages in a manuscript play called *The Booke of Sir Thomas Moore* have been ascribed to Shakespeare;

but apart from them, none of his literary manuscript survives. The texts of his works derive from the earliest printed editions; and for the sonnets and half of the plays, the modern editor must depend upon a single original edition. The sonnets were first printed in 1609, as the title page records, "By G. Eld for T.T." The entry of the volume in the *Stationers' Register* for May 20, 1609, identifies T.T. as Thomas Thorpe, who had "taken up the freedom of the Stationers' Company" about fifteen years earlier. The volume is entitled *Shake-speares Sonnets*. The sonnets end on recto K^1 and are followed by a poem of 330 lines called "A Lover's Complaint." Most scholars are reluctant to accept it as Shakespeare's, and it need not concern us here. The consensus is that Thorpe acquired a manuscript of the sonnets and published them without Shakespeare's permission, and there are enough printer's errors in it to make it clear that Shakespeare did not see the volume through the press. To this volume Thorpe contributed an enigmatic dedication, signing it with his initials. And so the mystification surrounding Shakespeare's sonnets begins with this first publication.

There are in all 154 sonnets. As printed in Thorpe's edition they fall into three groups: 1 through 126, which are addressed to, or are concerned with, a young man; 127 through 152, which are addressed to, or are concerned with, a young woman; and 153 and 154, which are free translations of a fifth century A.D. Greek poem. These last are undistinguished poems, unrelated to the preceding ones except for their common form and authorship, and they need not concern us further. Although many of the poems in the first group reproach the young

The Sonnets and the Commentators

man for his failings and weaknesses, the greater part are written in admiration and affection. The most common terms of address are "love" and "my love." In the second group the young woman is addressed as the poet's mistress. She is wooed, won, and rejected. It is possible that some of the sonnets in each group belong in the others, since—the English language being what it is—the references of pronouns do not always indicate gender; but whenever the references in the first group are clear, they are masculine, while those in the second are feminine. Several sonnets in the first group refer to another poet who is also addressing verses to the young man.

The sonnets therefore concern four people: Shakespeare, who writes in the first person; the young man, who is often known as Mr. W. H., even though this is only Thorpe's presumed designation of him; the young woman, who, because of her brunette beauty and the darkness of her deeds, has come to be known as the dark lady; and the other poet, often known as the rival poet. The attempted identifications of these persons has been a major task of the commentary on the sonnets. The conclusions reached depend in part on the critic's view of the circumstances under which the sonnets were written.

When the sonnets were published in 1609, the vogue of the Elizabethan sonnet sequence had passed, and the sonnet form itself was suspect. The later attitude taken to it is indicated by Ben Jonson's comparison of the sonnet to the bed of Procrustes "where some who were too short were racked; and others too long cut short." But in the 1590's, the sonnet was often considered pure eloquence itself. In mid-century France it had been the rallying flag of the poets of the Pléiade as they fashioned the new poetry, and it was the emblem of the new poetry when the same movement flowered in England at the end of the sixteenth century. The vogue of the sonnet sequence was kindled by the posthumous publication of Sir Philip Sidney's *Astrophel and Stella* in 1591, and in the next half-dozen years sonnet sequences appeared in rapid succession. It is argued that Shakespeare took advantage of this fashion to establish himself as a lyric poet, just as he had established himself as a narrative poet by the publication of *Venus and Adonis* and *The Rape of Lucrece* in 1593 and 1594 respectively. This, though plausible, is not established fact. We first hear of the sonnets in Francis Meres' *Palladis Tamia: Wits Treasury*, 1598, where we are told that Shakespeare's "sugred sonnets" were circulating in manuscript "among his private friends." This would have been according to the custom of the time whereby a gentleman could gain a reputation as a poet, as Sidney did, without descending to the vulgarity of print. How many of the sonnets were so circulating is not known. In 1599, however, two of the sonnets, numbers 138 and 144, were printed in a volume called *The Passionate Pilgrim*. In the first, the poet is the dark lady's contented and disenchanted lover; in the second, he suspects that the lady has betrayed him with his friend. If the sonnets are taken to reflect events in the poet's life, and to have been written while the events were in progress, then the affair with the dark lady was at its height by 1599 at the latest. Other internal evidence indicates an earlier date. The poet refers to himself as an unestablished writer; he fears that although his sonnets will survive, his name will be forgotten. And

The Sonnets and the Commentators

so on. But by 1598 Shakespeare was famous and could not seriously have written in that vein. Sonnet 104 tells us that the friendship with the young man has lasted for three years, indicating that the sonnets were written over a period of four or five years. In lieu of other evidence, most scholars accept 1592 to 1596 as approximate dates for their composition.

If, on the other hand, the events reflected in the sonnets are taken to be fictitious, we are free to assume that Shakespeare added to the sequence from time to time up to the date of publication, and we may attempt to date them by their references to historical events. Unhappily, such references are not clear. The fifth line of Sonnet 107 is a case in point: "The mortal moon hath her eclipse endured." "Mortal moon" is generally taken to mean Queen Elizabeth, and it is argued that the line refers to her death and the succession of James I in 1603; but it can also be taken to indicate her recovery from an illness in 1596. Samuel Butler and, more recently, Leslie Hotson in *Shakespeare's Sonnets Dated*, take "mortal moon" to mean the Spanish Armada, dating the poem in or shortly after 1588, before the vogue for sonnets had begun.

If the sonnets had not been forgotten thirty years after their first publication, their next editor, John Benson, could not have done what he did. In 1640 he reprinted them in an octavo volume, *Poems: Written by Wil. Shakespeare. Gent.*, interspersed them with other poems written by Shakespeare and others, gave them descriptive and often inept titles, and changed the pronouns in some of the sonnets addressed to the young man, making them appear to be addressed to a woman. After this the sonnets are little heard of in the seventeenth century, and the sonnet form itself, though put to brilliant use by Milton, was held in disesteem and largely disregarded. The four seventeenth-century folios of Shakespeare did not include the non-dramatic works, nor were they generally included in the eighteenth-century editions of his works. In 1710, when Charles Gildon reprinted the sonnets, he based his edition on Benson's. Others followed in his steps until, late in the century, editors returned to the 1609 edition. Basing his text on it, Edmond Malone in 1790 produced the first important critical text of the sonnets.

One of the changes Benson made in his reprinting of the sonnets was to vary the order of the 1609 edition. He may have been trying to cover his tracks, for he did not own the copyright, and an attempt to make the poems look fresh was clearly in order. In any case, the reordering of poems when reprinting them was a custom of the times. Malone re-established the order of the 1609 edition; but since this order may have been set down by Thorpe, it has occurred to others to question it. At times Thorpe's order is clearly right. Sonnets 73 and 74 comprise one poem, and Sonnets 1 through 17 are written on the same theme; but this is a coherence of parts rather than of the whole, and none of the many attempts to arrange the sonnets into a coherent whole has succeeded. The modern game of rearranging began in 1841 with the edition of Charles Knight, and it continues. Sometimes the motive is to make the sonnets tell a story, but they remain stubbornly lyric rather than narrative, a quality they share with other Elizabethan sonnet sequences. *The Variorum Edition* of the sonnets by Hyder Rollins lists the sequences of twenty rearrangements

The Sonnets and the Commentators

from Benson's to Tucker Brooke's in 1936. The present writer finds only the last helpful to a considerable degree in understanding the sonnets. Sir Denys Bray's rearrangement on the objective basis of rhyme-links separates some sonnets which obviously belong together. For the time being, the ardor for rearrangement has abated, but since 154 poems can be arranged in an almost infinite number of ways, the game will no doubt begin again; and while it seems unlikely that a series of poems written over a number of years on a variety of occasions could be made into a coherent whole, it is possible that the sequence of the 1609 edition will be improved.

Although sonnets were held in disesteem in the eighteenth century, they were written throughout the century in increasing if unimpressive numbers—not, however, because of the influence of Shakespeare. His rhyme scheme was not admired and seems hardly to have been distinguished from the then popular irregular forms of the sonnet. In his *Biographia Literaria,* 1817, Coleridge records that in his seventeenth year he was fascinated by the sonnet, but his admiration went to "the exquisite Bowles." In the same year he was taken to task by William Hazlitt for preferring Bowles' sonnets to Warton's, "which last we, in our turn, prefer to Wordsworth's, and indeed to any Sonnets in the language." The young Wordsworth thought that the sonnets to the dark lady were "abominably harsh, obscure, and worthless," but Coleridge recommended them to his son "to help explain the mind of Shakespeare." Elsewhere, however, Coleridge had little good to say about them; Shakespeare, he once remarked, is "never positively bad, even in his sonnets."

Wordsworth's magnificent mastery of the sonnet

began in 1802 under the influence of Milton, whom he followed in preferring the Italian sonnet form. But he did come in time to a full appreciation of Shakespeare's sonnets, writing in 1817 that "there is not a part of the writings of this Poet wherein is found in equal compass a greater number of exquisite feelings felicitously expressed." Keats read Shakespeare's sonnets with, in Caroline Spurgeon's phrase, "passionate interest and excitement" and wrote seventeen sonnets in imitation of them before his own interests shifted to the ode. In 1832 Edward FitzGerald wrote in a letter: "I have been reading Shakespeare's Sonnets, and I believe I am unprejudiced when I say, I had but half an idea of him, Demigod as he seemed before, till I read them carefully." In the same year the editors, under the influence of romantic enthusiasm, began to speak differently about them. Alexander Dyce, though ranking the sonnets below the plays, found that they "contain such a quantity of profound thought as must astonish every reader; they are adorned by splendid and delicate imagery; they are sublime, pathetic tender, or sweetly playful; while they delight the ear by their fluency, and their varied harmonies of rhythm."

The higher esteem in which the sonnets were then held reflected the progressively higher opinion being accorded the works as a whole. With the Victorians the romantic glorification of Shakespeare became a *magnificat*. To Carlyle, in "The Hero as Poet," "Shakespeare and Dante are saints of poetry; really if we think about it, canonized, so that it is impiety to meddle with them. . . . They dwell apart, in a kind of royal solitude; none equal, none second to them." And Shakespeare is greater

The Sonnets and the Commentators

than Dante: "He is the greatest of intellects." To Emerson, Shakespeare was "inconceivably wise; the others conceivably." And to Matthew Arnold, in his sonnet on Shakespeare, he is great beyond comprehension. We may see in this progression the amalgamation of comment on Shakespeare the poet and Shakespeare the man. Heretofore the sonnets were spoken of as poems; the commentary was judicial, its motive being to establish the worth of the poems. The judicial criticism continued, but the new and increasingly dominant mode of Shakespeare criticism was to consider the works in relation to the man and his time. This was especially true of the sonnets, for they speak in the first person and can be taken to be autobiographical in a degree to which the plays cannot. If the "I" of the sonnets is taken to be Shakespeare, who, it is inevitably asked, were the young man, the young woman, and the other poet?

The speculation on the identity of the young man began with the assumption that "the onlie begetter of these insuing sonnets" was the young man who inspired the greater part of them. Some scholars have supposed that "the onlie begetter" was the person who procured the manuscript of the sonnets for Thorpe, but this does not make so interesting a game, and relatively few scholars have played it. The attempts at identification began in the eighteenth century with Thomas Tyrwhitt (1730-1786) and Richard Farmer (1735-1797). Farmer proposed the name of William Harte, Shakespeare's nephew; but it turned out that Harte's mother was born in 1569 and could not have had a grown son in the 1590's. Tyrwhitt proposed a man named W. Hughes, basing his guess on a line in Sonnet 20: "A man in hue, all 'hues' in his controlling." No doubt there was someone named W. Hughes in Shakespeare's England, but there is no evidence for associating him with Shakespeare. Nevertheless, the ghost that Tyrwhitt created haunts us still. In Oscar Wilde's story, "The Portrait of Mr. W. H.," he turns out to be Willie Hughes, "a wonderful boy actor of great beauty" whom Shakespeare loved. This has found some acceptance, but in justice to Wilde it must be pointed out that "The Portrait" was presented as fiction, not as argument.

In *Shakespeare and His Times*, 1817, Nathan Drake presented a new candidate, Henry Wriothesley, Third Earl of Southampton, who is still a popular contender. The facts are that Southampton was twenty in 1593 when, it is held, the sonnets were being written. He was handsome and perhaps the most brilliant young courtier at Elizabeth's court. He was already a patron of poets, and there is a legend, which remains unsupported by evidence, that he was Shakespeare's patron too. Shakespeare, however, did dedicate his *Venus and Adonis* to him in 1593 and his *The Rape of Lucrece* in the following year. The more personal tone of the second dedication suggests to some an increasing intimacy between him and Shakespeare. The existence of the dedications makes it clear that Shakespeare had some connection with him, and, it is asked, why postulate another man when it is known that a man fitting the specifications was known to Shakespeare? But his initials are H.W., not W.H.

In 1832 the game became a contest when William Boaden announced that "Mr. W. H. was, in fact, William Herbert" who succeeded as Third Earl of Pembroke in 1601. As a young man, Herbert—like Southampton—

The Sonnets and the Commentators

was rich, sensual, averse to marriage, and a patron of literature. When in 1623 Shakespeare's associates in the theatre published the first collected edition of his plays, now known as the First Folio, they dedicated it to Herbert and his brother: "To the Most Noble and Incomparable Paire of Brethren." They go on to say that since their Lordships "have beene pleas'd to thinke these trifles some-thing, heeretofore; and have prosequuted both them, And their Author living, with so much favour: we hope, that . . . you will use the like indulgence toward them, you have done unto their parent." In Van Dyck's portrait of Herbert he appears as a handsome man. He has the right initials, and the dedication makes it clear that he had some connection with Shakespeare; but in 1593 he was only thirteen. The supporters of Herbert naturally prefer a late date for the sonnets.

Other contenders are William Hathaway, William Hall, William Hervey (Harvey), and others too numerous to mention, except, of course, for the person suggested by D. Barnstorff in 1860, William Himself.

It is possible that Benson in 1640 changed the pronouns in some of the sonnets in the first group because he wanted to avoid the appearance of homosexuality in the relation between Shakespeare and the young man. Clearly the sonnets were sometimes thought to disclose such a relationship. George Steevens, speaking of Sonnet 20 in 1780, found it "impossible to read this fulsome panegyrick, addressed to a male object, without an equal admixture of disgust and indignation." But the interest in the question would not be as widespread in our time as it is, had not the young man been taken to be a real person and the alleged liaison between him and Shakespeare to be, therefore, a matter of biographical interest. Edmond Malone in 1790 found it necessary to explain that in Shakespeare's time men often addressed each other in loving terms. Dyce in 1832 followed in this vein. They were of course right, and Shakespeare followed this practice in his plays; but not everyone was convinced. The rejoinder was made in 1861 by Franz Grillparzer that in the plays the affectionate terms of address between men do not arise from the speaker's awareness of the other person's beauty. To this it could be replied that in the sonnets the young man's beauty is far from being the sole source of the poet's affection and admiration. In 1890, Angelo Olivieri cited language used by Poliziano, Martelli, Bembo, and Michelangelo to indicate that Shakespeare's terms of address to the young man are only part of a literary tradition; but other commentators take the terms of address used by these poets to celebrate a love of a dubious character. In 1899, Samuel Butler's *Shakespeare's Sonnets Reconsidered* turned attention again to the question of homosexuality. Butler believed that the love of the two men was "though only for a short time, more Greek than English." But the extrapolation of vague references into specific events places his book among the more fantastic of those written about Shakespeare by famous men and reminds us that what Butler took to be the inimitably feminine touches in *The Odyssey* persuaded him that its author was a woman.

From Butler's time on, the charge of homosexuality has been alternately made and refuted. The disputants, up to 1944, are recorded in that mine of information about the sonnets, *The Variorum Edition* by Hyder

The Sonnets and the Commentators

Rollins. The present writer, in an appendix to *The Sense of Shakespeare's Sonnets*, 1952, considers the matter as a balance of probabilities. We know on indisputable evidence that Shakespeare had a hurried marriage at eighteen and was twice a father before he was twenty-one. This does not happen to a young man who is not heterosexual, but such a man may have a homosexual episode in his life. What is the probability that Shakespeare had? If we employ the arguments of those who take him to have had such an episode, we shall have to suppose that he was passionately in love with a young man at the same time that he was sexually enslaved to his mistress. This is, of course, possible, but how probable is it? Furthermore, the young man is not the only male designated as "lover." Shakespeare uses the phrase, "my lovers gone" (Sonnet 31) to indicate his dead friends, and the young man is told that if the sonnets endure he will live "in lovers' eyes" (Sonnet 55). If we take "lover" to indicate homosexuality, we shall have to extend the homosexuality back into the past on the part of Shakespeare and project it into the future on the part of the young man. This creates a morass of homosexuality incredible in its proportions. The charge of homosexuality can neither be proved nor disproved on the available evidence, but the balance of probabilities discredits it.

In *The Mutual Flame*, 1955, G. Wilson Knight regards the foregoing as oversimplification. The matter is, as he says, "finally a question of words. 'Homosexual' as I use the term, is not intended to signify physical intercourse, but it does involve, and I think Shakespeare's Sonnets do also, physical and sexual attraction. . . .

When Shakespeare as lover of the Fair Youth shows jealousy of the Dark Lady he is, in this regard, functioning as a female partner; we can say that the female element of his personality is engaged." This female element of the male is found to be an integral element of the male creative personality, which in the act of creation has the power of becoming woman. "Our greatest writers all have this share of supersexual understanding." And Shakespeare's female characters "may be said to represent the feminine aspect of Shakespeare's own self, or soul." This is a matter of the psyche and has nothing to do, as Knight makes clear, with Shakespeare's sexual practices. In *Shakespeare's Bawdy*, 1948, a glossary of Shakespeare's usage of sexual terms, Eric Partridge remarks in his introduction that throughout Shakespeare the sexual act is viewed from the masculine point of view, and that "had Shakespeare . . . been a homosexual, he would have subtly yet irrefutably conveyed the fact." As it is, there are no references to lesbianism in Shakespeare's works and few to homosexuality among men. Nowhere in Shakespeare's plays is there any indication that he considered homosexuality important in his interpretations of life.

The game about the identity of the dark lady began in earnest in 1797 when George Chalmers in *An Apology for the Believers in the Shakespeare-Papers* claimed that all 154 sonnets were addressed to Queen Elizabeth. "The queen," he remarks, "was often considered as a man." Samuel Neil, in *Shakespeare: a Critical Biography*, 1861, thought only some of the sonnets to be addressed to the queen. "Many were addressed to Anne

The Sonnets and the Commentators

Hathaway, as bride and wife, several to his daughter. . . ." E. I. Fripp, in *Shakespeare: Man and Artist*, 1938, said that she was "half a dozen 'ladies'—of the tavern, and the kitchen, and the drawing room." Some authorities consider her real but do not name her. Others refuse to admit her reality, among them Sir Sidney Lee, although he argues in his biography and elsewhere that the young man was Southampton. It is said that Sir William Davenant when in his cups liked to suggest that Shakespeare was his father—he seems to have preferred being thought Shakespeare's bastard to being known as the legitimate son of an innkeeper. Mistress Davenant has, then, been proposed as the dark lady.

But the identifications which have caught the imagination of Shakespeareans and others are Elizabeth Vernon and Mary Fitton. The first depends on the acceptance of Southampton as the young man, the second on the acceptance of Pembroke. In 1595 Southampton, having refused to be a party to Lord Burghley's plan to marry him to Burghley's granddaughter, began an intrigue with Elizabeth Vernon, a lady-in-waiting to the queen. They were married in May 1598, and their daughter was born early in November. The queen was furious, and for a short time Southampton was committed to prison. In 1595 a plan to marry Herbert to the daughter of Sir George Carey was broken off because of the prospective bridegroom's violent objections. He was fifteen at the time. In March 1601 his liaison with Mary Fitton, another of the queen's maids of honor, produced a son. He refused to marry her, and he too went to prison for a short time. Mary Fitton is the heroine of Shaw's *The Dark Lady of the Sonnets*, although

: 17 :

Shaw did not believe that she had in fact been the lady. We have here two young women who could conceivably have sat for Shakespeare's portrait, but apart from their connections with Southampton and Pembroke, there is no evidence for believing that either of them did. Lady Penelope Rich, the Stella of *Astrophel and Stella*, has also been nominated for the dubious honor, but only because she deserves it.

Thomas Tyler, whom Shaw described as "a gentleman of such astonishing and crushing ugliness that no one who had once seen him could ever thereafter forget him," was the father of the Fitton theory, which in 1897 received what to disengaged persons would seem a death-blow. It was pointed out that Mary Fitton did not marry until 1607, whereas the dark lady's infidelity to both her lover and her husband is one of her primary characteristics. Two portraits of her were reproduced by Lady Newdigate-Newdegate in *Gossip from a Muniment Room*. They showed her to have gray eyes, brown hair, and a fair complexion. Nevertheless, Tyler stuck to his theory, and William Archer asserted that the theory was strengthened by the portraits. Frank Harris in *The Man Shakespeare and his Tragic Life-Story*, 1909, found Mary Fitton recurring in play after play, and Arnold Bennett thought Harris' book both masterful and glorious.

As for the rival poet, he has been identified with almost every prominent poet of the time, and with some obscure ones. The sonnets make several references to his style. In Sonnet 85 he is said to write with "golden quill," "In polish'd form." This suggests Samuel Daniel to some, whereas "the proud full sail of his great verse" in

The Sonnets and the Commentators

the following sonnet suggests George Chapman to others. He clearly cannot be identified on the evidence the sonnets present. Needless to say, some commentators believe that more than one poet other than Shakespeare addressed verses to the young man.

By the end of the nineteenth century, historical criticism had become the dominant mode in Shakespearean studies. Its admirable motive was to achieve a greater objectivity by attempting to see a work of art through the eyes of the people for whom it had been created, and its method was to place the work against its historical background. The argument that, as used in the sonnets to the young man, the words "love" and "lover" mean "friendship" and "friend" is a case in point. The most prominent exponent of historical criticism of the sonnets was Sir Sidney Lee. Considering them in relation to the sonnets of Renaissance England and the continent, he found their themes to be repetitions of sonnet conventions, and therefore, in his view, lacking in conviction. What he overlooked is that the "I" of the sonnets is not necessarily the actual William Shakespeare of Stratford and London; it might well be his view of himself as lyricist, just as Colin Clout is Spenser's projection of himself as pastoral poet. Although illuminating and instructive, historical criticism turned out not always to have the objectivity its practitioners attributed to it.

In 1936 Caroline F. E. Spurgeon expanded her earlier studies in imagery into *Shakespeare's Imagery*. It deals with the "light thrown by the imagery . . . on Shakespeare's personality, temperament, and thought" and "on the themes and characters of his plays." It does not specifically consider the poems, but it was soon adapted to studies of them. Miss Spurgeon's method was largely statistical; but others who followed her did not count the images, for, since it is difficult to say how imagistic an image is, a series of images does not always add up. In this country the interest in imagery coincided with the emergence of what is called the new criticism. The new critics were, and are, too varied to constitute a school, but they can be said to concentrate on the analysis of the poem itself. They scrutinize its thoughts and emotions, its language and imagery, its rhythms, structure, and texture. Although they have not been notably concerned with Shakespeare's plays, they and their followers have illuminated many of the sonnets, and they have deeply influenced the criticism of poetry both in and outside the universities.

My own book, *The Sense of Shakespeare's Sonnets*, mentioned before, is concerned with what the sonnets say and not with the biographical authenticity of what is said. It attempts to clarify the sonnets by placing their themes and attitudes against both the tradition in which Shakespeare wrote and his use of them in his plays. It views the sonnets as Shakespeare's early lyric expression of his perceptions of friendship, of love and lust, of honor, of growth through experience, of sin and expiation, of mutability, plenitude, and the knowledge of good and evil. J. W. Lever's *The Elizabethan Love Sonnet*, 1956, is also concerned with what the sonnets say, though it is of larger scope than the preceding book. The greater part of it is devoted to the poetic vision of Wyatt, Surrey, Sidney, Spenser, and Shakespeare. In *The Shakespearean Moment*, 1954, Patrick Cruttwell finds that "the sonnets are a sort of embryo, in which the essential

The Sonnets and the Commentators

evolution of the whole of Shakespeare is carried out in miniature. . . . They widen in scope, till every interest of the writer's life is brought within their reach. . . ." They are the expression of a "multiple and divided" personality, and they share with the other great poetry of the end of the sixteenth and early seventeenth century the multiplicity of poetic vision on which their greatness in part depends.

In recent years, books, articles, and essays on Shakespeare have been published in Britain, continental Europe, and North America at the rate of almost a thousand a year. The indefatigable reader is referred to the annual bibliography published in the *Shakespeare Quarterly*.

NORTHROP FRYE

How True a Twain

Any critic of Shakespeare's sonnets will, to some extent, tell the world more about his own critical limitations than about his subject; and if he starts out with very marked limitations, the clear surface of the sonnets will faithfully reflect them. Many readers tend to assume that poetry is a record of a poet's experience. Those who tell us that Shakespeare must have been a lawyer to have known so much about law, or a nobleman in disguise to have known so much about aristocratic psychology, always start with this assumption as their major premise. The assumption is then used in value judgments. First-hand experience in life and second-hand experience derived from books are correlated with good and less good poetry respectively. Poem A is very good; therefore a genuine experience must lie behind it; Poem B is duller, so it must be a "mere literary exercise," where the poet's "real feelings" are not involved. Included in these assumptions, of course, is the view that convention is the opposite of originality, and the mark of inferior writers. It is particularly the lyric that suffers from such notions, as nobody can do much about the fact that every *play* of Shakespeare's tells a story that he got out of a book. And while experienced critics would repudiate all this in theory, still Shakespeare was an expert in keeping his personal life out of our reach, and we find this so tantalizing that any hint of more information about that life is apt to lower the threshold of a critic's discretion. The sonnets, therefore, still have power to release the frustrated Baconian who is inside so many Shakespearean scholars.

The first point to get clear is that if we read the sonnets as transcripts of experience, we are not reading them realistically but allegorically, as a series of cryptic allusions in which a rival poet may be Chapman, a mortal moon Queen Elizabeth, and a man in hue somebody named Hughes. Now if we approach the sonnets in this crude allegorical way, they become "riddles" of a most peculiar kind. They begin with seventeen appeals to a beautiful youth to beget a son. Rationalizing readers tell us that the poet is urging the youth to marry, but only one of these sonnets—the eighth—has any serious treatment of marriage. True, the youth is urged to marry as the only legal means of producing offspring, but apparently any woman will do: it is not suggested that he should fall in love or that there is any possibility of his producing daughters or even a son who takes after his mother, which seems curious when the youth himself does. In real life, one would think, the only possible reply from the youth would be that of Christ to Satan in *Paradise Regained:* "Why art *thou* solicitous?"

The poet then drops his appeal and falls in love with the youth himself. We next observe that although the poet promises the youth immortality, and clearly has the power to confer it, he does not lift a metrical foot to make the youth a credible or interesting person. He repeats obsessively that the youth is beautiful, and sometimes true and kind, if not overvirtuous; but in real life one would think that a poet who loved him so much would delight in telling us at least about his accomplishments, if he had any. Could he carry on a conversation, make puns, argue about religion, ride to hounds, wear his clothes with a dash, sing in a madrigal? The world's greatest master of characterization will not give him the individualizing touch that he so seldom refuses to the humblest of his dramatic creations. Of course, if we are predetermined to see the Earl of Southampton or some other witty and cultivated person in the youth, we may ascribe qualities to him that the poet does not. But considering him as a real person, and reading only what is there, we are forced to conclude that Shakespeare has lavished a century of the greatest sonnets in the language on an unresponsive oaf as stupid as a doorknob and as selfish as a weasel. Shakespeare expected the Earl of Southampton to be amused by his somewhat indecorous tale of a sulky urchin who was beloved by Venus herself and would not rise to the occasion. But the youth of the sonnets is more like the Adonis of that poem than he is like any appreciative reader of it.

Besides—who exactly is given immortality by the sonnets? Well, there was this Mr. W. H., except that some people think he was H.W. and that he wasn't a Mr. And how do we learn about this Mr. W. H., or this not-Mr. H. W.? Through one floundering and illiterate sentence, to call it that by courtesy, which was not written by Shakespeare, not addressed to us, and no more likely to be an accurate statement of fact than any other commercial plug. We are also referred to a story told in *Willobie his Avisa* about a certain H.W., who, "being suddenly infected with the contagion of a fantastical fit, at the first sight of A(visa), pineth a while in secret grief, at length not able any longer to endure the burning heat of so fervent a humour, bewrayeth the secrecy of his disease unto his familiar friend W.S." In short, a very literary story. As an account of something happening in real life, Polonius might believe it, but hardly Rosalind. We are not told that the youth of the sonnets wanted immortality, but if he did he would have done better to marry and beget a son, as he was advised to do all along. About all that one can get out of the sonnets, considered as transcripts of experience, is the reflection that pederastic infatuations with beautiful and stupid boys are probably very bad for practicing dramatists.

This conclusion is so grotesque that one would expect any critic who reached it to retrace his steps at once. But we often find such critics merely trying to save the face of the ridiculous creature that they have themselves created. Benson, the compiler of the 1640 edition of the sonnets, simply altered pronouns, but this is a trifle robust for the modern conscience. Coleridge disapproved of homosexual sentiments in poetry, and sneered at Vir-

How True a Twain

gil as a second-rate poet all his life because Virgil wrote the Second Eclogue; but Coleridge had practically signed a contract to endorse everything that Shakespeare wrote, so what to do? Well: "It seems to me that the sonnets could only have come from a man deeply in love, and in love with a woman; and there is one sonnet which, from its incongruity, I take to be a purposed blind." Another critic urges that the sonnets *must* be regarded as Shakespeare's earliest work, written in time for him to have got this affair out of his system, for if they are later, Shakespeare's personality must be considered "unwholesome." And what critic urges this? Samuel Butler, author of *Erewhon Revisited,* that genial spoofing of the eternal human tendency to turn untidy facts into symmetrical myths!

The same fate seems to pursue even the details of the allegorical approach. The line in Sonnet 107, "The mortal moon hath her eclipse endur'd," sounds as though it referred to Queen Elizabeth. If so, it means either that she died or that she didn't die, in which case it was presumably written either in 1603 or some time before 1603. Unless, that is, it is a retrospective allusion, of a kind that dilatory poets are only too apt to make, or unless it doesn't refer to Elizabeth at all, in which case it could have been written at any time between 1603 and its publication in 1609. Once again we feel uneasily that "Shakespeare the man" is slipping out of our grasp.

We should be better advised to start with the assumption that the sonnets are poetry, therefore written within a specific literary tradition and a specific literary genre, both of which were developed for specifically literary reasons. The tradition had developed in the Middle Ages, but would hardly have had so much vitality in Shakespeare's day without a contemporary context. In the Renaissance, anyone who wanted to be a serious poet had to work at it. He was supposed to be what Gabriel Harvey called a "curious universal scholar" as well as a practical expert in every known rhetorical device—and Renaissance writers knew many more rhetorical devices than we do. But learning and expertise would avail him little if he didn't, as we say, "have it." Have what? Have a powerful and disciplined imagination, to use the modern term, which, by struggling with the most tempestuous emotions, had learned to control them like plunging horses and force them into the service of poetry. True, the greatest moments of poetic *furor* and *raptus* are involuntary, but they never descend on those who are not ready for them. Could one acquire such an imagination if one didn't have it? No, but one could develop it if one did have it. How? Well, the strongest of human emotions, love, was also the most easily available.

The experience of love thus had a peculiarly close relation to the training of the poet, a point of some importance for understanding Shakespeare's sonnets. Love was for the Renaissance poet a kind of creative yoga, an imaginative discipline in which he watched the strongest possible feelings swirling around sexual excitement, jealousy, obsession, melancholy, as he was snubbed, inspired, teased, ennobled, forsaken, or made blissful by his mistress. The Renaissance poet was not expected to drift through life gaining "experience" and writing it up in poetry. He was expected to turn his mind into an emotional laboratory and gain his experience there under high pressure and close observation. Literature provided him with a convention, and the convention supplied the literary categories and forms into which his amorphous emotions were to be poured. Thus his imaginative development and his reading and study of literature advanced together and cross-fertilized one another.

Of course the experience of love is a real experience. It is not assumed that the youth trying to be a poet talks himself into a certain state of mind; it is assumed that, if normal, he will feel the emotion of love at some time or other, and that, if destined to be a poet, he will not fall in love tepidly or realistically but head-over-heels. But the experience of love and the writing of love poetry do not necessarily have any direct connection. One is experience, the other craftsmanship. So if we ask, is there a real mistress or does the poet merely make it all up? the answer is that an either-or way of putting the question is wrong. Modern criticism has developed the term "imagination" precisely to get around this unreal dilemma. Poetry is not reporting on experience, and love is not an uncultivated experience; in both poetry and love, reality is what is created, not the raw material for the creation.

The typical emotions inspired in the poet by love are thus formed into the typical patterns of literary convention. When the conventions of love poetry developed, the model for most of these patterns was the spiritual discipline of Christianity. In Christianity one may, with no apparent cause, become spiritually awakened, conscious of sin and of being under the wrath of God, and bound to a life of unconditional service to God's will. Much courtly love poetry was based on a secular and erotic analogy of Christian love. The poet falls in love at first sight, involuntarily or even with reluctance. The God of Love, angry at being neglected, has walked into his life and taken it over, and is now his "lord." His days of liberty are over, and ahead of him is nothing but unquestioning devotion to Love's commands. The first thing he must do is supplicate his mistress for "grace," and a mistress who did not demand long sieges of complaint, prayers for mercy, and protests against her inflexible cruelty was a conventionally impossible female. The mock-religious language, so elaborately developed in the Middle Ages, was still going strong in Shakespeare's day: Spenser's twenty-second *Amoretti* sonnet, for instance, moves at once from the Christian Lent into the Temple of Venus, where we find "saint," "image," "priests," "altar," "sacrifice," "goddess," and "relics."

The secular and erotic counterpart of the Madonna and Child was Venus and Eros, or Cupid. Cupid was a little boy shooting arrows, and at the same time he was, like his Christian counterpart, the greatest of the gods and the creator of the universe, which had arisen from chaos by the "attraction" of like particles. The domain of Eros included heat, energy, desire, love, and subjective emotion; Venus had the complementary area of light, form, desirability, beauty, and objective proportion. In a sense all lovers are incarnations of Eros, and all loved ones incarnations of Venus. One may express this by simple metonymy: thus Ovid, in a passage in the *Amores* which certainly caught Shakespeare's eye, remarks that while he prefers blondes, he can also get interested in a "Venus" with dark hair:

est etiam in fusco grata colore Venus.

The possible scale of themes in courtly love poetry is as broad as love itself, and may have any kind of relation-

How True a Twain

ship to its Christian model, from an integral part to a contrast or even a parody. We may divide the scale into "high" and "low" phases, using these terms diagrammatically and not morally. In the "high" phases love is a spiritual education and a discipline of the soul, which leads the lover upward from the sensible to the eternal world. In Dante, the love of Beatrice, announced in the *Vita Nuova*, is a spiritual education of this sort leading straight to its own logical fulfillment in the Christian faith. It not only survives the death of Beatrice, but in the *Commedia* the same love conveys the poet upward from the top of Purgatory into the divine presence itself. Dante's love for Beatrice was the emotional focus of his life, but at no point was it a sexual love or connected with marriage. The philosophy of Plato, where one moves from the body's attraction to the physical reflection of reality upward to the soul's union with the form of reality, provided a convenient framework for later treatments of the "high" version of the convention. We find this Platonized form of love in Michelangelo and in the speech of Cardinal Bembo at the end of Castiglione's *Courtier*.

Next comes what we may call the Petrarchan norm, a conflict of human emotions in which the main theme is still unswerving devotion and supplications for grace. In Petrarch the human situation in love is far more elaborately analyzed than in Dante, but as in Dante the poet's love survives the death of Laura and does not depend on sexual experience. In Christianity love for God is obviously its own reward, because God is love. The Petrarchan poet similarly often finds that it is love itself, not the female embodiment of it, which fulfills his desire, and such a love could logically survive the death of the beloved, or be content, as Herrick says his is, with a contact of almost unbearable refinement:

> Only to kiss the air
> That lately kissed thee.

In Petrarch, however, there is more emphasis placed on physical frustration than on spiritual fulfillment, and the same is true of most of his followers. At this point the relation between heavenly and earthly love begins to appear as a contrast, as it often does in Petrarch himself. Thus Spenser writes his hymns to Heavenly Love (Christ) and Heavenly Beauty (the Wisdom of the Book of Proverbs) as an alleged palinode to his courtly love hymns to Eros and Venus, and Sidney indicates in his famous "Leave me, O Love" sonnet a "higher" perspective on the story told in *Astrophel and Stella*.

In the middle of the scale comes the mistress as potential wife: this was still a rather rare form in love poetry, though of course normal for drama and romance. It is represented in English literature by Spenser's *Amoretti* sequence. We then move into the "low" area of more concrete and human relations, sometimes called anti-Petrarchan, the centre of gravity of the *Songs and Sonnets* of Donne, who remarks:

> Love's not so pure and abstract, as they use
> To say, which have no mistress but their Muse.

Here the poet is less aware of the dialectic of Eros and Agape, and more aware of another kind of dialectic es-

How True a Twain

tablished in the normal opening of the convention, when the poet first falls in love. When the God of Love enters the poet's life, the poet may regret his lost liberty of not having to serve a mistress, or he may contrast the bondage of his passion with the freedom of reason. He finds that in this context his love is inseparable from hatred—not necessarily hatred of the mistress, except in cases of jealousy, but hatred of the emotional damage done to his life by love. The God of Love in this situation is a tyrant, and the poet cannot identify the god's will with his own desire. Such moods of despair are often attached to palinodes, or they may be understood to be necessary early stages, where the poet is still establishing his constancy. But in "lower" phases the poet may get fed up with having so much demanded of him by the code and renounce love altogether; or the mistress may be abused as a monster of frigidity who has brought about her lover's death; or the poet may flit from one mistress to another or plunge into cynical amours with women of easy virtue—in short, parody the convention. Ovid, who as far as Shakespeare was concerned was by long odds the world's greatest poet, had a good deal of influence on these "low" phases of courtly love, as Platonism had on the "higher" ones.

It does not follow that the "lower" one goes, the more realistic the treatment becomes. This happens only to a very limited extent. The mistress normally remains almost equally uncharacterized at all stages: the poet is preoccupied with the emotions in himself which the mistress has caused, and with her only as source and goal of these emotions. Similarly with Shakespeare's youth: he is not characterized, in any realistic sense, because the conventions and genres employed exclude that kind of characterization. It is interesting to contrast the sonnets from this point of view with the narrative poem A *Lover's Complaint,* which, whoever wrote it, follows the sonnets in the 1609 Quarto, and presents three characters roughly parallel to the three major characters of the sonnets. Here what belongs to the genre is not so much characterization as description, which is given in abundance.

It was assumed that the major poet would eventually move on to the major genres, epic and tragedy, and from the expression of his own emotions to the expression of heroic ones. The young professional poet learning his trade, and the amateur too high in social rank to become a professional, both tended to remain within the conventions and genres appropriate to love poetry. The appropriate genres included the love lyric and the pastoral. In the love lyric the source of love was a mistress descended from the line of Laura; in the pastoral, following the example of Virgil's Second Eclogue, the love of two men for one another was more frequent. Here again the influence of Plato, in whose conception of love there are no mistresses, but the love of an older man for a younger one, has to be allowed for. Spenser began his career with the pastoral poetry of *The Shepheardes Calender,* because, according to his editor E. K., he intended to go on to epic, and pastoral was a normal genre in which to serve his apprenticeship. In "January," the first eclogue, Spenser represents himself as the shepherd Colin Clout, in love with one Rosalind, but also dearly attached to another shepherd named Hobbinol. E. K. explains in a note that such an attachment has nothing to do with pederasty (just as love for a mistress has no necessary,

How True a Twain

or even frequent, connection with adulterous liaisons). Spenser devoted the third book of *The Faerie Queene* to chastity, which for him included both married love and courtly *Frauendienst*, and the fourth book to friendship. In the Temple of Venus, described in the tenth canto of the fourth book, pairs of male friends are given an honored place, as friendship has a disinterested factor in it which for Spenser puts it among the "high" forms of courtly love. Examples include Hercules and Hylas, David and Jonathan, and Damon and Pythias. Such friends are called lovers, and it was conventional for male friends to use the language of love, just as it was conventional for a lover to shed floods of tears when disdained by his mistress. Similarly in Shakespeare the relation of poet to youth is one of love, but it is assumed (in Sonnet 20 and elsewhere) that neither the youth nor the poet has any sexual interest except in women. The "homosexual" view of the sonnets disappears at once as soon as we stop reading them as bad allegory.

After all the research, the speculation, and the guesswork, our knowledge of what in the sonnets is direct biographical allegory remains precisely zero. Anything may be; nothing must be, and what has produced them is not an experience like ours, but a creative imagination very unlike ours. Our ignorance is too complete to be accidental. The establishing of a recognized convention is of enormous benefit to poets, as it enables them to split off personal sincerity from literary sincerity, and personal emotion from communicable emotion. When emotions are made communicable by being conventionalized, the characters on whom they are projected may expand into figures of universal scope and infinitely haunting variety. Thus every syllable of Campion's wonderful song, "When thou must home to shades of underground," is pure convention, and no knowledge of the women in Campion's life could possibly have the least relevance to it. But it is the convention that has enabled him to realize so vividly the figure of the sinister underworld queen who has run through literature from Ishtar to the *femmes fatales* of our own day. Anyone who thinks he can write a better poem out of a "real experience" is welcome to try, but he cannot read Campion's poem with any understanding unless he realizes that the convention is not working against the emotion, but has released the emotion. The same principle applies to characterization. By suppressing realistic characterization, convention develops another kind, an archetypal character who is not individualized, but becomes a focus of our whole literary experience.

In Shakespeare's sonnets, the beautiful-youth group tells a "high" story of devotion, in the course of which the poet discovers that the reality of his love is the love itself rather than anything he receives from the beloved. Here, as in Petrarch and Sidney, the love proves to be an ennobling discipline although the experience itself is full of suffering and frustration. The dark-lady group is "low" and revolves around the theme of *odi et amo*. In the beautiful-youth group Shakespeare has adopted the disturbing and strikingly original device of associating the loved one with Eros rather than Venus, a beautiful boy who, like the regular mistress, is primarily a source of love rather than a responding lover. Other familiar landmarks of the convention can be easily recognized. The poet is the slave of his beloved; he cannot sleep for thinking of him; their souls are in one another's breasts; the poet protests his constancy and alleges that he has no theme for verse except his love; he is struck dumb with shame and bashfulness in the presence of his love; he ascribes all his virtues and talents to his love; his verse will immortalize the beloved; his love is triumphant over death (as the love of Dante and Petrarch survived the death of Beatrice and Laura respectively); yet he continually finds love a compulsory anguish.

It is a reasonable assumption that Sonnets 1 through 126 are in sequence. There is a logic and rightness in their order which is greatly superior to that of any proposed rearrangement (such as Sir Denys Bray's "rhyme-link" scheme), and this order is at least as likely to be the author's as the editor's, for Thorpe, unlike Benson, shows no signs of officious editorial meddling. Sonnet 126, a twelve-line poem in couplets containing a masterly summary of the themes and images of the beautiful-youth group, is inescapably the "envoy" of the series—any interpretation that attempts to remove it from this position must have something wrong with it. The repetition of "render," too, shows that it closely follows on the difficult but crucial Sonnet 125. If, then, Sonnets 1 through 126 are in sequence, the rationale of that sequence would be roughly as follows:

We begin with a prelude which we may call "The Awakening of Narcissus," where the poet urges the youth to beget a son in his own likeness. In Sonnet 17 this theme modulates into the theme of gaining eternal youth through the poet's verse instead of through progeny, and this in turn modulates into the main theme of the poet's own love for the youth. The poet then revolves around the youth in a series of three cycles, each of which apparently lasts for a year (Sonnet 104), and takes him through every aspect of his love, from the most ecstatic to the most woebegone. At the beginning of the first cycle the poet is confident of the youth's love and feels that his genius as a poet is being released by it, and the great roar of triumph in Sonnet 19 is its high point. Gradually the poet's reflections become more melancholy and more independent of his love. In Sonnet 30 the final couplet seems almost deliberately perfunctory, a perceptible tug pulling us back to the main theme. The poet's age begins to haunt him in 22; a sense of the inadequacy of his poetry enters in 32, and his fortunes seem to sink as the cycle progresses, until by 37 he is not only old but lame, poor, and despised. Already in 33 a tone of reproach has begun, and with reproach comes, in 36, a feeling of the necessity of separation. Reproach is renewed in 40, where we learn that the youth has stolen the poet's mistress. In 50 the poet has wandered far away from the youth, but in this and the following sonnet he is riding back to his friend on horseback.

The phrase "Sweet love, renew thy force" in 56 indicates that we are near the beginning of a second cycle, which starts in 52. The slightly effusive praise of the youth in 17 is repeated in 53; the feeling of confidence in the poet's verse, which we met in 19, returns in 55; and the sense of identification with the youth, glanced at in 22, returns in 62. As before, however, the poet's meditations become increasingly melancholy, as in 65 and 66, where again the final couplets seem to jerk us back with an effort to the theme of love. By 71 the poet is preoccupied with images of old age, winter, and death. His

How True a Twain

poetry, in 76, again seems to him sterile and barren, and in 78 the theme of the rival poet begins. This theme corresponds to that of the stolen mistress in the first cycle, and the two together form an ironic counterpoint to the theme of the opening sonnets. Instead of acquiring a wife and transferring his beauty to a successor, the youth has acquired the poet's mistress and transferred his patronage to a second poet. A bitter series of reproaches follows, with the theme of separation reappearing in 87. In 92, however, we have a hint of a different perspective on the whole subject:

I see a better state to me belongs
Than that, which on thy humour doth depend.

This second cycle ends in 96, and a third cycle abruptly begins in 97, with a great rush of coming-of-spring images. Once again, in 100 with its phrase "Return, forgetful Muse," the poet is restored to confidence in his poetry; once again, in 106, the youth is effusively praised; once again, in 107, the poet promises the youth immortality in his verse. Again more melancholy and introspective reflections succeed, but this time the poet does not go around the cycle. He replaces reproach with self-reproach, or, more accurately, he replaces disillusionment with self-knowledge, and gradually finds the possession of what he has struggled for, not in the youth as a separate person, but in the love that unites him with the youth. In 116 the poet discovers the immortality of love; in 123 his own love achieves immortality; in 124 the phrase "my dear love" refers primarily to the poet's love; in 125 the poet's heart is accepted as an "oblation," and in 126 the youth, now only a lovely mirage, is abandoned to nature and time. Thus the problem stated in the opening sonnets, of how to perpetuate the youth's beauty, has been solved by poetic logic. It is the poet's love, not the youth's marriage, which has created a new youth, and one capable of preserving his loveliness forever. This at any rate is the "argument" of these sonnets whether they are in sequence or not, and we reach the same conclusion if we disregard sequence and simply study the imagery.

If Shakespeare himself had identified a specific person with the beautiful youth of the sonnets, that person would have had much the same relation to the youth that Edward King has to Lycidas. Milton tells us that *Lycidas* was written to commemorate the drowning of a "learned friend." But *Lycidas*, as a poem, is a pastoral elegy about Lycidas, and Lycidas is a literary and mythological figure, whose relatives are the Adonis and Daphnis of classical pastoral elegies. Similarly, the beautiful youth, though human, incarnates a divine beauty, and so is a kind of manifestation of Eros: "A god in love, to whom I am confined." Just as other love poets were fond of saying that their mistress was a goddess to rival Venus or the Platonic form of beauty that had fallen by accident into the lower world, so the youth is the "rose" (in its Elizabethan sense of "primate") or "pattern" of beauty, a kind of erotic Messiah to whom all past ages have been leading up (17, 53, and 106, or what we have called the "effusive" sonnets), whose death will be "Truth and Beauty's doom and date." In short, he is a divine man urged, like other divine men, to set about transferring his divinity to a younger successor as soon as he reaches the height of his own powers. And whether

How True a Twain

the sonnets are in sequence or not, he is consistently associated with the spring and summer of the natural cycle, and winter and old age are associated with absence from him. His moral character has the same associations: it is spring or summer when he is lovable and winter when he is reproachable.

The poet cannot keep the resolution announced in Sonnet 21 of detaching the youth from nature. A human being is a microcosm of nature, and the most obvious and conspicuous form of nature is the cycle. In the cycle there are two elements of poetic importance. One is the fact that winter and summer, age and youth, darkness and light, are always a contrast. The other is the continual passing of one into the other, or the cycle proper. The first element suggests an ultimate separation of a world of youth, light, and "eternal summer" from its opposite. This can never happen in experience, but it would be nice to live in the paradisal *ver perpetuum* that the youth's beauty symbolizes (Sonnet 53), and poetry is based on what might be, not on what is. The second element suggests universal mutability and decay. Thus if a final separation of the two poles of the cycle is conceivable, the lower pole will be identical with the cycle as such, and the world of winter, darkness, and age will be seen as the wheel of time that carries all created things, including the blossoms of spring, away into itself.

Time is the enemy of all things in the sonnets, the universal devourer that reduces everything to nonexistence. It is associated with a great variety of eating metaphors, the canker eating the rose, the festering lily, the earth devouring its brood, and the like, which imply disappearance rather than digestion. Death is only a small aspect of time's power: what is really terrifying about time is its capacity for annihilation. Hence the financial metaphors of "lease," "audit," and similar bargains with time are continually associated with the more sinister images of "expense" and "waste." The phrase "wastes of time" in Sonnet 12 carries the heaviest possible weight of brooding menace. Nature itself, though a force making for life as time makes for death, is capable only of "temporary" or time-bound resistance to time. Behind the daily cycle of the sun, the yearly cycle of the seasons, the generation cycle of human life, are the slower cycles of empires that build up pyramids with newer might, and the cosmological cycles glanced at in Sonnets 60 and 64, with their Ovidian echoes. But though slower, they are making for the same goal.

Nature in the sonnets, as in many of the plays, is closely associated with fortune, and the cycle of nature with fortune's wheel. Those who think of fortune as more substantial than a wheel are the "fools of time," who, whatever they are in Sonnet 124, include the painful warrior who is defeated and forgotten and the makers of "policy, that heretic"—policy, in contrast to justice or statesmanship, being the kind of expediency that merely greases the wheel of fortune. Royal figures are also, in Sonnets 7, 33, and perhaps 107, associated with the cycle of nature: they pass into "eclipse" like the sun and moon turning down from the height of heaven.

The nadir of experience is represented by the terrible Sonnet 129, which, starting from the thematic words "expense" and "waste," describes what a life completely bound to time is like, with the donkey's carrot of passion jerking us along its homeless road, causing an agonizing wrench of remorse at every instant. Directly above is "the heaven that leads men to this hell," and which includes in its many mansions the fool's paradise in which the youth is living in the opening sonnets. Here we must distinguish the poet's tone, which is tender and affectionate, from his imagery, which is disconcertingly sharp. As Sonnet 94 explains in a bitterer context, the youth causes but does not produce love: he is a self-enclosed "bud," contracted to his own bright eyes like Narcissus. As with a child, his self-absorption is part of his charm. He does not need to seek a beauty in women which he already contains (Sonnet 20, where all the rhymes are "feminine"). He lacks nothing, so he is never in search: he merely attracts, even to the point of becoming, in Sonnet 31, a charnel-house of the poet's dead loves. He is therefore not on the side of nature with her interest in "increase," "store," and renewed life, but on the side of time and its devouring "waste." He is his own gradually fading reflection in water, not "A liquid prisoner pent in walls of glass," or a seed which maintains an underground resistance to time. The poet's arguments in Sonnets 1–17 are not intended to be specious, like the similar-sounding arguments of Venus to Adonis. The youth is (by implication at least) "the tomb of his self-love," which is really a hatred turned against himself, and has no future but "folly, age, and cold decay."

It would take a large book to work out in detail the complications of the imagery of eyes and heart, of shadow and substance, of picture and treasure, around which the argument of the beautiful-youth sonnets revolves. We can only try to give the main point of it.

Above the self-enclosed narcissistic world of the youth of the opening sonnets, there appear to be three main levels of experience. There is the world of ordinary experience, a physical world of subject and object, a world where lover and beloved are essentially separated. This is the world associated with winter and absence, with the "lower" elements of earth and water (Sonnet 44), with the poet's age and poverty which increase the sense of separateness, with the reproach and scandal that separate them mentally and morally. This is also the world in which the poet is a busy actor-dramatist, with a capacity for subduing his nature to what it works in unrivalled in the history of culture, a career which leaves him not only without a private life but almost without a private personality.

Then there is a world above this of lover and beloved in contact, a quasi-paradisal world associated with the presence and kindness of the youth, with spring and summer, with air and fire in Sonnet 45, with content, ecstasy, forgiveness, and reconciliation. It is in this world that the youth appears like a god of love, associated with the sun and its gift of life, the spirit who appears everywhere in nature (Sonnet 113), the god of the spring flowers (99), all hues in his controlling. But even in this world he is still a separate person, contemplated and adored.

There is still another world above this, a world which is above time itself. This is the world in which lover and beloved are not simply in contact, but are identified. The union symbolized by the "one flesh" of Christian marriage is a sexual union: this is the kind of union expressed in the light-hearted paradoxes of *The Phoenix*

How True a Twain

and the Turtle, where reason is outraged by the fact that two souls are one and yet remain two. In the sonnets the union is a "marriage of true minds," but the symbolism and the paradoxes are much the same. All through the sonnets we meet metaphors of identification and exchange of souls: these are, of course, the regulation hyperboles of love poetry, and in their context (as in Sonnet 39) are often harshly contradicted by the reality of separation. But in the 116-125 group they begin to take on new significance as a genuine aspect of the experience.

Sonnet 125 begins with adoring the youth's external beauty, expressed in the metaphor of bearing the canopy, and thence moves into the youth's heart, where an "oblation" and an exchange of souls takes place. The final consummation carries with it the expulsion of the "informer" or accuser, the spirit of the winter-and-absence world of separation, with all its scandals and rumors and misunderstandings and reproaches. Thus the lower world is left behind, and the higher paradisal world still remaining is dismissed in its turn in Sonnet 126. Here the "lovely boy" is seen in the role of a mock king, invested with the regalia of time, and the poem ends in a somber warning tone. From our point of view it is not much of a threat: he is merely told that he will grow old and eventually die, like everyone else. But the lovely boy from this perspective has nothing to him but what is temporary: what faces him is the annihilation of his essence.

It is not hard to understand how the selfish youth of the winter-and-absence sonnets, whose beauty is as deceitful as "Eve's apple," can also be the divine and radiant godhead of Sonnet 105, an unexampled trinity of kind, true, and fair. Love and propinquity work this miracle every day in human life, and Sonnet 114 shows it at work in the poet's mind. But what relation does the youth have, if any, to the "marriage of true minds"? There is little enough in the sonnets to show that the youth *had* a mind, much less a true one. We can hardly answer such a question: even Christianity, with all its theological apparatus, cannot clearly express the relation of whatever it is in us that is worth redeeming to what we actually are. And Shakespeare is not turning his theme over to Christianity, as Dante does in the moment at the end of the *Paradiso* when Beatrice gives place to the Virgin Mary. In these sonnets the poet assumes the role of both redeemer and repentant prodigal son. His love enables him to transcend himself, but in the instant of fulfillment the object of his love vanishes, because it is no longer an object. A straight Platonic explanation would be that the lover leaves behind the beautiful object as he enters into union with the form or idea of love: this is true enough as far as it goes, but we should not infer that the poet has achieved only a subjective triumph (he is no longer a subject) or that the world he enters is devoid of a beloved personality. However that may be, one thing is made clear to us: the identity of love, immortality, and the poet's genius or essential self. As Chaucer says:

> The lyf so short, the craft so long to lerne,
> Th' assay so hard, so sharp the conquering,
> The dredful joye, that alwey slit so yerne,
> Al this mene I by love.

How True a Twain

Just as Sonnet 129 is the nadir of experience as the sonnets treat it, so Sonnet 146 is its zenith. Here there is no youth, only the poet's soul, which is told, in the exact imagery of the opening sonnets, not to devote all its attention to its "fading mansion" which only "worms" will inherit, but (in an astonishing reversal of the eating metaphors) to feed on death until death disappears. The poet's soul in this sonnet is a *nobile castello* or House of Alma, to outward view a beleaguered fortress, but in itself, like the tower of love in Sonnet 124, "hugely politic," reaching clear of time into a paradise beyond its cycle, as the mountain of purgatory does in Dante. In this sonnet, near the end of the series, Shakespeare takes the perspective that Petrarch adopts in his first sonnet, where he looks down at the time when he was another man, when he fed his heart with error and reaped a harvest of shame. But Shakespeare is not writing a palinode: nothing in the previous sonnets is repudiated, or even regretted. Love is as strong as death: there is no wavering on that point, nor is there any tendency, so far as we can see, to change from Eros to a "higher" type of love in mid-climb.

The second group of sonnets, 127 through 154, though a unity, can hardly be in strict sequence. Two of the finest of them, 129 and 146, have already been discussed: they indicate the total range of the theme of love as Shakespeare handles it, including this group as well as its predecessor. Some seem expendable: the silly octosyllabic jingle of 145 does not gain any significance from its context, nor do the last two, which really do come under the head of "mere literary exercise," and for which the models have been discovered. Two other sonnets in this group, 138 and 144, appeared in *The Passionate Pilgrim* in 1599, along with three poems from *Love's Labour's Lost*, two of which are also sonnets. *Love's Labour's Lost* is a play which cries out for—in fact practically announces—a sequel, and Meres' reference to a *Love's Labour's Won* suggests that a sequel was mooted, if not written. I sometimes wonder if these sonnets were not originally thought of as potentially useful for some such play: if so, Sonnet 144 may have become the germ of the two great cycles after the play was abandoned. Perhaps the conception of an original dramatic context might be stretched to accommodate that social climber Sonnet 145. Every writer on the sonnets is entitled to one free speculation.

Most of these sonnets, of course, revolve around a dark female figure, who, unlike the youth, can be treated with irony and detachment, even playfulness. The basis of the attachment here is sexual, and the slightly ribald tone of 138 and 151 is appropriate for it. This ribald tone never appears in the first group except in the close of Sonnet 20, an exception which clearly proves the rule. In the first group the youth takes over the poet's mistress, and the poet resigns her with a pathetic wistfulness ("And yet it may be said I loved her dearly") which is not heard in the second group. In the second group the poet has two loves, a fair youth and a dark lady, in which the former has the role of a "better angel"—hardly his role in the other group, though of course he could be called that by hyperbole. It is natural to associate the mistress of Sonnet 42 with the dark lady and the "man right fair" of 144 with the beautiful youth. But it is simpler, and not really in contradiction with this, to think of the two groups, not as telling the same story, but as presenting a contrast of two opposed attitudes to love, a contrast heightened by a number of deliberate resemblances—"Minding true things by what their mockeries be," as the chorus says in *Henry V*.

The word "fair" in modern English means both attractive and light-complexioned, and Shakespeare's "black" has a similar double meaning of brunette and ill-favored. The same pun occurs in *Love's Labour's Lost* in connection with the dark Rosaline, and in *The Two Gentlemen of Verona* the fickle Proteus says that his new love for Silvia makes his old mistress Julia seem like a "swarthy Ethiop," though Julia herself tells us that her hair is "perfect yellow." The uniting of the two meanings suggests an involuntary attachment: involuntary means against the will, and the theme of the imprisoned will leads to more puns on the poet's name.

The center of gravity of the dark-lady sonnets is Sonnet 130, which corresponds to Sonnet 21 in the other group, where the poet stresses the ordinary humanity of his beloved. As we saw, he could not keep this balance with the youth. The youth is either present or absent: when present he seems divine, when absent he turns almost demonic. In the dark-lady group the poet again cannot keep the human balance, and the tone of affectionate raillery in 130 (and in 128) is not heard again. In striking contrast to the earlier group, the dark lady is both present and sinister. She takes on divine attributes up to a point, but they are those of a "white goddess" or what Blake would call a female will. Like   Blake's Gwendolen or Rahab, she can be fitfully maternal (143) and more than fitfully meretricious (142), but her relation to her love is ultimately destructive. Thus these sonnets deal with what we have called the "low" dialectic of bondage and freedom in its sharpest possible form, where the lover is held by a sexual fascination to a mistress whom he does not like or respect, so that he despises himself for his own fidelity.

The dark lady is an incarnation of desire rather than love; she tantalizes, turning away "To follow that which flies before her face," precisely because she is not loved. The youth's infidelities hurt more than hers, but they do not exasperate: they touch nothing in the poet that wants only to possess. The assertion that her "face hath not the power to make love groan" indicates that she is a projection of something self-destructive in the lover, a death as strong as love, a "becoming of things ill" which ends, not in a romantic *Liebestod*, but in a gradual desiccation of the spirit. It is a very Proustian relation (though the role of the captive is reversed), and it is significant that the imagery is almost entirely sterile, with nothing of the former group's emphasis on store, increase, and rebirth.

What one misses in Shakespeare's sonnets, perhaps, is what we find so abundantly in the plays that it seems to us Shakespeare's outstanding characteristic. This is the sense of human proportion, of the concrete situation in which all passion is, however tragically, farcically, or romantically, spent. If the sonnets were new to us, we should expect Shakespeare to remain on the human middle ground of Sonnets 21 and 130: neither the quasi-religious language of 146 nor the prophetic vision of 129 seems typical of him. Here again we must think of the traditions of the genre he was using. The human middle ground is the area of Ovid, but the courtly love tradition, founded as it was on a "moralized" adaptation of Ovid, was committed to a psychological quest that sought to explore the utmost limits of consciousness and desire. It is this tradition of which Shakespeare's sonnets are the definitive summing-up. They are a poetic realization of the whole range of love in the Western world, from the idealism of Petrarch to the ironic frustrations of Proust. If his great predecessor tells us all we need to know of the art of love, Shakespeare has told us more than we can ever fully understand of its nature. He may not have unlocked his heart in the sonnets, but the sonnets can unlock doors in our minds, and show us that poetry can be something more than a mighty maze of walks without a plan. From the plays alone we get an impression of an inscrutable Shakespeare, Matthew Arnold's sphinx who poses riddles and will not answer them, who merely smiles and sits still. It is a call to mental adventure to find, in the sonnets, the authority of Shakespeare behind the conception of poetry as a marriage of Eros and Psyche, an identity of a genius that outlives time and a soul that feeds on death.

LESLIE A. FIEDLER

Some Contexts of Shakespeare's Sonnets

I. THE OTHER SEQUENCE

Any reflections on Shakespeare's sonnets must begin from the disconcerting awareness that we do not possess them in a text which the poet himself ordered and oversaw. There are, in fact, three quite separate collections, printed within less than fifty years of each other, which contain all or some of the poems we conventionally speak of as "the sonnets"; but none of these collections is made up entirely of sonnets in the narrow definition of the term, and all three include poems whose authorship has been challenged. Certainly none provides us with a narrative arrangement of Shakespearean short poems which has struck critics as entirely satisfactory.

The first collection did not appear until 1599, a year after Francis Meres has already alluded in print to Shakespeare's "sugred sonnets among his private friends."

Leslie A. Fiedler

It is a quite slim volume which was called *The Passionate Pilgrim* and which contained not only the poems we now refer to as Sonnets 138 and 144, but three poems from *Love's Labour's Lost,* plus four sonnets on Shakespeare's favorite theme of Venus and Adonis, as well as eleven other verse pieces, making a total of twenty—a convincing and shapely number. The volume was printed for William Jaggard, and carries, apparently without authorization, Shakespeare's name on the title page. The Jaggard collection has been examined and questioned and probed by generations of scholars with quite inconclusive results; so that the strongest challenge one recent editor can make to the authenticity of its text is to observe that "at least one" of the poems included is known not to be Shakespeare's.

A much larger edition was printed for Thomas Thorpe in 1609 and was called simply *Shake-speares Sonnets.* This edition, which contains 154 "sonnets" (the last two of which are variant englishings of a Greek epigram and have little to do with what comes before) plus a long rather inept poem entitled *A Lover's Complaint,* provides the basis for modern editions of the Sonnets and for the confusion which has been confounded by centuries of explanation and counter-explanation. An even fatter volume, however, succeeded this one in 1640, appearing under the auspices of John Benson, who called his selection *Poems: Written by Wil. Shake-Speare, Gent.* Later editors have been scornful of Benson, though his is the first attempt to make sense of the provocatively cryptic array of poems we call the sonnets—which he swelled out with borrowings from elsewhere in Shakespeare as well as from other poets.

Some Contexts of Shakespeare's Sonnets

Benson tried to give apt descriptive titles to individual poems, to emend obvious errors, and to deal for the first time with the problematical nature of the affection expressed by the poet in the sonnets to his friend. To be sure, Benson's solution to the ambiguity of the homoerotic poems is cowardly enough (it consists largely of changing embarrassing "he's" to "she's"); but he wanted to sell books and to do this felt he had to assure potential readers that Shakespeare was "normal" as well as "lucid." To make the latter point, he depended less on emendation than on a preface which guaranteed that the poems he was offering for sale contained "no intricate or cloudy stuffe to puzzell intellect. . . ."

There would be little point in making a detailed examination of Benson's padded and cautious collection; for his volume appeared after the death of Shakespeare and is interesting chiefly as the start of a concerted effort, still maintained with varying degrees of self-awareness, at making Shakespeare safe for philistines. The Jaggard version, however, appearing as it does ten years before what we have come to regard as the standard version of the sonnets, ten years closer to the conception and writing of most of them, might well be expected to reflect—in trim and simplified form—if not Shakespeare's own view of what he was after, at least that of his contemporaries, of someone perhaps privy to the circle of "private friends" for whom his "sugred" erotica was intended.

Jaggard's title in itself carries assurance that the compiler was aware of one key image in the sequence, that of the poet whose mind even from afar travels toward the beloved, as in the sonnet numbered 27 by Thorpe:

Leslie A. Fiedler

*For then my thoughts, from far where I abide,
Intend a zealous pilgrimage to thee, . . .*

It is encouraging further to find that of the two sonnets included in the 1599 collection out of those printed ten years later for Thorpe, one is 144—the poem most commonly considered the thematic key to the entire sequence, the single poem which explicitly joins the praise of the fair friend, central to Sonnets 1 through 126, with the outpouring of self-torturing lust for the dark lady, expressed in 127–152. As printed in *The Passionate Pilgrim*, this sonnet runs as follows:

*Two loves I have, of comfort and despair,
That like two spirits do suggest me still;
My better angel is a man, right fair,
My worser spirit a woman, colour'd ill.
To win me soon to hell, my female evil
Tempteth my better angel from my side,
And would corrupt my saint to be a devil,
Wooing his purity with her fair pride.
And whether that my angel be turn'd fiend,
Suspect I may, yet not directly tell;
For being both to me, both to each, friend,
I guess one angel in another's hell:
    The truth I shall not know, but live in doubt,
    Till my bad angel fire my good one out.*

These fourteen lines contain the essential fable of the whole poem, the main narrative line, perhaps as much obscured as developed in the other 152 (plus two) sonnets of the Thorpe collection. If all the sonnets except 144 were to disappear tomorrow, we would be left in

Some Contexts of Shakespeare's Sonnets

possession not only of the story Shakespeare tries to tell—the account of a poet who, seeking to divide his love in two, directing all that is ennobling in it toward one object, all that is vile toward another, ends by suspecting his two loved ones in each other's arms—but also of the moral significance that story is intended to convey: a comment on the ambiguity of passion, the eternal danger that the best which man makes of the force drawing flesh to flesh can be corrupted by the worst to the worst. But 144 contains more even than this, for it suggests the unconventional symbolism through which Shakespeare chose to project his plot and theme, the image of Two Loves, embodied, not as in our world by wife and mistress, but by friend and mistress, boy and whore.

Moreover, in this sonnet, fable, moral, and symbol alike are rendered in a special tone, a tone also sustained by the second of Thorpe's sonnets included in the Jaggard collection, number 138, with its Donne-like opening in which the show of brittle cynicism betrays an undercurrent of profound nausea:

> When my love swears that she is made of truth
> I do believe her, though I know she lies, . . .

The suggestion contained in the last word is picked up in the concluding couplet—much more clearly in the later version than in the somewhat muddled lines of *The Passionate Pilgrim*:

> Therefore I lie with her and she with me
> And in our faults by lies we flatter'd be.

Appropriately enough, the double tone encompasses not only the poet's reaction to sexual infidelity but also his attitude toward the discrepancy between his own age and the youth of both his loves, fair and foul alike. In the whole sequence, the note struck here is sustained, Shakespeare using the theme of "crabbed age and youth" to cast a note of comic anomaly on his relationship with the lady and of hopeless melancholy on that with the fair youth.

In both 138 and 144, the doubleness of tone finds expression in the dirty pun, the *double entendre;* and reading *The Passionate Pilgrim* in which they stand first, we are aware of how important this device is in determining the final sense and *feel* of the sonnets. They help us to recall a sizable group of poems which tend to get lost in the later collection, a kind of sonnet which must have been especially fashionable (it is to the fashion they represent that Jaggard tries to appeal) among both members of the larger audience lucky enough to hear them whispered and the young aristocrats for whose amusement their off-color wit was in the first instance provided. The kind of humor they exploit must have been a staple amusement for noblemen, contrived on demand by such privileged entertainers as Shakespeare, who made the mistake in fact (or fancy) of falling (or imagining he fell) in love with one of his elegant benefactors; and who thereafter made love rather than mockery his essential theme. There seemed, indeed, no contradiction—at least at first—for his love was directed toward a male, while the cynicism demanded of him by fashion was directed toward the female.

It is woman's sexuality that Shakespeare's puns ex-

Some Contexts of Shakespeare's Sonnets

coriate: the play on "lie" and "lie" in 138 equating women's facility at falsification with the ease with which they can be persuaded to go to bed; the two meanings of "hell" in 144 equating the vagina with the place of eternal punishment; while the quibble on "fire" attributes to the dark lady the power both to damn and venereally infect the youth. In light of this, it is not surprising to discover that such *double entendres* abound in the latter, the dark-lady, segment of the Thorpe sequence, reaching one climax in the pair of sonnets (134 and 135) which ring the changes on the several meanings of "Will"—volition, carnal desire, the name of the poet and perhaps also of the friend:

> So thou, being rich in Will, add to thy Will
> One will of mine, to make thy large Will more.

Another appears at the very end of the sequence, Thorpe preferring to close as Jaggard began (except for the pair of Alexandrian fancies which serve as a coda), not only choosing from Shakespeare's naughtier verse a series of bitter sonnets exploiting the lie–lie conceit (the sequence proper ends with that word), but interweaving with them a second series of puns referring to the male erection.

The couplet which concludes 150 first suggests the double meaning ("If thy unworthiness raised love in me, /More worthy I to be beloved of thee") then made explicit in 151 (". . . flesh stays no farther reason,/But, rising at thy name, doth point out thee/As his triumphant prize. . . .") and confirmed wryly in the couplet:

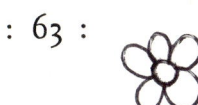

Leslie A. Fiedler

> No want of conscience hold it that I call
> Her 'love' for whose dear love I rise and fall.

We have, oddly enough, moved via an obscene pun toward a religious conclusion; for if "rise" is erotic in its implication, "fall" is quite Christian. Indeed, in any ideal order of the poems, 151 would be followed not by the present 152, which ought to be shifted back some three or four places, but by 129, which opens with a *double-entendre* of the kind we have been examining, proffered in a tone no longer fashionably cynical but deeply troubled.

> The expense of spirit in a waste of shame
> Is lust in action; . . .

Shakespeare begins; and we are expected to know that "spirit" has the second meaning of "semen," and "waste" is also to be read "waist." But the poem rapidly becomes a typical Renaissance palinode, a vehement Christian denial of the flesh; and though it ends on the very pun we have noticed in 144, this time the equation of hell and the pudenda is intended to stir not the snigger but the shudder:

> All this the world well knows; yet none knows well
> To shun the heaven that leads men to this hell.

This kind of wit, however, trembling always on the verge of nausea and self-hatred, is not found exclusively in the second part of the Thorpe sequence. There are traces of it, revealed by the sort of punning with which it

Some Contexts of Shakespeare's Sonnets

is typically associated, in Sonnet 20, whose close has occasioned so much soul-searching among the critics and which, despite its position among the sonnets of praise, is quite as anti-feminist as any poem specifically directed to the dark lady. "And for a woman wert thou first created; / Till Nature, as she wrought thee, fell a-doting, . . ." this eulogy of the Friend begins its sestet, and ends:

> But since she prick'd thee out for women's pleasure,
> Mine be thy love and thy love's use their treasure.

The couplet involves a play not only on the word "prick'd" but also on "use," which means, besides "employment," "usury" or "interest" and "the sex act." The latter is a quibble of which Shakespeare is particularly fond, speaking in *Measure for Measure* of the "two usuries," by which he means money-lending and copulation; and making throughout *The Merchant of Venice* an implicit contrast between the consummation of love and the extortion of interest. It is clear which usury Shakespeare prefers, but it is also clear that ideally he would choose neither. His peculiar way of playing on "use" tended to identify the carnal love of women with what his age still regarded as "unnatural" sin. In Dante—more orthodoxly—it is homosexuality which is associated with usury, the sins of Sodom and Cahors being punished in the same circle; but in the sonnets, the guilt by association is attributed to heterosexual consummation.

If a third one of the Thorpe sonnets had been included in *The Passionate Pilgrim*, it might well have been number 20—and not on grounds of tone alone; for it continues to develop the theme of "Two Loves" in its comparison of the friend to women in general, women whose hearts are given to "shifting change" and whose eyes are practiced in "false . . . rolling." What 20 makes clearer than anything in Jaggard is the epicene character of "the master-mistress of my passion" ("passion" meaning song *and* suffering *and* libidinal love), *i.e.*, what the friend shares with women as well as what distinguishes him from them. What differentiates him is, according to the poet, double: the male organ (alas!) and purity of heart (thank God!). What makes him like the despised sex is his physical beauty, his womanly face and eye and air.

The notion is touched on again here and there, in 106, for instance, in which the boy's living beauty is compared with literary accounts of both "ladies dead and lovely knights"; and in 53, where he is likened to the two legendary charmers, Adonis and Helen. It strains the contemporary reader a little to try to empathize with an ideal of male good looks and sexual charm identical with that applied to the female; and the allusion to Adonis in particular suggests that the roots of that ideal are to be sought in what had become of the pederastic element in Greek culture by Hellenistic times. But that allusion also refers us once more to *The Passionate Pilgrim*, in which the poems numbered IV, VI, IX, and XI are sonnets by a single hand, all retelling the story of Venus and Adonis.

Some Contexts of Shakespeare's Sonnets

II. STAIN TO ALL NYMPHS, MORE LOVELY THAN A MAN

Whether the hand that composed the four Adonis sonnets was Shakespeare's remains still undecided. There is certainly no clear-cut case against their being his, though one of them was claimed as his own by Bartholomew Griffin in 1596. They represent, at any rate, another treatment of the Ovidian tale which Shakespeare has rendered in his long erotic poem, *Venus and Adonis*, a treatment which, like that by Shakespeare, combines Ovid's account of Venus' passion for Adonis with the same poet's version of the love of Salmacis for Hermaphroditus—a grafting found also in Marlowe's *Hero and Leander*. Their presence in *The Passionate Pilgrim* serves to remind the reader that the sonnets, if they are to be fully understood, must be placed in a larger context than Thorpe provides for them—a context which includes not only *Venus and Adonis* but also, as we shall see, *Love's Labour's Lost*, *Two Gentlemen of Verona*, *The Merchant of Venice*, *Henry IV*, etc., etc.

The fable of *Venus and Adonis* is, like the fable of the sonnets, merely one in a series of analogous reworkings of a compulsive Shakespearean theme: the encounter between a passive male and an aggressive female, between modest reason and shameless lust, symbolized respectively by a boy and a woman. In *Venus and Adonis*, the poet who makes this encounter a triangle in the sonnets is lacking; and there are, therefore, strange equivocations as Shakespeare is driven to embody in Venus—whom he basically distrusts and fears for the nakedness of her lust—his own desire for epicene beauty. He actually puts into her mouth the argument that great beauties have a special obligation to marry and reproduce ("Seeds spring from seeds, and beauty breedeth beauty") which in the sonnets he speaks through the poet who is his mask. We may, indeed, agree with a recent editor of the poems that "there is more of Shakespeare himself" in Venus than in Adonis, as there is more of him in Cleopatra than in Antony, in Falstaff than in Prince Hal; but we remember, too, that Venus remains for him always the representation of all he fears in passion and the female sex.

As late as *The Tempest*, he is still dreaming of a world in which "increase" is possible without lust, a world without prenuptial or extramarital passion, in which Ceres and Juno preside chastely over weddings from which Venus has been banned. It is Ceres who speaks for the poet against her sister goddess at the pageant prepared by Prospero to honor Ferdinand and Miranda:

> . . . *Since they did plot*
> *The means that dusky Dis my daughter got,*
> *Her and her blind boy's scandal'd company*
> *I have foresworn.*

No wonder, then, that the end of *Venus and Adonis* is a catastrophe more unmitigated than the conclusion of the sonnets themselves, involving not mere corruption of a boy by a woman, but the death of that boy—a death

Some Contexts of Shakespeare's Sonnets

which Adonis seems all along to have felt as preferable to seduction, and which is followed by Venus' curse on the love which she embodies:

> It shall be fickle, false and full of fraud
> Bud, and be blasted, in a breathing while.

In the four Venus–Adonis sonnets of *The Passionate Pilgrim*, neither the rich, almost cloying texture of Shakespeare's long poem nor its underlying tragic tone are present; and the note of ambivalence toward sex represented in the Queen of Love is absent, too. The poems rather affect the brittle, detached irony of the two sonnets with which Jaggard opened his collection; their meanings are simple, their puns obvious and undisturbingly obscene—one is tempted to say childishly obscene. The last three lines will do by way of illustration, foreshadowing as they do the goring and death of Adonis, but all in the guise of a joke.

> "See in my thigh," quoth she, "here was the sore!"
> She showed hers, he saw more wounds than one,
> And blushing fled, and left her all alone.

Similarly, the desire of Venus for Adonis as he stands naked on the edge of a pool is rendered with jocular detachment in Jaggard's poem VI, which combines Ovid's story of Venus' passion with that poet's account of the lust of Salmacis for Hermaphroditus. The association suggests that if in order to understand the fair youth of the sonnets we must see what in him is derived from the myth of Adonis, we must also be clear about how much of Shakespeare's Adonis is Hermaphroditus—that son of Hermes and Aphrodite whose body was blended into one with the body of the water-nymph Salmacis when she perceived that only thus could she attain the union she desired with him.

In Ovid, it is *not* Adonis but Hermaphroditus who struggles against love, adamantly preferring his own beardless beauty to that of a woman; and it is Hermaphroditus in his final transformation who provides the prototype of the anomalous beauty attributed to the "master-mistress" in Sonnet 20:

> And the two bodies seemed to merge together,
> One face, one form . . .
> So these two joined in close embrace, no longer
> Two beings, and no longer man and woman,
> But neither, and yet both . . .

In the museums of half the world, there are to be found to this day Alexandrian images in marble and alabaster of the boy–woman Hermaphroditus, images worked in love by the craftsmen of a culture which considered pederasty a grace of civilized life. The beholder who comes upon the mythical figure sees him first from the rear, half-curled up as if in sleep; and noting the long, lovely sweep of back and flank takes him for a woman, a mistake confirmed when that beholder peers around the hyacinthine head into the beautiful face. But looking lower he discovers, surprised, that the body is "prick'd . . . out for woman's pleasure" and knows he stands before the Hermaphrodite.

Just such an image seems to have possessed the

Some Contexts of Shakespeare's Sonnets

imagination of the Renaissance, in Italy first, in England afterward; and it is this image which, projected in the theatre by the boy actors of women's parts, gave sensual substance to the Cult of Friendship and the literary tradition of the Praise of Lovely Boys. That the Elizabethans had no suspicion of the homosexual basis of the cult in which they participated seems unlikely, particularly since any grammar-school boy of the time was likely to have parsed the legend of Hermaphroditus in class. He therefore knew that, like Shakespeare's *Venus and Adonis* but unlike Ovid's, that story ended with a curse—a curse no less terrible than Shakespeare's though somewhat different. It is Hermaphroditus who speaks after his transformation in the pool where Salmacis has trapped him, crying out his cruel prayer in "a voice whose tone was almost treble":

> . . . *O father and mother, grant me this!*
> *May every one hereafter, who comes diving*
> *Into this pool, emerge half man, made weaker*
> *By the touch of this evil water!*

It is hard to believe that the group of Shakespeare poems which includes *Venus and Adonis* and the sonnets does not deal centrally with this problem of unmanning, with the price paid for diving into the pool of Salmacis in an attempt to escape the cult of Woman. And one's suspicions are further strengthened when one turns from Book Four of the *Metamorphoses*, from the tale of Hermaphroditus, to Book Ten and the story proper of Adonis, in search of some clue as to why Shakespeare made over an Adonis quite willing to be loved by Venus into the image of a reluctant Hermaphroditus. Book Ten opens with the legend of Orpheus and Eurydice, but as Ovid recreates the myth it serves chiefly as a preface to a group of songs sung by the bereaved Orpheus. Overwhelmed by grief for his lost wife, the poet has disowned women and turned for love to boys.

> *His love was given*
> *To young boys only, and he told the Thracians*
> *That was the better way: enjoy that springtime,*
> *Take those first flowers.*

Orpheus is not content, moreover, merely to celebrate pederasty; he dedicates himself, too, to the vilification of women, invoking Jove, lover of Ganymede, to inspire him:

> *. . . for I would sing of boys*
> *Loved by the gods, and girls inflamed by love*
> *To things forbidden, and earned punishment.*

He would sing, in short, of boys like Adonis–Hermaphroditus and of women like Venus; describe, as Shakespeare was to describe, Two Loves—one idyllic, one disgusting. Shakespeare's hermaphroditic revision of Adonis' character makes him all the more appropriate to the general tenor of the homosexual apology attributed to Orpheus in Book Ten, more at home with Ganymede and Hyacinthus and Cyparissus, who drew the gods from Olympus to the earth; while his version of Venus associates her with "the foul Propoetides" whom Ovid

Some Contexts of Shakespeare's Sonnets

portrays as the first whores, or with Myrrha, who, seducing her father, begot Adonis, doomed to die beneath the boar's tusk. Ovid is not seldom as melancholy as he is sensual; and over Book Ten falls the shadow not only of the death of beloved boys but of the singer of their loveliness, of Orpheus, who, as Book Eleven opens, is destroyed by women, a wild female pack urged on with the cry, "Look there!/There is our despiser."

In his own time and among the "private friends" for whom the sonnets and *Venus and Adonis* were written, Shakespeare surely assumed he could evoke with a passing allusion any section of the *Metamorphoses*. So Marlowe seems to have assumed, when in the concluding speech of the damned Dr. Faustus, he inserted the improbable tag from Ovid's account of Jove's night of love with Alcmene, "*Lente, lente, currite, equi noctis.*" All the more so might the poet contemporaneously described as Ovid reborn ("The sweete wittie soul of Ovid lives in mellifluous and hony-tongued Shakespeare . . .") feel free to evoke by allusion an aspect of Ovid's retelling of the Orpheus myth which we commonly expurgate these days, we who require ponderous historical studies to make us aware of Shakespeare's living connection with a text we know casually if at all.

III. THE WORDS OF MERCURY ARE HARSH . . .

The first two sonnets of the Venus–Adonis sequence are numbered in *The Passionate Pilgrim* IV and VI, and are framed by two other sonnets extracted from *Love's*

Leslie A. Fiedler

Labour's Lost and numbered III and V. The first of these is attributed in the play to Longaville, the second (in hexameter lines) to Berowne, who acts as *raisonneur* for Shakespeare in that strange "highbrow" un-comedy. Both represent (along with Dumain's song which Jaggard prints as number XVI) bootlegged attempts at erotic verse, shamefacedly produced by aristocratic young men who earlier have abjured love out of a desire to set up a kind of neo-Platonic Academy. In the all-male community which they dream, they plan to eschew women and the flesh for the sake of "study" and the fame which devotion to study brings. Thus, they boast, they will, having triumphed first over themselves, triumph also over "coromant devouring Time."

The poems themselves are thoroughly undistinguished, meriting the scorn visited on them in the text both by the pedant Holofernes, who finds Berowne's effort mere "numbers ratificd" (referring his hearers for the true "golden cadence of poetry" to Ovidius Naso—of course), and by Berowne himself, who says of Longaville's rhymes what he surely knows bears also on his own:

> This is the liver vein, which makes flesh a deity;
> A green goose a goddess; pure, pure idolatry . . .

But they fit, in their vain rationalizing of apostacy to reason, their defense of foreswearing oneself in the name of love, with the tone and terror of the gloomier sonnets. *Love's Labour's Lost*, though presumably written to be played for a select audience rather than in the commercial theatre, is still more guarded than those sonnets composed to be read in private by readers close to the

Some Contexts of Shakespeare's Sonnets

events they describe. In certain love scenes of the play, however, particularly in those in which Berowne pays his begrudged and witty court to an equally bitter Rosaline, there are clear analogues to the relationship of the poet and the dark lady of the sonnets. Not only is Berowne's beloved described as being black as "the school of night" and his own commitment to her qualified as "toiling in a pitch," but their relationship refuses to be contained within the compass of a romantic happy ending. The play which presents it can only close (not end—there is no end, happy or otherwise) after the acceptance by Berowne, half bitter, half orthodox, of his own helplessness before passion:

> We cannot cross the cause why we were born;
> Therefore, of all hands must we be forsworn.

What is added, finally, by *Love's Labour's Lost* to the complex of ideas defined by the image of the Two Loves and the myth of Adonis-Hermaphroditus is a kind of homoerotic version of the Fall of Man—in which woman and the serpent are identified with each other; and the fallen Adam is condemned to leave the Garden of the King of Navarre's "little academe" arm in arm with his temptress—if she will have him. It is a variant form of a theme found throughout Shakespeare's work: men bound together by ties of friendship are sundered by the love of woman (as in *Two Gentlemen of Verona*, for instance, or *The Merchant of Venice*) and must somehow make a new, more fragile compact or sadly learn to part. Sometimes it is a political crisis which destroys the homoerotic bond, as in *Julius Caesar* and *Henry IV, Part*

II, where political considerations persuade a younger man to destroy his older benefactor and friend; but usually what causes the rift is the intervention of the female principle in one form or other. Certainly that is the case in *Love's Labour's Lost* as in the sonnets themselves, though in the former the demands of the theater require that the ensuing queasiness at the threat of female sexuality be played out in lighthearted wit-combats. Only in occasional sonnets and in certain of the later tragedies (including *Lear* and *Hamlet*) is that queasiness fully indulged; and in one soliloquy of Posthumus Leonatus in *Cymbeline* it erupts at such an hysterical pitch that genteel nineteenth-century editors were moved to deny that the speech was written by Shakespeare:

>   . . . Could I find out
> The woman's part in me! For there's no motion
> That tends to vice in man, but I affirm
> It is the woman's part: be it lying, note it,
> The woman's; flattering, hers; deceiving, hers;
> Lust and rank thoughts, hers, hers . . .
> All faults that may be named, nay, that hell knows,
> Why, hers, in part or all; but rather, all . . .

In *Love's Labour's Lost,* this shrill note is avoided, though for one moment, as the play moves toward its climax, it is the women who seem to have triumphed, the men who appear to have been made fools, in a tangle of disguises and counter-disguises, masks and pleasant confusions of identity—quite Mozartian in complexity

Some Contexts of Shakespeare's Sonnets

and lightness of tone. What is being mocked, it seems clear, are male pretensions to immunity from passion, perhaps even the specific all-male "academy," around whose members charges of atheism and homosexuality floated during the time of Shakespeare: that circle of "soul-loved friends" which included noblemen like Derby, Northumberland, and Sir Walter Raleigh and which boasted as its poet-laureate George Chapman, favored candidate for the role of rival poet in Shakespeare's sonnet sequence. Speculation about this circle is lost in scholarly attempts to reconstitute literary history out of ancient gossip and veiled allusions; but it is not unlikely that it, or some similar "academy," must have seemed to Shakespeare an attractive butt for satire, competing as it did with the Essex-Southampton group in which he apparently was permitted to play the part accorded Chapman in the first.

Condemning one "academy," however, Shakespeare could not easily avoid condemning the other; caricaturing Chapman and his beloved intellectual dandies, he caricatured himself and the lords he served—even the one lord he loved. The ironies of *Love's Labour's Lost*, that is to say, are not all directed outward at some detested other; and to read the play so is to reduce its complexity and mitigate its appeal. Self-hatred is everywhere an undercurrent, reflected especially in the self-tormenting wit of Berowne, who seems from time to time another version of the poet in the sonnets. Only read together and illuminated by each other are the sonnets and *Love's Labour's Lost* fully comprehensible, and this the editor of *The Passionate Pilgrim* appears to have known. Shakespeare's most "highbrow" and personal play does not conclude, however, any more than the sonnets themselves, with the mere triumph of women over men's vows of dedication to study and chastity and each other. As the title itself tells us, no kind of love triumphs in the end; for even as the irrational desire for the female has driven out reason, so the shadow of death cools irrational desire.

The play concludes, not in a series of embraces or a mass wedding, but in the departure of the ladies and the imposition on their lovers of certain unforeseenly grim tasks. Berowne, for instance, is commanded by his beloved to remit his suit for a year and in the interim to visit hospitals where he is bidden:

> With all the fierce endeavour of your wit
> To enforce the pained impotent to smile.

Not only does the evocation of pain and impotence seem to us an odd ending for what had promised to be a comedy, but the suggested necessity to seek an antidote to wit undercuts—as well as the character to whom it is directed—the witty play in which he appears and its jesting author. The net effect is that of a palinode, of such a denial of love and joy as Shakespeare entrusts to Sonnets 129 and 146.

In *The Passionate Pilgrim*, that note of denial is sustained in poems like X, XVII, and XX, and especially in XIII, which begins "Beauty is a vain and doubtful good . . ."; but its most intriguing embodiment is found in the single stanza quoted from the answer to Marlowe's "Live with me and be my love," which was signed originally *Ignotus* and later was attributed to Sir Walter Raleigh.

Some Contexts of Shakespeare's Sonnets

> If all the world and love were young,
> And truth in every shepherd's tongue,
> These pretty pleasures might me move
> To live with thee, and be thy love.

If these lines are, indeed, not Shakespeare's but those of a member of the rival group he presumably satirized in *Love's Labour's Lost*, the fact should serve to remind us of how many assumptions (imported from Italy, perhaps, and become the mode) were shared by the antifeminist "academies." Shakespeare or Raleigh, it makes little difference; either might have spoken the final hermetic word. "The words of Mercury are harsh after the songs of Apollo" reads the tag which closes *Love's Labour's Lost*; and this line, too, the scholars hesitate to give to Shakespeare, taking it instead for the comment of a reader distressed by the final turn of the play—in which its comic characters return after the failed happy ending to represent the debate of the cuckoo and the owl: a debate without a difference, in which spring is presented as the season which brings fear to married men, and winter as a time presided over by red-nosed and greasy kitchen wenches.

IV. WHEREFORE LOVE IS OF IMMORTALITY...

There is finally only one major theme of the sonnets unrepresented in *The Passionate Pilgrim* and this is the notion of the Two Immortalities which underlies that of the Two Loves. Yet the perplexity in response to which this theme is generated is already suggested in the *Ignotus* stanza. "If love is based on beauty and beauty depends on youth, how can it survive in a world which, like ourselves, from moment to moment grows old? One answer passionately asserted by Venus herself in *Venus and Adonis* is restated somewhat more objectively (more coldly and formalistically, some readers would argue) in Sonnets 1 through 17. The young man must, the poet contends, recreate the beauty with which nature has endowed him and which time strips away, by marrying and begetting, by "breed." This is a pagan idea to be sure; and however Christian Shakespeare's sequence may finally become, in its long forepart it conceives of immortality—naturalistically—as endless propagation.

Beauty, the sonnets begin by stipulating, since it exists in the flesh must seek its perpetuity in the flesh; but before long it is further suggested (in number 15 first of all) that beauty can survive transformed into art, recreated in the enduring poetic image. In either case, love must be the spur—either the love which attracts man to woman, body to body, and ends in marriage and the family, or the love which draws man to man, soul to soul, and ends in—literature. Shakespeare apparently does not find it easy to believe that poetry is a sufficient guarantee of the beloved's immortality, and in Sonnet 16 cries out:

And fortify yourself in your decay
With means more blessed than my barren rhyme . . .

Yet in the long run, he decides that the immortality of art is superior to that of "breed," abandoning the plea to marry in favor of repeated asseverations that:

Some Contexts of Shakespeare's Sonnets

His beauty shall in these black lines be seen,
And they shall live, and he in them still green.

Behind the poet's quarrel with himself, or the conclusion to which he comes, survive—at one remove or another—certain arguments out of the *Symposium*: Pausanius' distinction, for instance, between "the Love which is the offspring of the common Aphrodite" and "is apt to be of women . . . and of the body rather than the soul . . ." and the Love which is "the offspring of the heavenly Aphrodite . . . a mother in whose birth the female has no part . . .", "that Love which is of youth." It is worth pausing over the phrase "in whose birth the female has no part . . .", for it represents an obsessive concern of Shakespeare throughout his entire career. In *Macbeth*, the point is made that only the man not born of woman (like Posthumus Leonatus to whose despairing cry "Is there no way for men to be but women/ Must be half-workers?" we have already alluded) can triumph over evil; and in the last plays, girls like Miranda, motherless as the Uranian Aphrodite, pure daughters of the Father, subdue lust and strife in mankind and the world.

It is in the speech of Diotima, however, as reported by Socrates, that the essential Shakespearean attitudes toward love's triumph over time can be perceived. What object do lovers have in view, the prophetess asks, and answers herself, "The object . . . is birth in beauty, whether of body or soul . . . Wherefore love is of immortality." The final phrase might well stand as the motto of the sonnets; and the meaning of the whole sequence is further illuminated as Diotima continues: "Those who are pregnant in the body only, betake

Leslie A. Fiedler

themselves to women and beget children . . . but souls which are pregnant . . . conceive that which is proper for the soul . . . And such creators are poets . . ." Here, then, is the second classic context of Shakespeare's theorizing about love: the homosexual apologetics as the *Symposium*, derived via various Italian middlemen (Michelangelo, Bembo, Bruno, Florio, etc.) and already given, before reaching Shakespeare, an anti-Petrarchan or anti-courtly love cast. Where the Orphic attack on women, learned from Ovid, and the neo-Platonic espousal of an all-male *amor razionale* meet, the theme of Two Loves as summarized in Sonnet 144 is transformed into that of the Two Immortalities.

Shakespeare's Sonnets can be read biographically despite all of the difficulties and confusions inherent in such an approach. There is, indeed, much in them too specific to be explained away by any general reading: the class difference between the two male lovers, for instance, and the clear indication that the older one is involved one way or another in the debased profession of the theatre. Such things obviously are in the poems because they happen to have happened. But there is much else which is only completely meaningful on the level of the general, the symbolic, or even the allegorical; and in the end one reads the complete sequence not as the mere confession of an erotic misadventure but as a study of love itself as understood in Western Europe toward the end of the sixteenth century. The sonnets, that is to say, record one man's attempt to reconcile certain contradictions inherent in the courtly love codes as well as certain difficulties arising where those codes confronted Christianity.

Shakespeare begins by undermining the idealization of woman and the pseudo-sanctification of adultery

Some Contexts of Shakespeare's Sonnets

which lie at the roots of courtly love; and he is not alone among his English contemporaries in this strategy. Both Donne and Sir Walter Raleigh have recorded cynical reservations about women and love not very different from his; and even Wyatt, who imported into England the courtly love mythos in its Petrarchan form, also undercut from time to time the image of the adored lady as angel and saviour. The convention and the anticonvention grow up together; and neither necessarily arises from a deeper or more honest perception of the world. When Shakespeare writes the well-known sonnet which begins "My mistress' eyes are nothing like the sun . . .", he is inventing nothing new, only providing an already expected titillation. Yet his sonnets are unique, though not in their anti-feminism.

What is peculiar to Shakespeare's sequence is its attempt to preserve much of the mystique of courtly love along with much of the traditional imagery of poems written in its name—by transferring that mystique and that imagery to a male rather than a female beloved. Like the poets of ancient Provence—and like that slippery and ironical codifier of their assumptions, Andreas Capellanus—like Dante himself, Shakespeare seems to have believed that love is suffering, "a certain inborn suffering," but that it is a suffering which redeems. Like his predecessors, he further seems to have believed that *only* love redeems, makes a gentleman, refines a poet, improves manners, and refreshes the soul; he, therefore, like them, pretends to find in the joy which loving imparts to the lover a sufficient counterweight to the pain inflicted by fate, the world, even the indifference or aloofness of the beloved.

Like the earlier theorists of courtly love, he seems to

have discriminated between two kinds of love, *amor purus* and *amor mixtus*, the latter involving a final consummation, the former precluding it; but like those theorists, he thinks of even "pure" love as physical, beginning in the eye and implying, in addition to the communion of souls, sensual delight in the cheek, lip, all the lovely flesh of the loved one. To Capellanus, for example, even the contact of naked bodies in bed did not impugn love's purity, so long as there was no actual penetration of flesh by flesh, no expenditure of seed. Finally, like the Provençals themselves, Shakespeare thought of the higher kind of love as being necessarily outside of marriage (Spenser in the *Faerie Queene* was contemporaneously attempting a Protestant, bourgeois synthesis of redemptive passion and marriage), in some sense, therefore, adulterous. No more than any love poet of the Middle Ages would Shakespeare have considered addressing an erotic poem to his wife.

Like his traditional prototypes, Shakespeare was accustomed to refer to his beloved as a rose, a muse, an angel; like them, he compared that beloved to such great beauties of antiquity as Helen of Troy; but unlike them, he found his muse–angel–rose–Helen in a boy (as Orpheus preached and Diotima urged) rather than in a woman. There is no use asserting that such a procedure is, in the history of English society or in that of English sonnet sequences, either "normal" or "conventional." It is extraordinary, even a little disturbing; and there is something more honest in Benson's attempts to bowdlerize the sonnets by changing "he's" to "she's" than in the pretense that one has dealt adequately with the problem once he has "proved" by an analysis of Sonnet

Some Contexts of Shakespeare's Sonnets

20 (it is possible in our emancipated age for even a Shakespearean scholar to admit that Shakespeare was playing on the street meaning of the word "prick") that Shakespeare did not actually have physical relations with boys. The point is that the poet admits to, even boasts of, sleeping with women and considering it filthy, while chastely (but passionately) embracing an idealized male beloved.

How was Shakespeare driven, fictionally at least, to advocate so extraordinary a splitting of love, to endure such a profound division between sentimentality and desire? What ends as division begins with a dream of synthesis, a desire to reconcile Christianity and Love, the lesson of the Scriptures and the burden of vernacular secular poetry as written in Europe for some six hundred years before his time. To comprehend the problems posed for Shakespeare by courtly love, one must first understand its effect on the soul of the West, the sense in which what began as a pastime for idle courtiers became a counter-religion to the reigning orthodoxy. Between the elevation of the lady to a kind of godhead by the advocates of *amour courtois* and the Christian teaching that such adulation is idolatry or worse, there can be no compromise. This Shakespeare perceived and entrusted to Berowne to express for him in *Love's Labour's Lost*, in what starts as the criticism of a friend's sonnet. The voice which identifies courtly verse as "the liver vein," a sign of "idolatry" is a good deal closer to the wisdom expressed by Andreas Capellanus in his recantation ("No man through any good deeds can please God so long as he serves in the service of love.") than to the ecstatic poet of Provence who sang, *Nuls om ses amor*

Leslie A. Fiedler

res no vau, "Without love, no man is worth aught."

Even more dangerous to the orthodox than the deification, half in sport, half in earnest, of Woman, is the view that human love is a source of grace, a rival to the love of God. What courtly love poet, pledged to this belief, could doubt—if he pretended also to be a Christian—that his soul was in jeopardy? But what could he do without denying either his muse or his God? On the one hand, he could live as men have lived during the last two thousand years by compartmentalizing his allegiances, serving woman until the ebbing of animal vigor left him nothing but the pleasures of recantation. Or he could try to have it both ways at once by idealizing, which is to say, decarnalizing, human love; but this way was likely to leave its practitioners with a conflict compounded rather than resolved. Idealized love demanded the pure worship of a mistress remote and unsought; the flesh required sexual satisfaction; the love of God demanded the renunciation of both. The love of another man's wife remained adulterous whether consummated in the flesh or not; and super-adding a pseudo-religious note merely complicated the original sin with an overlay of idolatry.

It was the Italians who completed the "sanctification" of passion. From Frederic II of Sicily, who learned from the Arabs to keep a harem and from the Provençals to sing the praise of women, the tradition was transmitted to the *Vita Nuova* of Dante, where what had already been transformed from passion to art became theology. For every man, Dante suggests, there is somewhere a woman who is his personal mediator, a "miraculous" avenue to salvation. The name "Beatrice" provides

Some Contexts of Shakespeare's Sonnets

tempting opportunities for puns on "she who beatifies"; and Dante cannot resist extending his quibbles until he has hinted that Beatrice represents, in some sense, Christ! At this point the Inquisition moved in to expurgate his little book. Beyond the mystical symbolism of the *Vita Nuova* lies the allegory of the *Comedy*, which makes of Beatrice Divine Theology, and the game is saved: not an actual woman but only that for which she stands is the source of salvation. It is a solution which leaves unresolved the contradiction with which it began, leaves to the soul of the West an institutionalized schizophrenia. So Petrarch, who followed Dante, after a lifetime of singing his passion could only disavow it in his old age. *Vergogna e 'l frutto!*—"Shame is the fruit!"

Shakespeare's theory of two loves, one angelic, the other diabolic, is at least a new way of stating the old problem, especially since he directs the first impulse toward a fair youth (loved as purely as any Italian poet of the sweet new style longed for his lady) and the black woman (lusted after in self-hatred and disgust). Love as grace is attached to the homoerotic Beatrice, love as sin to the dark lady; but this means that sentimental salvation is attributed to the male, passionate damnation to the female. Shakespeare has thus resolved one contradiction at least, that between the popular-orthodox conception of Woman as tempter and the courtly concept of her as Saviour. It is the boy, Shakespeare insists, in loving whom one can find salvation, not the daughter of Eve. But the taint of homosexuality clings to such a suggestion; and Shakespeare himself is painfully aware of the proverbial fickleness of boys, declaring through the Fool in *Lear* that "He's mad that trusts . . . a boys loue, or a whores oath." After all, he had lived with boys in the theatre, watched them offstage as well as on; and though he can praise his fair youth with a tenderness so genuine that generations of men have read his words to their mistresses, the fable of the sonnets does not end on a note of tenderness.

The poet, troubled from the first by doubts as to whether generation in the flesh through marriage is not superior to "birth in beauty" through poetry, is further tormented by doubts about the worth of his own verse, by the threat of a rival lover–poet to win away his friend (there are *two* triangles in the sonnets), and is dismayed at last when his two loves fall into each other's arms—the untainted boy betrayed by the embrace of a gonorrheal whore. "Boy" and "whore," the very words have a special affinity for each other in Shakespeare's imagination, as illustrated by the passage from *Lear* and by Cleopatra's speech foretelling the actor who will someday "boy my greatness i' the posture of a whore." In the world of Shakespeare's work, boy actors daily put on and doffed the allure of women, played women for him; and who can doubt that their sometimes blatant homosexuality travestied behind the scenes the pure and rational love of males that he dreamed of—or that mincing little "queens" caricatured those ambiguous boy–girl heroines so essential in their transvestite loveliness to plays like *As You Like It* and *Twelfth Night*.

For Shakespeare himself, apparently, the system of Two Loves did not hold up, since they tend to fall together when the youth, longed for as a symbol of innocence, lusts after the female symbol of concupiscence. In the end, for Shakespeare, too, there remains only the terrible cry, as old as Christianity itself:

Some Contexts of Shakespeare's Sonnets

*The expense of spirit in a waste of shame
Is lust in action . . .*

It becomes clear finally that the seed of corruption was in the friend from the first, already present in the chaste relationship between him and the poet. There is no pure masculine principle, no male immune to the evil element represented by the female. Only the legendary "man not born of woman," the motherless man, can break out of the trap of sin. The youth, however, is very much his mother's child; and the poet desiring him has no way of being sure that he has not desired in him the "woman's part," the "motion that tends to vice . . .". The poet cannot even be sure that he has not himself played the woman's part, has not been the Venus who, in fantasy at least, has assailed the virtue he loves. When the youth falls, the poet cannot be certain that he has not wished that fall, somehow collaborated in it; for the dark lady is a projection of his deepest imagination, too, and he is the link between her and the fair friend. The guilt which the poet discovers in his mistress and in the youth, he finds also in his own deepest heart.

Certainly, in the plays which deal with analogous love affairs, in *Henry IV, Julius Caesar, The Merchant of Venice*, there is not only a pervading sense of melancholy, a feeling that the relationship which joins youth and age, man and boy, is doomed; but there is also a suggestion of guilt, the feeling that the relationship should never have existed. In Shakespeare's imagination, the older lover does not escape unscathed but is condemned, as in *Julius Caesar*, to be stabbed to death; or destined, as in *Henry IV*, to be cast off to die of a broken heart; or permitted, as in *The Merchant of*

V*enice*, to make the gesture which hands over his friend to women forever. Shakespeare, in any case, at the time of writing the sonnets could not condone in himself the highest love he could conceive, but foresaw its dissolution in betrayal and lust, felt that it deserved to be so dissolved. And so he falls back (like Capellanus or Chaucer or Petrarch himself) into the Christian palinode.

The Uranian strategy does not finally work; and the poet in the end abandons the solution of the *Symposium*, the dream of Diotima, in favor of the Christian doctrine that there is no rebirth of beauty except in God, that here on earth all beauty must be yielded up in order to ransom it from time.

> *Buy terms divine in selling hours of dross;*
> *Within be fed, without be rich no more:*
>   *So shalt thou feed on Death, that feeds on men,*
>   *And Death once dead, there's no more dying then.*

Yet the palinode is not quite the final word; for we are aware that the recantation itself is part of a poem whose beauty survives its own denial, a poem which works and reworks in its text the quite un-Christian sentiments of Ovid's valedictory verses in the *Metamorphoses*:

> *Now I have done my work. It will endure,*
> *I trust, beyond Jove's anger, fire and sword,*
> *Beyond Time's hunger . . .*
> *I shall be read, and through all centuries,*
> *If prophecies of bards are ever truthful,*
> *I shall be living, always.*

STEPHEN SPENDER

The Alike and
the Other

T<small>HE</small> <small>GREAT</small> <small>DIFFICULTY</small> confronting the reader of Shakespeare's sonnets is to discriminate among the different kinds of truth they reveal. Polonius might have called them tragedy, history, psychology, poetical-historical, platonic-psychological, tragical-historical-autobiographical-platonic, and a good deal else. There is truth on several levels.

A theory which can be rejected is the one taken up from time to time by defenders of Shakespeare's good name: that the narrative of a poet who loves a young man with whom he shares a mistress, and who is jealous both of friend and mistress, is fiction. This cannot be so: there are too many glancing references at people and events that must have existed. We feel sure that these are real because, if they were not, the "other poet" (for example) would be more fully invented. *Venus and Adonis* and *The Rape of Lucrece* are full of precise characterization. If Shakespeare had invented the young man, he would have described his gestures and the clothes he wore. The story has every appearance of bitter, frustrating, unrewarding truth, out of which an extraordinary blossoming and harvest have been wrung.

However, a generally rejected theory may have something to offer. If the sonnets are about real things, Shakespeare nevertheless brought to bear on them his invention and imagination as poet and dramatist. This does not mean that they are exaggerated, but that the logic of fulfillment and frustration, the lessons of love and the world, may have been developed from experiences or feelings in themselves transitory. This would help explain why so many readers read themselves into the sonnets. What may to Shakespeare have been the margin of his experience—explored, analyzed, and recreated in the poetry—may, differently interpreted, seem to each reader the truth about himself.

The sonnets may, then, tell us more of events, situations, and feelings that the poet lived and felt and analyzed to conclusions, than of what he *was*. This would elucidate, I think, another difficulty: that they express things so completely, and yet seem strangely indecisive. It is difficult to think of these loves having a future beyond the period covered by the actual writing of the sonnets. One cannot cast the dark lady for the role of Beatrice or Laura, and the relationship with the young man seems of a kind sustained exactly by the amount of faith and imagination the poet puts into it. Shaw

The Alike and the Other

suggests (in the preface to *The Dark Lady of the Sonnets*) that Shakespeare, in the manner of marrying men, stopped writing sonnets when he and his mistress settled down together and lived happily ever after. This seems a Shavian extravagance.

So perhaps the ever-fixed marks of love which the sonnets chart are not derived from extension in time but from insight into life. They tell more of how Shakespeare could penetrate into the logic of experience than of his own nature. The sonnets are an intermittently-kept poetic diary covering a period, supposedly, of three years. If they had been kept over twenty or thirty, we might form a different picture of the poet's psychology. All we have is a section which may well be of the exception rather than the rule. Whatever conclusions we draw from them should be with this in mind.

Many questions of fact arise which I shall not confront: they will be discussed with more authority by other contributors to the volume. So I shall not choose between the claims of Southampton and Pembroke as candidates for the role of the friend. All I shall say is that, from reading the sonnets themselves, I agree with those who think that the friend was well born, though perhaps of a recently elevated *arriviste* family. I cannot think that he was a play actor. The reference to "Hues" in Sonnet 20 could more easily be explained as an allusion to someone called Hewes or Hughes over whom the friend exercised his power of fascination than as meaning that the friend himself was called Hewes. I have no theory about the identities of the "other poet" and the dark lady.

I shall begin from the relationship between the poet

and the friend and the mistress. It is one (or should I say two? or three?) where, although there is rivalry, there is also connivance. The ideal requirements of the friendship are "arranged" by the poet, and he often uses the poetry to hold up to the young man the terms of the arrangement. In the triangle of poet, friend, and mistress, the love between the friends is sharply distinguished by the poet from the lust which draws both to the woman. The difference between the relationship of the friends with one another, and of the poet with the mistress, is of identification between the friends and of otherness with the mistress. The poet and the friend are one, the mistress is "other." Yet the poet fears that when the friend and the mistress are together they are one, and that, for them, the poet is then the "other." This crucial fear is expressed in 144 with its pun on the word "angel":

> To win me soon to hell, my female evil
> Tempteth my better angel from my side,
> And would corrupt my saint to be a devil,
> Wooing his purity with her foul pride.
> And whether that my angel be turn'd fiend
> Suspect I may, yet not directly tell;
> But being both from me, both to each friend,
> I guess one angel in another's hell:
>   Yet this shall I ne'er know, but live in doubt,
>   Till my bad angel fire my good one out.

Relations with the mistress are with hell; those with the friend are with a heaven which, unfortunately, being of this world, is subject to betrayals, treachery, the fall.

The Alike and the Other

The ground of union with the woman is love inseparable from lust, and indeed from hatred. Bernard Shaw, in the same preface, reasons that the cruelty with which the poet writes of the dark lady is the language of sexual passion, thus proving—that which for Shaw and Frank Harris scarcely needs pointing out—Shakespeare's normality; whereas "the language of the sonnets addressed to Pembroke, extravagant as it now seems, is the language of compliment and fashion . . . unmistakable for anything else than the expression of a friendship delicate enough to be wounded, and a manly loyalty deep enough to be outraged."

That the imaginative world of Shakespeare is one of normal relations between men and women is not in doubt. The question is whether he did not, in this section of his life which is the sonnets, enter into an abnormal relationship, and show a profound understanding of it.* There is a further question which arises: is not the poet's love–hate for the dark lady related to the disgust for physical sex which is a feature of the last plays, and of *King Lear*? And although the idealized relation with the friend may involve sexual feelings which come into consciousness in certain passages, may not this relationship—considered as a whole and not just in the light of certain guilt-ridden sonnets—be a sublimation of sex, an escape from that kind of relationship which leads to revulsion and disgust with the shared mistress?

---

* Mr. Martin Seymour Smith, in his introduction to his commentary on the sonnets, the typescript of which he has generously shown me, argues that Shakespeare was a normal man who for some months or years fell in love with a boy.

Shaw's argument that the language of the sonnets to the friend is simply a convention of the time, has, of course, been used by other critics and commentators. It is both true and untrue. Of course the sonnets belong to their time, when hyperbolic expressions of feeling between friends were not considered compromising. There were conventions of feeling which obsessed writers during the Renaissance, such as the idea, worked out with elaboration in Sonnet 24, of the perfect exchange between kindred spirits. Moreover, as J. B. Leishmann has recently pointed out, many passages in the sonnets are derivative of Horace, Ovid, and Italian and French models. But he also emphasizes how original in mood and feeling they are. No other sequence is anything like this one.

Reading the scholars on "influences," conventions of manners, and the like, the common reader may begin almost to think that all poetry is the result of previous poetry and contemporary manners, feelings, and beliefs, the poet being a kind of sensitive instrument synthesizing these attitudes. But the conventions of manners at a particular time, and the fashions at that time in past literature, are really only the outer circumference of the forms that poets use, which are also conventions. To rhyme or not to rhyme, the meters in which a poet writes—these are only aspects of an agreed politeness between poet and reader or hearer, and have something to do with the general manners and tone of the age. Sometimes, of course, the poet may be simply reflecting the conventions of feeling and manners of his time, just as sometimes his poetry may be the vehicle of the form, rather than the form that of the poetry. But when

The Alike and the Other

the poetry uses the form to convey experiences which are individual to him, then we may take it that we are in the presence of unique experience, as we often are with Shakespeare's sonnets.

As a matter of fact, the argument about conventions of polite language cuts both ways. For if it is true that the exaggerated tone is due to the conventions of polite expression in the past, it is also true that feelings may be inhibited in their expression by conventions. If it is convention which makes it "normal" for Shakespeare to call his friend "dear my love" in 13, it may be the same convention which prevents him from being more outspoken in 20. In fact it is unlikely that at any time in post-Christian Europe a poet—one who did not set out, like Marlowe, or like Rimbaud, to be *maudit*—could have confessed to that carnal act which Sonnet 20 is taken to repudiate.

Sonnet 20—this declaration of love for the "master-mistress of the poet's passion" who has "A woman's face with Nature's own hand painted," and this renunciation of "love's uses"—comes even earlier in the series than the number would indicate. For the first seventeen sonnets, being concerned with exhorting the poet's friend to get married and have an heir, are frequently taken to have been commissioned by Lady Pembroke, in the interest of William Herbert, her son. Thus this sonnet has the important position of third of the series in which the poet is advocating his own love. In 20, Shakespeare declares his love and makes, wittily, a physiological alibi.

. . . for a woman wert thou first created;
Till Nature, as she wrought thee, fell a-doting,

> And by addition me of thee defeated,
> By adding one thing to my purpose nothing.
>   But since she prick'd thee out for women's pleasure,
>   Mine be thy love and thy love's use their treasure.

The meaning is conveyed not just by what is said but by the tone. The argument may serve to clear Shakespeare of the charge of a "serious offense," but the tone seems hardly that of indignant repudiation. Perhaps, one might argue, it is a kind of light-hearted kidding-on-the-level made possible because such a consummation is quite out of the question. Probably this is what Shaw means when he refers to Shakespeare's innocent quips. However, from what we soon learn about the friend, with his "sensual fault" and lasciviousness, it seems unlikely that, to him, such a relationship would be unthinkable. However else one considers the friend, one can hardly read the sonnets without coming to the conclusion that to love him—if not to know him even—was compromising. Very shortly after the twentieth sonnet, the poet writes in the vein of pleading with him on behalf of his better and purer nature. Retrospectively then, this sonnet seems to suggest a kind of connivance with faults which the poet, at this stage of their relationship, perhaps did not take seriously.

A thing that is often forgotten by writers about the sonnets is that they are not a monologue. They are one side of a dialogue, or a speech (as is most touchingly evinced in 26, "Lord of my love to whom in vassalage"), or they are letters. Looked at as part of such a dialogue, Sonnet 20—a letter from an older man to a younger—does not read as simple repudiation. The older man writes to the "master-mistress of his passion" that

The Alike and the Other

he considers him more beautiful, more constant, and more virtuous than women. He follows this with an ambiguous reference—"A man in hue, all 'hues' in his controlling"—to his success with men. He goes on to imply that if the "lovely boy" were a girl, he would make love to him, but, deprived of the means for this physical consummation, he claims the friend's love, leaving to women the use of his sex. The poet condemns the falsity of women, attacking them in especial—like Hamlet—for their use of make-up. What would the reader, if he did not know the writer to be Shakespeare, think of such a letter? Surely, an unprejudiced view would be: 1) that it is a declaration of the writer's love for the youth; 2) that the writer attempts, by flattery and cajoling, to influence the youth against the other sex; 3) that supposing the writer were, in fact, having an affair with the young man, he could scarcely have written more openly—the law, and the "politeness of the time," would not have permitted him to do so.

What concerns us here is not what "happened" but the kind of feeling involved. It is of course difficult to judge whether what would seem compromising today would have seemed so to the Elizabethans. But what is surely not just of its time in this and other sonnets is the insistence on the quality of the young man's beauty. John Donne, who was only seven years Shakespeare's junior and who, in his Satires and Epistles, is a close observer of the society in which he lived, comments in *The Progresse of the Soule* (the poem that contains the memorable line "Is any kinde subject to rape like fish?"):

Sinnes against kinde
They easily doe, that can let feede their mind

Stephen Spender

*With outward beauty; beauty they in boyes and
beastes do find.*

There is much insistence on the outward beauty of the lovely boy in the sonnets.

Writers about conventions of polite and courtly language forget that even within polite society there is more than one convention. There are also the conventions of cliques, conventions within conventions, conventions of private jokes. The idiom which Shakespeare mimics in the conversation of Osric in *Hamlet* is an example of disagreeably cliquish idiom. If, as I think likely, the last six lines of 20 were written during an early stage of the infatuation ("Nature . . . fell a-doting") when the poet caught up the tone of the young man and his circle—then these last lines might conceal a veiled sexual approach or, equally, a refusal (in its context tactfully and lightly made) to an approach made by the poet.

I don't want to advance either of these possibilities as what happened. But writers who see the sonnet as a simple "clearing" by Shakespeare, read it as though it were addressed by the poet to himself or to a bardolatrous posterity. When one remembers that it was written to a young man of lascivious faults, one has to consider that the poet was anticipating some reaction, the nature of which we can only guess.

Sonnet 20 is, however, unique in the series for its particular kind of sophistication. And even here the apposition is maintained between falsity (women) and truth (the friend) which is such a serious theme of the sonnets. Perhaps it is conversationally written in the

The Alike and the Other

voice, not of the poet, but of the frivolous young man, at a time when the poet was charmed by his naughtiness, and before his eyes had been opened—as they so soon were to be—to its serious consequences.

Whether or not the poet shared some guilty awareness with the young man, it is clear that the young man committed "sensual sinnes" with others, and that the poet, knowing of these, had complicated reactions. He felt betrayed: not just personally betrayed (though there is something of this in 33, 34, and 35) but more deeply so in that the young man, betraying himself, betrayed also their shared world, the light in which both moved, the "glorious morning" and the "beauteous day." The identification of their mutual life with the life of nature was complete: guilt of the friend was both their guilt and the guilt of life itself (33): "Suns of the world may stain when heaven's sun staineth."

When the friend betrayed him with others, then, not sharing the offense with his body, the poet nonetheless became involved in the guilt with his mind (35):

> All men make faults, and even I in this,
> Authorizing thy trespass with compare,
> Myself corrupting, salving thy amiss,
> Excusing thy sins more than thy sins are;
> For to thy sensual fault I bring in sense. . . .

The poet here is not just being noble, assuming a burden of guilt that is not his own. He is arrogating to himself the right to feel his own nature contaminated by the fault of the young man. The betrayal is disloyal to a claim which the poet feels he has over the friend, "that sweet thief which sourly robs from me," whether or not he exercises it. A claim for a shared life is here, surely implicit.

My argument is that there is a dark and guilty side of the relationship between the two men, perhaps on account of certain acts with one another, perhaps through the moral involvement which made the poet suffer the friend's guilt as his own, perhaps through the sharing of the mistress, perhaps simply as the price of mutuality and the relation of patronage.

The whole effort of the poet is to convert this darkness of separation into the light, identified with the springing and golden and ripened seasons, which returns to the one theme of ever-fixed love, affirming it, burying in it all defects. "Why write I still all one, ever the same?" he asks (76); and the answer is, "you and love are still my argument; /So all my best is dressing old words new, /Spending again what is already spent."

Many readers have been puzzled by Keats' "Beauty is truth, truth beauty, that is all /Ye know on earth, and all ye need to know." One reading of Shakespeare's sonnets might be the application of this sentiment to the relationship between the friends. The young man is beautiful and his beauty is identified with inner qualities of virtue and truth (22):

> For all that beauty that doth cover thee
> Is but the seemly raiment of my heart.

Beneath the perhaps conventional machinery of identification of the palpable presence of the young man with

The Alike and the Other

the poet's own life (in the sonnets of absence when they are physically separated) there is a much deeper realization of the ideal of identity within the poetry itself. It might be expressed as an equation: the friend's beauty = his inner truth and virtue = the poetry = the shared life of the friends = the world of the poet's imagination.

The progress of the friendship is not unlike that of a legend in which tests are applied to a truth invented by magic (the wand, corresponding to Prospero's, being here the picture of the relationship held up before the young man by the poet in his poetry). The magic garden is the shared life between the friends, in harmony with nature, but separate from the world. But the world intervenes with tests which lead to bitter disillusionment, and awareness of sin and evil. Perhaps it would not be altogether fanciful to suggest that on the outskirts of the magic garden the dark lady signifies the fall of both into the same evil in which they share their separateness: but whereby they become really separated.

Apart from that finality of separation which is the shared mistress, all the tests prove opposite things—act, as it were, in two ways. If they prove that the friend has faults, they also test the ability of the poet's love to accept such faults and transform them into the believing imagination, or to exorcise them by producing parallel faults of his own.

The friendship, idealized, provides a system of judging, pardoning, reconciling, transforming, the young man and the poet. I don't mean that what priests and neighbors might call evil is their good, but that they can, ideally, absorb evil within good, so that bad acts, although they provide the relation with severe tests, need not count as proving that they themselves are bad or that their relationship has failed. Indeed, they may do the opposite, as in 120:

> *That you were once unkind befriends me now, . . .*
> *. . . your trespass now becomes a fee;*
> *Mine ransoms yours, and yours must ransom me.*

The sonnets have religious feeling, but being concerned with a world totally transformed into the poetry, there is almost no feeling of an external judge who condemns, say, sensual faults. It is an Eden invented by the poet's imagination into which external values are not disregarded, but have been absorbed and re-invented.

If the poet reports that he has sinned, and that his sin is the equal of the young man's, the reader does not really believe this, because the world of the poet's imagination is profoundly moral, and encloses and reaches beyond any sin that he might commit. It is inevitably self-forgiving because it is self-created. By the same token, the friend's real failure is failure of imagination. He chooses the worst because he cannot imagine the best.

"There is nothing good or bad, but thinking makes it so," and "I could be bounded in a nut-shell, and count myself a king of infinite space," says Hamlet. The sonnets are dominated by such a thinking and controlling imagination. At the center of the world there is the simple awareness of the bare "I am." The poet is aware of primary naked existing behind all the externals of place and reputation, acts and station. This sense of simple being, separate from what the neighbors say

The Alike and the Other

about him, and even from his own actions and formed character, is elaborated in 121, where the poet seems to address his own soul:

> No, I am that I am, and they that level
> At my abuses reckon up their own:
> I may be straight, though they themselves be bevel;
> By their rank thoughts my deeds must not be shown;
> Unless this general evil they maintain,
> All men are bad, and in their badness reign.

At a first reading, the poet may appear simply to be saying that others' gossip about him is false, being a projection onto him of their own faults. This misses though the admissive opening:

> 'Tis better to be vile than vile esteem'd,
> When not to be receives reproach of being,
> And the just pleasure lost which is so deem'd
> Not by our feeling but by others' seeing:
> For why should others' false adulterate eyes
> Give salutation to my sportive blood?
> Or on my frailties why are frailer spies,
> Which in their wills count bad what I think good?

A disclaimer which seems to say that if the poet is ill thought of, he would best enjoy the pleasure for which he is blamed, and to which he therefore has a just claim, seems cynical. But here again the tone has from the first line onward a more somber color than the meaning. As the sonnet proceeds the meaning catches up, as it were, with the music, and the force of the irony is evident. The contrast is really between "false adulterate eyes" and "sportive blood"—that is to say, between those whose awareness is the object of their vices, who are evil, think evil, and see evil, who have become what they do—and the poet who spontaneously is his sportive blood. The sense of the sonnet is somewhat as follows: "If people blame me for what they think I do when I don't do it, then I might as well do it and enjoy the justice of my bad name. But what I do—or what they think I do—is something quite apart from what I am, and therefore my way of doing, which is to act out of my being, is different from theirs when they do the same thing: because they have become identical with their acts. They have no standard to judge me by but their lives, which are so tainted by their deeds that they and their deeds are identical. But whatever I do I remain what I am: and therefore my deeds may not be twisted to make me look as if I am the same as they. I should add that, if nevertheless I am bad, this is because the very quality of existence may be tainted at the source."

One has the sense of concentric circles of bad and less bad, the outer circle of which is the proposition "all men are bad." But at the center of all, that which maintains him is "No, I am that I am," the final inviolable fortress of an awareness of his own being, separate from the actions which he shares with all, and therefore not at all to be condemned or fixed down by others' opinions because forever escaping into unscathed, ever-renewed, and renewing existence.

It is frequently pointed out that Shakespeare's view of life is aristocratic. In the sonnets, what this means is clear. Aristocracy is original being which has purity and

The Alike and the Other

integrity. It is perhaps the result of birth, but at any rate contains intrinsic virtue (symbolized by the rose) which he who *is*, must not corrupt or betray. Original virtue is planted truth and where there is external beauty, its only value is to correspond to this. There is the idea of continuity that runs from root, through bough, to flower and fruit, through the seasons, through history, through individual human life. "Ripeness is all."

Aristocracy of being is the inherited pride and virtue of living in a way that remains true to origins—origins which reach back to a supposed antiquity, when men lived close to their own natures and in harmony with external nature. It is originality, not in the smart modern sense, but in the sense of remaining true to origins. The rose symbolizes the confluence of natural being with human breeding: this is realized as external beauty, aristocratic worth, and virtue in a person. It signals as it were the vision of a journey back to unadulterated times, "When beauty lived and died as flowers do now,/ Before these bastard signs of fair were born" (68).

Some of the most searching sonnets are those which explore worldliness, or society, or tasks that vitiate being, making it the object of what it does and undertakes. We hardly believe the poet when he tells us he has transgressed, but we can believe in his mood of self-doubt when he chides the fortune that

> . . . did not better for my life provide
> Than public means which public manners breeds.

Here is the difference between transgression which is active and does not necessarily taint being, and occupation in the world, society, routine, which may do so.

Religion in the sonnets is an aspect of that wholeness, that continuum of the natural, benevolent forces which derive from the past and reach in an unbroken line toward the future. It is of the universe of the "star that guides my moving" and "points on me graciously with fair aspect." It is at least one aspect of the truth that is realized in the beauty of the friend, love for whom, as J. B. Leishmann points out, is embued with religious feeling. That this love should be spontaneously devout emphasizes the extent to which Shakespeare's *pietas* includes the religious as part of the universe, a correctness of feeling rather than as external authority—though sometimes religion is authority, as in 146, "Poor Soul, the centre of my sinful earth." Here, in a mood curiously suggesting a religious sonnet of Donne, the poet turns away from human love, and seeks the divine in Death, that "feeds on men."

The religious mood is more often what I would call adjectival. With a tact that depends on a kind of sleight of hand whereby, when he is comparing his love to the divine, he keeps our attention on the holy, he surrounds his human love sometimes with Christian trophies, sometimes pagan ones. Sonnet 68 refers to pre-Christian antiquity, pursuing the theme that the friend reincarnates through the truth of his being, within a false present, the ideal past:

> *In him those holy antique hours are seen,*
> *Without all ornament, itself and true.*

The Christianly devout 31 employs the same theme to different effect. Now the friend is strangely and marvelously seen as "the grave where buried love doth live."

The Alike and the Other

All those whom the poet has loved and mourned are discovered in the bosom of the friend. This fulfillment is orchestrated with imagery and music so solemn, ceremonious, and devout that the poetry produces a sense of religious awe. We do not have time to reflect that the lines beginning, "How many a holy and obsequious tear /Hath dear religious love stol'n from mine eye," leading to the cult of the young man in whom these things are supposed to lie hidden, are almost idolatrous. In 105, Shakespeare takes up, not very seriously, the charge that his love is idolatrous and dismisses it, ingeniously, by discovering in it a metaphor for the Trinity, illustrated by the three virtues—"fair, kind, and true"—which are present in the one being of the young man. "Three themes in one, which wondrous scope affords."

The love for the young man may verge on idolatry but it is not blasphemous. That he should call it religious love, and that he should return so often to the theme of the one, the only one, shows clearly that his love for the friend was of a kind in which there was belief: perhaps one kind of belief fortified by other kinds. He believed in the friend's virtue corresponding to his beauty; and this virtue opened onto the universe, antiquity, and religion. Also there was the belief which wrestles with unbelief: belief that, despite all bad appearances, the beauty of the friend did not lie, or that beneath the lie it still corresponded to deeply submerged truth which could be exhumed. Perhaps the idea of redemption helped here, and religious belief comes in again in a different way.

It is necessary to consider the young man more closely. Clearing our minds of preconceptions, if we read the sonnets simply accepting what they tell us about him, what impression would we get? The first thing that would strike us is, I think, that he has opposite characteristics. He is divided between his ideal nature, corresponding to his outward beauty, and his actual behavior, which is shown to be cold, self-seeking, proud, and corrupt.

On the one hand the poet reiterates the theme of "kind and true" and "For nothing this wide universe I call, /Save thou, my rose; in it thou art my all" (109). On the other hand the rose is cankered (95):

> How sweet and lovely dost thou make the shame
> Which, like a canker in the fragrant rose,
> Doth spot the beauty of thy budding name!

On the one hand the young man is pure essence; on the other hand he is essence tainted at the source.

Shakespeare was, of course, addressing the sonnets to the friend. He was not making a word portrait of him, and we attempt to deduce his character from things written to him, about him. What we see are two things, characteristics which the poet doubtless found present in the real young man, but which are so idealized that it is difficult to form a realistic picture from them: and, opposite to this, references to the friend's lasciviousness, sensual faults, coldness, falsity, and his ill reputation, a kind of counter-image held up before his eyes as a terrible example. One cannot but be reminded of the scene in which Hamlet holds up before his mother's eyes "the counterfeit presentment of two brothers," one with "a station like the herald Mercury," the other "like a mildew'd ear."

The Alike and the Other

From reading the sonnets and making my own deductions—which may be very different from those of other readers—the picture I have is of a person who produced in the minds of others the double impression of the self-fixated. The doubleness in such people consists essentially in their being loved, but being unable to love back in return, through the cold self-sufficiency and self-attachment which is the result of their very beauty. They like to be loved partly because being loved is reflected self-admiration, but partly also because they would themselves perhaps like to love and think that through being loved they may learn to do so. The combination of beauty, coldness, and desire to learn to love, gives them a kind of purity. But in their behavior they may be corrupt because they accept, with involuntary indifference, whatever love they get, though they retain the air of perpetual seeking. What they are genuinely seeking is those qualities which they lack. When such a person is loved by an artist, he has the attraction of being an empty vessel, a blank page into which the admirer can read his own ideal.

Shaw points out that however much Shakespeare may have suffered on account of the dark lady, it is wrong to regard him as a victim. She can hardly have been happy reading about herself in 127, 130, and 138. The same holds good for the young man, whose behavior the sonnets analyze and excoriate. From the internal evidence of the sonnets he sometimes tried to answer accusation with counter-accusation. In 120 the poet admits in lines close to doggerel:

> For if you were by my unkindness shaken
> As I by yours, you've pass'd a hell of time,

Stephen Spender

> *And I, a tyrant, have no leisure taken*
> *To weigh how once I suffer'd in your crime.*

There are critics who idealize the young man and others who abhor him. But the poet's attitude to the friend is hardly discussed; and there is surely an element of unfairness in putting pressure on him to be something that he is not, and of then turning on him because he has failed to be the ideal. The poet seems often as much in love with the picture in his mind of the arranged relationship of complete mutuality as with the young man, who has to fit into this picture.

Yet so long as the poet continued to write sonnets I think that he must have believed in some ultimate quality of pure being which resided in the young man, under the misbehavior and the falsity. Even after bitter disillusionment he reverts to the purity of the original concept; in 105, for example:

> *Kind is my love to-day, to-morrow kind,*
> *Still constant in a wondrous excellence.*

So the sonnets express the conflict between idealization of the young man as the living equal of the poet's imaginings, and the realization that he is different from this. Sometimes the difference is analyzed as betrayal, sometimes the poet endeavors to find a basis on which he can accept it and yet retain the relationship. Sonnet 36 is an extreme example of acceptance of difference, in which he admits that their ways must be separate: "Let me confess that we two must be twain" and yet their "undivided loves are one." He invents metaphors for the

The Alike and the Other

relationship which suggest a rethinking of what it really is or must be. In 37, it is of father and son, and, indeed, where the young man fails, it tends to shift from the pattern of mutuality to that of a son whose errors are seen and suffered and forgiven by a loving father. In 33, contemplating the withdrawal of the "sun" into the "region cloud," the poet resumes the pun in the couplet with:

Yet him for this my love no whit disdaineth;
Suns of the world may stain when heaven's sun staineth.

In 93, desperation drives the poet to the metaphor of a "deceived husband"; and frequently he is a slave who tends upon, and waits for, his lord.

Whether one thinks, as I do, that Shakespeare continued, in spite of everything, to love and (like a forgiving father) believe in the young man, or that the disillusionment of realization led to his regarding him only (or with very little qualification of charitable feeling) as a subject for irony, affects one's interpretation of the very important 94, "They that have power to hurt and will do none."

After a very close analysis, William Empson concludes (in *Some Versions of Pastoral*) that this sonnet expresses almost total contempt for the friend. The contempt is qualified only by the poet discovering, through his pretending to praise what he does not admire, "a way of praising W. H. in spite of everything."

It is not possible here to argue my way through Empson's close analysis, for which I have great respect. My disagreement with him is not in disputing his interpretation of references and complexities of meaning in particular phrases, but because I think that, through the irony and the realization, there seems to me a note of exhortation which still clings to belief, and which arises from a love that endures. In a word, I would say the sonnet found "a way of *loving* in spite of everything," rather than, or as well as, a way of praising. The love is cruel, but praise would be nothing except cruel and contradictory, since it means praising what the poet did not regard as praiseworthy. If it is praise, the sonnet is, as Empson notes, an "evasion." But if it is love, it is more in the nature of a desperate warning.

My argument is clear if I say that the two last lines of the previous sonnet (93), "How like Eve's apple doth thy beauty grow, /If thy sweet virtue answer not thy show!" are more exhortatory than condemnatory. The poet still clings to the hope that even if while the young man's face shows nothing but sweet love (". . . heaven in thy creation did decree /That in thy face sweet love should ever dwell") his heart (unlike others whose false hearts show in the "wrinkles strange" of their faces) may be false—that even so, he can, by an effort of willing truth, make inner being conform to the outward appearance of love. The kind of exertion required is not of making a lie true, but of making what is true, which has for some perverse reason become falsified, revert to its real nature, become true again. It is an argument based on love which appeals to the imagination to realize in action the truth which exists. It is a creative attitude different from a modern irony, though of course it uses irony. In fact it is very much the type of argument which Hamlet uses to his mother when, showing her the pictures of her two husbands, he appeals to her to use her eyes (her inner eyes) in

The Alike and the Other

order to make a choice which is imposed on her simply by her seeing which is false and which is true.

Condensing the argument of 94, the desperate appeal, based on a cool appreciation of the young man's nature, seems to me of this kind: "If you are cold and self-centered as I have now come to realize you are, then you may perhaps participate in the power, justice, and virtue of those who are detached from passion, but who nevertheless control the lives of others; but to be like them, you must have the virtue of coldness which is chastity. You are, after all, more like the funereal lily than the generous rose; but remember that when the cold are false, their corruption is far more evil than that of the warm." The thought is perhaps that the warm, being essentially more alive (and not like stone) go on being capable of self-renewal and repentance.

This is very much the attitude that a father, himself believing in the personal values of human relations and love and imagination, might feel toward a much-loved son, whom he discovered to be of a cold nature, but possessed of beauty and power to entrap others. The father does not cease to love his son, but begins to realize that his moral character will be ruined, unless he match his power with scrupulousness, his coldness with chastity. Otherwise the corruption of his personality will be worse than that of a person who is lascivious but warm-hearted, and because warm-hearted, capable of contrition and change.

The sonnet expresses, of course, a change of attitude, coming—as 93 and 95, the sonnets on each side of it, show—from a shock of realization of the deep corruption of the young man.

That the powerful are praised has surprised many

readers. Previously, although a world of power has been taken for granted, it has not been discussed; it has remained the background to personal relations. But suddenly the poet expresses his admiration for the cold and powerful. If one remembers once again that the sonnets are one side of a dialogue, this is not so surprising. Number 94 was written perhaps during a phase when the poet was most critical of the friend's character. Surely, the friend may have said to the poet: "The truth is that your sorts of people are not mine. The people I admire are the great and powerful, and I want to belong to them." In this case the sonnet may be seen as taking up the theme, accepting, with whatever undertones of bitterness and despair, that the friend might belong to this other world, but using the acceptance as another way of hammering in the lesson of pure being.

Although 94 expresses such a shift from personal to public values, from the imagination to the world of power, the thematic material introduced in the sestet, which indicates the presence of the young man, remains the same as in earlier sonnets.

In fact the poem takes the form of a general statement about the virtues of the great and powerful, in the octave and then, in the sestet, applies this to the young man.

The octave is, as it were, a different voice, not quite that of the poet, but to which the poet assents, indeed lends his gift, stating a case in the strongest and most favorable terms.

The case is that those who are great and powerful and who, although they might do so, do not use their power to cause others pain—those who, while making others act, remain immovable themselves, and are un-

The Alike and the Other

tempted, incorruptible—merit their position. There is a feeling of rendering unto Caesar that which is Caesar's. There is irony, but there is also assent. Angelo, in *Measure for Measure*, is admired so long as he remains cold and powerful. It is when he becomes lascivious and corrupt that he appears far worse than the carnal sinners on whom he sits in judgment.

In the first line of the sestet the young man appears in a guise with which we have been made familiar very early on, in fact in the first sonnet, where we read of the young man, ". . . thou, contracted to thine own bright eyes, /Feeds't thy light's flame with self-substantial fuel." Here he is the summer's flower, "to the summer sweet, /Though to itself it only live and die." * The position is restated. In the first sonnet the self-sufficient lovely boy is asked to marry. Later he is asked to love the friend. Now he is being warned that perhaps he would do well to model himself on the coldly powerful, since he is himself cold. But if he does so, let him remain like them, solitary, chaste. If he does not do so, the lily (which he has chosen to become rather than the rose to which he has previously been compared) will, festering, "smell far worse than weeds."

Doubtless there is irony here, and bitterness, but what seems to me the strongest feeling is a despairing acceptance of the young man's coldness combined with an equally despairing warning.

---

* The "summer's flower" is, surely, the rose. I cannot agree with Empson when he suggests that "the summer's flower" is the apple blossom of Eve's apple, referred to in the couplet of 93. For one thing, apple blossom is not a summer flower.

Stephen Spender

The first seventeen sonnets are usually, as I have noted above, regarded as being outside the main series. They are so, but they are also a kind of prelude, and throw light on the character of the friend.

Here, when the poet is exhorting the friend to marry, he also makes very apparent the reasons why he should not do so. They are that he is concentrated on, almost married to, his own image. The arguments used to persuade him to marry are that a son would provide, as it were, a mirror projecting the image of that beauty which culminates in his face now, into the future (13):

> O, that you were yourself! but, love, you are
> No longer yours than you yourself here live.

So while the friend is warned of the dangers of "having traffic with thyself alone," the poet nevertheless shares with him the view that he is the paragon. The poet puts himself at the young man's side fighting for the cause which is that a means should be found to perpetuate his beauty exactly as it now is. The poet offers two means of achieving this result. One is fathering a child, and the other, which plays an even more persistent part in the sequence, is the poetry. Sonnet 17 unites these two themes in the culminating couplet:

> But were some child of yours alive that time,
> You should live twice; in it and in my rhyme.

So that while the poet dutifully uses the poetry to urge the friend to marriage, his verse itself is advertized as a means of achieving the same result as a son might do. In

The Alike and the Other

a manner of speaking, both child and poetry are mirrors of the young man's own face.

The modern reader may well be tempted to condemn the obvious narcissism of the friend, which Shakespeare exploits so much as argument. But it should be noted that Shakespeare does not appear to condemn it, though he may, later, deplore its callous effects. But he is in complete agreement with the friend as to his beauty, as though it is a value which both share, the young man having his face, and the poet having his poetry, which he identifies with the lovely boy. The poet has an attitude towards the young man's beauty which seems exactly the same as that of the young man himself. Both regard it as a unique value which must by every means possible be preserved.

The young man's narcissism—which, versed in modern psychology, we are apt to condemn—may indeed have been precious to the poet. For it is very difficult in the world of the sonnets to draw a line between the young man's self-regard—which the poet supports—and the claims that the poet makes for his immortal verse. To us, the readers, they may seem very different, but given the extraordinary aesthetic cult of the young man's external appearance, which is central to the sonnets, they may seem the same thing. Again and again the argument is put forward that the poetry is the immortalization of the young man's beauty. The boy's beauty has the inestimable virtue of being life. The virtue of the poetry is as a perpetuating mirror which freezes on its bright surface the fleeting image which will die. The attraction of the young man is that of all life, made incarnate in an incomparable beauty of form.

Stephen Spender

Narcissus fell in love with himself, but the water in which he gazed at his reflection surely also fell in love with his image. The mirror is in love with the mirrored because it becomes the gazer—that which the gazer never succeeds in doing himself. The poet through his poetry can retain the beauty which the friend himself is bound to lose. Moreover, the poet is changed into the beauty of the youth by virtue of retaining that image in his heart (22):

> My glass shall not persuade me I am old,
> So long as youth and thou are of one date . . .

Most critics are puzzled by the insistence of the poet on the contrast between his "chopped antiquity" and the young man's beauty and youth. Nothing is really less surprising. For a relationship which is based on the idea of identity is inevitably upset by dissonances. So the great and perhaps excessive insistence on the immortality of the poetry in these poems is a claim made not for the poet but for the friend. It is he who is going to survive in these lines, we are told through many variations (63):

> His beauty shall in these black lines be seen,
> And they shall live, and he in them still green.

So the poet was occupied in giving back, by the means of his poetry, the image of the friend to himself. To us this bargain seems unequal, because all we have of the young man is the written words, which are Shakespeare's self. We should remember, though, that for the poet, the

The Alike and the Other

matter was different. He was taking life in its miraculous complexity and giving back words. The fact that the words are so marvelous is due (or may have seemed to him due) to the fact that the living reality was of such extraordinary value. Occasionally, for example, in 53, we experience the impact of million-faceted flesh, worshipped as the moment of beauty never matched in all past time:

> What is your substance, whereof are you made,
> That millions of strange shadows on you tend?

The mirror image constantly occurs in the sonnets. There is also implicitly the idea of two mirrors reflecting one another with rays that reach into infinity. When the "lovely boy" looks into the friend's poetry, he sees not only his own image, but that the physical presence of the poet has been changed into that beauty.

Perhaps the significance of the narcissism of the friend may be that if the narcissist has a character that requires a mirror, the artist also requires a mirror of life in which to see his art. As Hoelderlin observed in *Socrates and Alcibiades*, "often in the end the wise pay homage to the most beautiful." The world of art or thought which fills the mind of genius is essentially lonely. He finds it least of all reflected in the minds of other artists, and the public. He seeks it therefore in the beautiful, particularly among those in whom nature seems to have flowered spontaneously without the interruption of too much intellectual process. The narcissist, in his self-cultivation (Montherlant describes the poet as one who gives himself up to "noble self-cultivation") may appear to have an affinity with the artist. The narcissist might be described as a living poem going in search of a poet.

At the same time, the discovery that the narcissist is vulgar, that his self-absorption and isolation do not prevent his belonging to the "region cloud," that he will look in any broken fragment of glass to see the same reflection of himself, is inevitable. But there was a time in the sonnets when the young man's beauty seemed of the season which is fresh in nature and which was also incomparably fresh in Shakespeare's poetry.

The failure was that of the poet to discover his own inner being mirrored—as it should have been—in the young man's external beauty, and leading there to the love in which they shared their being. The poetry is a plea to him to be true to his own appearance, and in doing this, true to the poet's imagination.

In one way, the sonnets may be regarded as a dramatization of the theme that—wherever it appears—seems to spring more directly than any other from the heart of the poet—the theme of simple truth standing alone against the world of lies. It is the cry of Troilus:

> *I am as true as truth's simplicity,*
> *And simpler than the infancy of truth,*

echoed in Sonnet 82, where comparing his claims with those of the other poet, and of other admirers, he strikes to the heart, which should be both their hearts, but remains only his own:

> *. . . yet when they have devised*
> *What strained touches rhetoric can lend,*

The Alike and the Other

*Thou truly fair wert truly sympathized
In true plain words by thy true-telling friend.*

Sonnet 66 ("Tired with all these, for restful death I cry") is a complex statement of the case of simple truth against worldliness. "Desert a beggar born," "needy nothing trimm'd in jollity," "purest faith unhappily forsworn," "gilded honour shamefully misplaced,"—the world is characterized as that place where the tares flourish, the good seed is choked at birth. Even stronger than the idea of injustice is that of *contra naturam*, that human beings are surrounded by the example of a benevolent nature whose rightness they acknowledge, but which they deny, pervert, destroy. There is of course an unnaturalness of nature, which is the bad seed, the withered tree, and it is exactly this which is reflected in most human institutions. Through the whole sonnet there runs the suppressed metaphor of a plant which grows naturally from seed to branches, leaves, flowers, and fruit where the natural should attain its just fulfillment but everywhere the world denies such an unstunted growth.

The relationship with the dark lady is corruption of, or being raped by, the world. That with the friend is the struggle to share with another the poet's vision of true being. To the reader, coming four hundred years later, who knows that the poet is a supreme genius and who sees the character of the friend exposed to examination under the withering light of that gift, the attempt may seem doomed, and he may even come to think of the sonnets as an ironically intended exposure of the young man's folly and corruptibility. Myself, I cannot, as I have pointed out, accept this view, because I think that it is to misunderstand the relation of the poet to surrounding life, which is often exemplified in the relationship of a particular artist to a particular person (Keats and Fanny Brawne would provide a parallel example). The poet may be conscious of his outstanding genius in employing the techniques of his art, he may feel that his formulations endow his name with immortality, but nevertheless the purpose to which he puts his talents is to create the unique awareness of simply being alive in a world of other living beings. Anyone endowed with sufficient consciousness would, ideally, share the awareness of the life that is realized by the artist. Since the expression of awareness of life is what he is concerned with, he will feel that he could share that awareness with a truthful person who was made similarly conscious of the significance of existing. This is the truth that Shakespeare tries to inculcate into the young man. So long as he loves his friend, he loves in him that external beauty and potentiality for inner truth which he believes to be alive. His so-called irony is simply his concern with tearing away the veils of lies which cover over the truth of the ultimately real being of the young man.

The poetry is concerned with the continuum of true and simple being, and it is this which the poet seeks in other people. There are two places where it might be found. One where the truth that is beauty is reflected in the virtue of the inner life which is the boy. The friend is praised as that being who in terms of physical appearance matched by inward virtue corresponds to the life of the imagination.

The other place where the poet might escape from

The Alike and the Other

the paradoxical solitude of life which everywhere is repudiated in living, might be through the very opposite: the evil, the lustful, the damned, the dark lady.

In the event, however, that the friend and the dark lady, in one another's arms, are, in their relation to the poet, the same, both of them are the other. Both of them are the world. In neither of them does he discover that identity which is his imagination, that life which made Keats exclaim, "What shocks the virtuous philosopher, delights the camelion poet."

Does not the quotation from Keats' letter to Woodhouse throw light on the relationship of Shakespeare with the young man and the dark lady? "A Poet is the most unpoetical of anything in existence; because he has no identity—he is continually in for—and filling some other body—the Sun, the Moon, the Sea and Men and Women who are creatures of impulse and poetical and have about them an unchangeable attribute—the poet has none; no identity—he is certainly the most unpoetical of God's creatures."

The paradox that Keats here explores is that to the poet the supreme value is being, whereas other people become the objects of their ambitions and impulses. The poet is concerned with the essential nature of being, and he seeks this in the nature and the other lives around him. It is just this which Shakespeare, in the sonnets, does not, in the long run, find in the young man, who ought but does not have a soul which reflects the marvelous life revealed by nature in his physical appearance.

The negative capability that seeks to enter into all the aspects of life, lives in a perpetual solitude. Hence the greatest sonnets are those of generalized truth, lessons plucked from experience, which lead beyond the young man or the dark lady to tell us of the power of the image of beauty pondered by love to resist the ravages of time (19, 55, 64, 65); or to upbraid the incorrigible vice of societies which is to subject the just demands of humble individual being to those of institutionalized or powerful interest (66); or to analyze coldly, devastatingly, and finally the degradation of lust separated from love (129); and greatest of all to uphold the impregnable power of a contract freely entered into by lovers whose minds are equal in truth and in trust (116).

When one considers these themes and a few others, questions about the nature of the relationship between the three protagonists tend to evaporate in the truths beyond questions gained. The autobiographical element reduces itself to what it simply is: the price paid in bitter experience by the poet for his knowledge, wrested out of such opportunities and conditions as were provided by his time, and extending the territories of the live imagination.

R. P. BLACKMUR

A Poetics
for Infatuation

THERE WILL never be, I hope, by some chance of scholarship, any more authoritative order for Shakespeare's sonnets than that so dubiously supplied by the 1609 Quarto. It is rather like Pascal's *Pensées*, or, even better, like the *order* of the Psalms, as to matters of date or interest. No one can improve upon the accidentally established order we possess; but everyone can invite himself to feel the constant interflow of new relations, of new reticulations—as if the inner order were always on the move—in the sonnets, the *Pensées*, the Psalms. Thus the vitality of fresh disorder enters the composition and finds room there with every reading, with every use and every abuse we make of them. Each time we look at a set of things together but do not count them, the sum of the impression will be different, though the received and accountable numerical order remains the same. If we complain of other people's perceptions, it is because we feel there is greater vitality in our own; and so on; we had better persist with the received order as a warrant that all of us have at least that point in common.

That point is worth a good deal more with Shakespeare's sonnets than with Pascal or the psalmist. It is thought that the text follows that of original manuscripts or fair copies, and no intuition bids me think otherwise. Furthermore, till private interests rise, the sequence we have seems sensible with respect to their sentiments, and almost a "desirable" sequence with respect to the notion of development. Anyone who feels weak about this should try reading the sonnets backwards all the way; they will turn themselves round again from their own force. At any rate numbers 1 to 17 make a preparatory exercise for the theme which emerges in number 18 and continues through number 126. With number 127 there is a break, not to a new theme, but to a new level or phase of the old theme which lasts through number 152. The remaining pair of sonnets sound a light echo on an ancient model, but with fashionable rhetoric, of the devouring general theme.

That theme is infatuation: its initiation, cultivation, and history, together with its peaks of triumph and devastation. The whole collection makes a poetics for infatuation, or to use a slight elaboration of Croce's phrase, it gives to infatuation a theoretic form. The condition of infatuation is a phase of life; not limited to sexual attraction, though usually allied with it, it also modifies or exacerbates many matters besides—espe-

A Poetics for Infatuation

cially, it would seem in these sonnets, matters having to do with the imaginative or poetic powers. The story of Pygmalion is one of several ultimate forms of infatuation, and Pygmalion is a name for sonnet after sonnet because the problem of personal infatuation is turned into a problem in poetics. If I cannot have my love, I will create it, but with never a lessening, always an intensification of the loss, the treachery, the chaos in reality; to say this is to say something about what is over-riding whenever we think either of infatuation or poetics. The maxim was never made overt but it was latent—in the undercurrent of the words—throughout much of the Renaissance: If God is reality, I must contend with him even more than I accept him, whether as lover or as poet. So it is in the sonnets. Like all of Shakespeare, they contain deep grasping notions for poetics; and this is precisely, as we master these notions, how we make most use of his poetry. We beset reality.

Let us see. The first seventeen sonnets are addressed to a beautiful young man who seems unwilling to settle down and have children. They could be used by any institute of family relations, and they must have been a great nuisance to any young man who received them. The most they tell him is that he cannot stop with himself (which is just blooming), that he cannot conquer time and mortality and reach immortality (which do not now concern him), and indeed that he can hardly continue to exist unless he promptly begets him a son. If these sonnets were paintings by Titian they would swarm with naked children—little Eroses, or putti—but Venus would be missing; there is no bride in the marriage. The argument of these first sonnets proceeds with an end in view; the prudent member speaks; but there's no premise, and no subject. There was no real "young man" in these poems—though he could be invited in. As they stand, Shakespeare was addressing, not a young man, but one of his unaccomplished selves; the self that wants progeny addressing one of the selves that does not. The voices of the children in the apple trees can be heard whenever this set of the sonnets stops in the mind: a deep strain in us all. Perhaps it is this strain in the feelings that makes Shakespeare the poet address the other fellow as the unwilling father—the chap who never answers. Montaigne's thoughts on the affections of fathers for their children (II–VIII) reach the same sort of points Shakespeare dandles a little, but cannot yet accept, in Sonnets 15 to 17. "And I know not whether I would not rather have brought forth one child perfectly formed by commerce with the Muses than by commerce with my wife." Sonnet 17 goes only so far as to offer both immortalities, the child and the rhyme.

In 18 ("Shall I compare thee to a summer's day?") there is a rise in poetic power and the poetic claim is made absolute. At the same time the "young man" gains in presence and particularity, and the emotion begins to ring. The "other" self has been changed. Where the lover had been using verses around a convention, now the poet is using love both to master a convention and to jack up his self-confidence. This is of course only the blessed illusion of *poiesis:* that what *poiesis* seizes is more certain (as it is more lasting) than any operation of the senses. The couplet illuminates:

> So long as men can breathe or eyes can see,
> So long lives this and this gives life to thee.

A Poetics for Infatuation

There is a burst of splendor in the tautology of "this." Every essence is eternal, but Shakespeare wants his eternity in time (which, as Blake says, is the mercy of eternity). He keeps both "thy eternal summer" and his own "eternal lines," and these are the tautology of "this." But the sonnet contains also premonitions of the later Shakespeare, especially in the seventh and eighth lines where *we cannot trim sail to nature's course,* and it is this sentiment which haunts the whole poem, its special presence which we get by heart. Shakespeare hung about not only where words were (as Auden says the poet must) but also where sentiments were to be picked up. A good poem (or bad) is always a little aside from its particular subject; a good (or bad) hope from its object; or fear from its horror. Shakespeare could take the nightmare *in* nature as an aspect of unaccommodated man—whether on the heath in *Lear* or in the waste places of private love. At any rate, in this "this" sonnet there is a change in the theoretic form one makes in order to abide nature, a change from convention to *poiesis.* Poetry seizes the eternal essence, and the substance (here the poem) ceases to matter. We *give up* the fertile self; one illusion succeeds another, one self another self. The last illusion would be to create or find the second self of second sight. For this a poem is our nearest substitute and furthest reach.

Sonnet 19 ("Devouring Time, blunt thou the lion's paws") comes, for this argument, as a natural digression, where Shakespeare announces and explicates the doctrine of rival creation (creation not adding to but changing God's creation). If in this sonnet we understand time to be God in Nature, the matter becomes plain. We save what is ours, we save what we have made of it: beauty's *pattern* to succeeding *men.* Only the pattern saves and salves. Even the phoenix burns in the blood; only in "my verse" shall the phoenix of my love "ever live young." Perhaps this is to take this sonnet too seriously, for it may be only an expression of vanity —yet vanity may be as near as we come to expressing our doctrine, and vainglory, in this world of time, as near to glory. Poetry is a kind of vainglory in which we are ever young.

Sonnet 19 is not only a digression, it is a nexus to number 20 ("A woman's face with nature's own hand painted") where the notion of verse—or love—ever-young sets up a fright. That in us which is immortal is never free of time's attainder. Nothing in us is free, for there is no necessity with which we can cope. We cope with what passes away, necessity leaves us behind. Whenever immortal longings are felt, one begins to learn dread of the immortal. Who has not seen this in the pupils of his beloved's eyes?—that if the immortal is the ultimate form of paradise, it is the immediate form of hell. *One's firmest decision is only the early form of what transpires as a wrong guess.* In the sonnets Shakespeare deals with the reckless firmness of such untranspired decisions, and I would suppose this sentiment to be in vital analogy to the puzzle-phrase of Sonnet 20— "the master-mistress of my passion"—and is a phrase at the very heart of the dialectics of infatuation (which is a lower stage of poetics, as our master Plato shows in his *Phaedrus*). Master-mistress of my passion! It is the woman in me cries out, the smothering cry of *Hysterica Passio,* which Lear would have put down as a climbing sorrow. The notion is worth arresting us. Poetics, hysteria, and

A *Poetics for Infatuation*

love are near together—and the nearer when their mode is infatuation. In Sonnet 20 Shakespeare "found" (we may find) the *fabric* of what we call his sonnets—his second-best bed—the fabric, the chinese silk or Egyptian cotton or West of England cloth or Scotch voile or some animal fur to your choice—some membrane to your touch. Shakespeare is *il miglior fabbro* in another sense than either Dante or Eliot had in mind; he found the fabric of raised feeling. But when I say "found" I do not mean that Shakespeare (or we) thought it up. It was the other side of the lamp post or when you opened the bulkhead of the cellar in your father's house. I cannot speak of the particulars: but I fasten for one moment on the rhyme (lines 10 and 12) of "thee fell a-doting" and "my purpose nothing." What is that aspirate doing there in that completing rhyme? Is it the breath of doting in nothing? It was behind the lamp post and in the cellar; and what did Hamlet say to his father's ghost? If that is not enough to get from a rhyme, let us go back to the distich of lines 7 and 8. Here bawdiness is compounded with metaphysics in the new simple: the master-mistress:

A man in hue all 'hues' in his controlling,
Which steals men's eyes and women's souls amazeth.

There is a rhyme of meaning here if not of sound between "controlling" and "amazeth," and the one confirms the other; it is one of the many places where Dante and Shakespeare rhyme—I do not say they are identical —in what they signify. In Canto XIX of the *Purgatorio* Dante converts a thought into a dream of the Siren, and in that dream things change as he wills, all hues are in his controlling, for the object of attention changes complexion or color—*colors*—as love wills: *come amor vuol, così le colorava*. The second line in Shakespeare's distich is the confirmation. The hues attract, draw, *steal* men's eyes, but penetrate, discombobolate, *amaze* the souls or psyches of women. There are infinite opportunities but no direction. A minotaur lives at the heart of this dream which if it lasted would become bad, but the dream wakes in the last line: "Mine be thy love, and thy love's use their treasure."

If you do not like the minotaur with Theseus and Ariadne, then let us repeat that word which superbly rhymes with itself: Narcissus. If so we must leave Narcissus at once and come again to Pygmalion. Narcissus and Pygmalion are at the two extremes of every infatuation. Of Pygmalion alone we had a hint in Sonnet 9 and again in 15 to 17; but in Sonnet 21 we begin to move toward the poetic Pygmalion making not Galatea but Narcissus. In short we come on Pygmalion and the rival poet, the poet who cannot tell the truth but only its convention. Pygmalion works in private on the making of his Narcissus.

If we follow the rival poet, he can only be the will o' the wisp of another self—in reality the anticipation of this self, and so on. We are among the executive hypocrisies by which we get along. Treachery becomes a fount of insight and a mode of action. Indeed, there is a honeypot of treachery in every loving mind, and to say so is no more than a mild expansion of these lines:

> And then believe me, my love is as fair
> As any mother's child, . . .

A Poetics for Infatuation

When there is infatuation of soul or body in it, love is always my child. Sonnet 22 has two examples, one of the child, the other of the treachery. There is:

> For all that beauty that doth cover thee
> Is but the seemly raiment of my heart

where the child exaggerates, perhaps corrects, certainly gets ahead of, the father; and, for the treachery,

> O, therefore, love, be of thyself so wary
> As I, not for myself, but for thee will;

—lines which tell that wonderful, necessary lie without which we could not tolerate the trespass we know that our affections make upon others: I love you on your account, not mine, for yourself not myself: a lie which can be true so far as Pygmalion and Narcissus make it so. When I say love, I speak of Eros and Philia but not of Agape who is with the sun and moon and other stars, and under their influences torn to other shreds. I think, too, of Rilke's Prodigal Son who ran away because he could not abide the love around the house. Shakespeare, however, in the couplet, lets the pride of lions loose—the very first *terribilità* in the sonnets:

> Presume not on thy heart when mine is slain;
> Thou gavest me thine, not to give back again.

In short, you are nothing but what I created. Put out that child.

However accidentally it is achieved, the sonnets proceed, at least from Sonnet 23 through Sonnet 40, in an order wholly appropriate to the natural consequences of the position reached in Sonnet 22. If we insist on what we have made ourselves, nothing else can serve us much. As we find this and that unavailable we find ourselves subject to the appropriate disorders that belong to our infatuation and the worse disorders—the order of the contingent or actual world—which seem to attack us because we think we have no part in them. The disorders are all familiar; it is the condition of infatuation that makes it impossible for us to ignore them and undesirable to understand them: our intimacy with them frights us out of sense, or so to speak raises the temperature of sense a little into fever. So we find Shakespeare, in his confrontation of the young man, feeling himself the imperfect actor, inadequate to his role and troubled by himself and the world, and all for fear of trust—of himself or of others.

> So I, for fear of trust, forget to say
> The perfect ceremony of love's rite . . .

The rival poet is in the twelfth line, "More than that tongue that more hath more express'd"—where "more" becomes an ugly accusation indeed from a man "o'er charg'd with burden of mine own love's might." To self-inadequacy is added, as if it were a double self, a new, and worse, and inextinguishable self-love, which at one moment asserts eternal strength and at the next fears im-

A Poetics for Infatuation

potence and cries out for fresh "apparel on my totter'd loving." Infatuation does not fill every moment and would not exist at all if one were not half the time outside it. The *miseria* of infatuation is in the work necessary to preserve it *together* with the work necessary sometimes to escape it; and *ennui* is always around the last and next corner—the last and next turning—of *miseria*. It is *ennui* that gives infatuation its sharpest turn. Sonnet 29 ("When in disgrace with fortune and men's eyes") is a poem of *ennui*, but is also (and perhaps consequently) a true monument of self-pity—of ambition, career, profession, as well as infatuation: all places where one finds oneself "desiring this man's art, and that man's scope." It is in T. S. Eliot's *Ash Wednesday* —*his* monument to self-pity—that this line is used with the word "art" changed to "gift." Love is only a refuge as it was only an excuse for percciving all this. It may be less Christian of me but I prefer Shakespeare's word and if I had to make a substitution, I would use "deep skill." Sonnet 30 ("When to the sessions of sweet silent thought") carries on this theme of self-pity which no writer of the first rank—and I think no composer—has been able to avoid, and makes in the first quatrain a human splendor of it. The splendor was so great that nothing could be done with it; so he made a couplet. One engages in self-pity to secure an action or to preserve a sentiment. The sentiment is in the second quatrain, the action in the third, but the human splendor is in the first. As for the couplet, its force is much better expressed in the third quatrain of Sonnet 31, which otherwise fits poorly in this set, unless as a digressive generalization.

> Thou art the grave where buried love doth live,
> Hung with the trophies of my lovers gone,
> Who all their parts of me to thee did give;
> That due of many now is thine alone.

It seems an accident of *expertise* that the next sonnet should be a complaint—the special complaint of the lover as poet—that this poet cannot join the decorum of style with the decorum of love. Who knows better than the man aware of his infatuation that style is impossible to his love? The content of infatuate love, while one is in it, is of a violence uncontrollable and changeable by a caprice as deep as nature, like the weather; which one might not have thought of did not the next sonnet deal with violent change in actual weather, the one after that with changes in moral and spiritual weather; and the third, (number 35) making something of both weathers, brings us to the civil war of love and hate, from the sense of which we are hardly again free in the course of the sonnets, whether those to the young man or those to dark lady. It is that civil war of love and hate, no doubt, which inhabits Sonnet 36 ("Let me confess that we two must be twain") but appears in the form of the perennial guilt felt in any unrequited love. This kind of guilt is what happens to the motive for action that cannot be taken.

> I may not evermore acknowledge thee,
> Lest my bewailed guilt should do thee shame.

The next batch of sonnets (37 through 40) make something like a deliberate exercise in poetics on the

A Poetics for Infatuation

analogy of substance and shadow, with love (or the young man) as the tenth muse who brings presence to the other nine. But they also show (in 40) the first dubious form of the jealousy that is about to rage at large, quite as if it had been what was being led up to all along. Jealousy is perhaps the tenth muse, and has the advantage that she can be invoked from within, the genie in the jar of conscience, needs no help from outside, and operates equally well on both sides in the civil war of love and hate, outlasting both. Jealous, it should be remembered, was once an active verb in English (as it still is in French) having to do with an intense, usually unsatisfiable, craving, especially in its defeated phase. It is the right verb for infatuation in its later and virile stages when all but the pretense of the original force of love is gone. It is of this sort of thing Thomas Mann is thinking when he speaks (in *The Story of a Novel*) of "the motif of the treacherous wooing" in the sonnets, and of their plot as "the relation of poet, lover, and friend"—a relation made for jealousy.

Indeed from Sonnet 41 on there is little left truly of love but infatuation and jealousy in a kind of single distillation, sometimes no more than a flavor and sometimes the grasping substance of a poem. Jealousy becomes a part of clear vision and by the special light it casts alters the object of the vision. The three-fold relation makes jealousy thrive and encourages her to create. There is an intermittence of life as well as of the heart, and it takes place in those moments when jealousy reigns absolutely, which it succeeds in doing more frequently than any other of the emotions under love. But the moments of sovereignty are never long; she never rules except by usurpation, and by pretending to powers and qualities not her own—as truth and necessity. In her bottom reality she is a craving, zeal without a proper object, and indeed as sometimes in English the words jealous and zealous have been confused, so have what they signify. In the sonnets the occasional return to the purity of infatuation is almost like becoming whole-souled. Again, as before, the accidental order of the sonnets provides a fresh reticulation. After the jealousy of 41 and 42, there is the invocation of dreams and day-dreams in 43 and the invocation of thought in 44 and 45, with, in 46, "a quest of thoughts, all tenants to the heart." These remind us that there is a desperation of condition, deeper than any jealousy.

Dreams are a mode and daydreams are the very process of creation. Nathan Sachs' remark which ought to be famous, that "day-dreams in common are the form of art" can perhaps be amended to read "the form of life" —especially when connected with an infatuation which, as in these sonnets, takes over so much else in life than its asserted object. There is much to be said about daydreams as the poetic agent of what lasts in poetry, but not here; here the point is to emphasize that dreams and daydreams—"darkly bright, are bright in dark directed"—show a deep poetic preference at work; this sonnet does not wish to *change* reality so much as to rival it with another creation. Similarly, addressing ourselves to Sonnet 44 ("If the dull substance of my flesh were thought"), there is a great deal to be said about the way the poetic process illuminates the nature of thought; here the immediate interest, and it should not be pushed much out of its context, is in the ninth line: "But, ah!

A Poetics for Infatuation

thought kills me that I am not thought." May not this be pushed just enough to suggest that thought and daydream are in the very closest sort of intimacy? Shakespeare seems to grasp what I assume to be the fact that thought takes place elsewhere than in words, though there may be mutual impregnation between them. I believe there is some support for such a notion in Prospero's phrase: "Come with a thought; I think thee, Ariel: come." This is rival creation triumphant.

The three sonnets 49 through 51 could be taken to represent that awful *ennui* in infatuation when both thought and daydream fail. The idea—image, not thought—of suicide seems at hand, the only refuge from the *ennui* of the unrequited. The idea lurks between the words, lending a thickness. But the *ennui* itself get bored into a return to the old actions and the old patterns of action, together with the doubts and stratagems appropriate to each, in the contrary stages— the breathless ups and exhausted downs—in the history of any grasping infatuation. Consider the variety—the disorder pushing into order, every created order dropping away—in Sonnets 53 through 65. The paradox of substance and shadow presides, but is constantly recognizing other speakers. It is essential to infatuation that it cannot feel sure of itself except by assertion, and every assertion carries its own complement of doubt and therefore its need for reassertion. In one's love one makes, or finds, the ideal in the beloved; and at once the ideal draws on, breathes in, everything in the lover's mind; then the beloved, so to speak, is surrounded, attended or ignored as the case may be. It is certain among all uncertainties that when Shakespeare speaks of the constant heart (at the end of Sonnet 53), what is signified is the pulsing shadow of the veritable ideal. But, to repeat: consider the variety of these assertions. There is the poetics of beauty and truth, where my verse distills your truth, and with this belongs the immortality of ink. Then there is the feeling of apathy in perception, that slipping off of infatuation where one *knows* it to be self-sustained if not self-created; but to know this is to feel the pinch that sets one going again, when we get infatuation fully occupied *and* conscious of itself. This releases the possibility, which Sonnet 57 seizes, that one may so rejoice in jealousy that it becomes a masochistic generosity, a martyrdom for love of the enemy and the self—not God. Surely then there is the need to ad lib at the edge of love, playing with eternal recurrence, with the poetics of time, and risking the assertion of self-love (in argument to the beloved) as a form of objective devotion. Then comes the most familiar recurrent assertion of inky immortality, with the poetics of history and ruin and the mutability of Nature herself (as we might say in the second law of thermodynamics) as new modifiers. Such is a summary account of the variety of pattern and shifting pattern. The next sonnet (66) speaks sharply to the whole procession, what is past and what is to come. It is the center of the sequence.

It is better at the centre than it would have been at the end, for as it is now the reader can put it in wherever he arrests a particular reading of the sonnets. It is a center that will hold, I think, wherever it is put. "Tired with all these, for restful death I cry." In form it is not a sonnet, nor is it so as a mode of thought, but it exists formally to the degree that it is among sonnets, and as mode of thought it depends on,

A Poetics for Infatuation

and is in answer to, the feelings that inhabit these sonnets: it is like a principle issuing order for their values. It is an advantage that the poem had also an independent existence as a catalogue and a naming of the convertibility of goods and ills in the world that makes us—a convertibility to downright domination. The lines are in the Roman sense classic in their modeling and so familiar in their sentiment that we can nearly ignore them as one more cry: All that's upright's gone! But let us look at the lines not as familiars but as strangers—or if as familiars, as familiars we detest. Each line from the second to the twelfth exhibits clichés for what in any other form we could not tolerate and as clichés can dismiss if we read lightly. But once we bend our attention we see that these are insistent clichés, like the ornamental dagger on the desk which suddenly comes to hand. The cliché insisted on resumes its insights, and perhaps refreshes and refleshes itself as well. To re-expand the cliché, so that it strikes once again upon the particular and the potential experience it once abstracted and generalized, may well be a part of the process of wisdom; it is certainly the business and use of serious poetry—a business and use of which Shakespeare was prime master, a mastery our sense of which only redoubles when we remember what we can of the powerful clichés his work germinated in our language. In the present poem the clichés were not germinated by him but were modified by the order he gave them and by the vocabulary—mastery of the force in words—of the last four in the catalogue.

And art made tongue-tied by authority,
And folly doctor-like controlling skill,

R. P. Blackmur

> And simple truth miscall'd simplicity,
> And captive good attending captain ill.

Do not these items precipitate us at once from the public life which presses us so much but in which we are actually so little engaged directly into the actual life which absorbs both our private momentum and all our free allegiance? These are lines where our public and private lives meet and illuminate, even judge, each other. They strike our behavior down with all its inadequacies to our every major effort; yet this behavior, and its modes, are how we keep alive from day to day though it is how we should die lifetime to lifetime. The reader may gloss as he will the generals of these lines into the privates of his life; but I think he might well gloss in the light they cast on the secret form of the mastering infatuation we have been tracing in these sonnets. These are the circumstances of any love which makes a mighty effort. Here it seems better to gloss only the apposition of "simple truth miscall'd simplicity." What is truly simple is only so to those who are already equal to it; a simple is a compound, like a compound of herbs, of all that we know which bears, into the nearest we can manage of a single substance. Here, in this line, a truth achieved is miscalled perception not begun. Hence the rightness of Shakespeare's couplet.

> Tired with all these, from these would I be gone,
> Save that, to die, I leave my love alone.

Love is the simple truth achieved, and not to be able to love is to be in hell. This sonnet is a critique of love infatuated.

A Poetics for Infatuation

It is a pity not to arrest these remarks now, but there are other themes, and new developments of old themes in the remainder of the sonnets, both those to the young man and those to the dark lady, which will fatten further into fate the truth of the love and of the infatuation here paused at in "Tired with all these." A few will do for comment, and the first will be one of the sonnets (number 73, "That time of year thou mayst in me behold") having to do with the imminence of death. I remember H. Granville-Barker talking at great length about the first quatrain of this sonnet. It illustrated his notion of why we need no scene painting when producing the plays. I do not know if these remarks got printed, or I would send the reader to them. Here are lines 2 through 4:

*When yellow leaves, or none, or few, do hang
Upon those boughs which shake against the cold,
Bare ruin'd choirs, where late the sweet birds sang.*

The reader will remember that the second quatrain is an image of sunset fading into dark and sleep, and that the third develops the notion that the ashes of our youth make our death bed and ends with the trope that haunted Shakespeare throughout his work, the trope that something may be "consum'd with that which it was nourish'd by." These two quatrains have no particularity in their imagery or their syntax, and are indeed vague generally, a sort of loose currency. But the quatrains are lent particularity and the force of relations by the extraordinary particularity (barring perhaps the word "choirs") and syntactical unity of the first quatrain. If the reader cannot see this, and see where he *is*, indefeasibly, let him read the lines over till he does, noting especially the order of "yellow leaves, or none, or few." Perhaps it will help if he remembers an avenue of beech trees with nearly all the leaves dropped, and the rest dropping, on a late November afternoon toward dusk; then even the "bare ruin'd choirs" become enormously particular. These words are the shape of thought reaching into feeling and it is the force of that thought that was able to achieve particularity and order in the words. It is to achieve the eloquence of presence, and it is this presence which interinanimates the whole poem, so that what was merely set side by side cannot now be taken apart. I suggest that this is a model in something near perfection for how the order and particularity are reached in the sum of the sonnets if they are not counted but taken by the eloquence of full presence as one thing.

In support of this, the set of eleven sonnets (numbers 76 through 86), which are frankly on poetics, may be brought into consideration as studies of the interinanimation of poetry and love. One begins to think that one of the things to be said about poetry is that it makes an infatuation out of life itself: the concerns of the two seem identical. At any rate these sonnets are concerned with style—where "every word doth almost tell my name"—with style whereby we both invoke and control the violent talents of the psyche. Grammar and glamor, as the dictionaries will tell you, are at some point one and the same; the one is the secret art, the other the public show; the one is the Muse, the other the Love. The rival poet—the "other" way of writing—also inhabits these sonnets, and I think his shadowy presence suggests that he never existed save as an aid to Shakespeare's poetics.

A Poetics for Infatuation

He makes possible, this rival poet, along with the mistress shared by the lover and the young man, the seeking of humiliation and hatred and personal falsity, and that very grace of shame (Sonnet 95) which discloses what Dostoevsky's Dmitri Karamazov calls the beauty of Sodom together with the harshness of love in action. But he does not make possible, except as something to turn aside from, as a prompt to a reversal of momentum —the deepest change of tide, yet only possibly its fall— these two sonnets of transumption. (I will not say transcendence; it is not a word that belongs in Shakespeare's poetics, and I prefer Dante's Latin adjective *transumptivus* to describe this aspect of Shakespeare's sonnets.) I mean Sonnets 105 ("Let not my love be call'd idolatry") and 108 ("What's in the brain that ink may character") The first sonnet is a Phoenix and Turtle poem, with these last six lines:

'Fair, kind, and true,' is all my argument,
'Fair, kind, and true,' varying to other words;
And in this change is my invention spent,
Three themes in one, which wondrous scope affords.
   'Fair, kind, and true,' have often liv'd alone,
   Which three till now never kept seat in one.

I will not gloss the three words, except that they have to do with belonging and that together they make a mood which does not gainsay or transcend but is a crossing over from other moods by the ritual of repetition. The ritual is necessary and superior to the mere words—like Pascal's unbeliever who if he takes the devout posture may find belief—and when ritual is observed the distinction disappears between the hysterical and the actual.

This, in effect, is the commentary Sonnet 108 makes on the text and practise of Sonnet 105.

> . . . like prayers divine,
> I must each day say o'er the very same.

To cultivate one's hysteria and to cultivate the numen may often turn out to be the same thing, and the ritual for the one may be the observance of the other. In the end how far can the human need be from the power that moves it? And how different should be the approach? We repeat and repeat—almost as much as in music in the elsewhere of poetry we repeat—for the secret presences in words are felt, if not revealed, in repetition, and this is so whether it is the Lord's Prayer or the prayer that intensifies personal infatuation. As the good father who would convert us says, we cannot escape prayer. The immediate object of the prayer tends to disappear as the presence presses; fair, kind, true.

Only one other sonnet (number 116, "Let me not to the marriage of true minds") makes a comparable transumption, and again it comes with a reversal of the tide that has been flowing. That tide was undermining and reductive, subduing the lover's nature to what it worked in, reducing love at last to a babe in the couplet of number 115, as if this were the last form the hovering, transmuting eye of infatuation could show. But from Love is a babe we come in number 116 to "Love's not Time's fool." Like Cleopatra's speeches in acts IV and V of her play, we need the right syntax of feeling to see how this sonnet escapes nonsense: it is a nonsense we would all speak—and many of us have said it *again*—as

A Poetics for Infatuation

notably Goethe—at the next epiphany, whether of the same person or another. Such nonsense is the only possible company for the mighty effort to identify the ideal of love in the individual. It is the last accommodation of man alive, its loss its deepest discomfort. The second quatrain knows both:

> O, no! it is an ever-fixed mark,
> That looks on tempests and is never shaken;
> It is the star to every wandering bark,
> Whose worth's unknown, although his height be taken.

Some say the star is the North star, but I think it may be any star you can see, and lose, and find again when you use the same way of looking, the very star "whose worth's unknown, although his height be taken." It is only the angle of observation that we have learned of the one thing always there. The pang is in the quick.

Beyond this there is nothing in hope or faith; but in cheated hope and bankrupt faith, there are the sicknesses and nightmares of love infected by the infatuation it had itself bred. So it is with the remaining sonnets addressed to the young man. It is not the sickness of love-longing, it is the sickness when the energy has left the infatuation, though the senses are still alert and vanity still itches, and indifference has not supervened. The nightmare is double: the trespass of the actual beloved upon the lover, and the trespass of the actual lover upon the beloved. These are the trespasses that bring us to ruin—if anything of the ever-fixed mark can still be seen —and the amount of ruin in us is inexhaustible until we are exhausted. "O benefit of ill!" Nightmare is how we assess the trespass of one individual upon the other (which is why trespasses in the Lord's Prayer are nearer our condition than debts), and if we have dreams and daydreams in common, as Montaigne and Pascal thought then it may be that in the terminal stages of an infatuation we sometimes have nightmares in common. Then the general becomes our particular. Let the first quatrain of Sonnet 119 stand for these trespasses:

> What potions have I drunk of Siren tears,
> Distill'd from limbecks foul as hell within,
> Applying fears to hopes and hopes to fears,
> Still losing when I saw myself to win!

Number 126, the last of the verses to the young man, is not a sonnet but six rhymed couplets. Had it become a sonnet, or even added a couplet, it must have become a curse or even an anathema. Nothing is so mortal as that which has been kept too long in one stage of nature; we have horror even of a beauty that outlasts the stage of nature to which it belonged. Not even an infatuation can be maintained more than one and a half times its natural life. There is no relief so enormous as the surrender of an infatuation, and no pang so keen as the sudden emptiness after. Such is the curse, the anathema, upon Pygmalion and Narcissus these sonnets show; but they would show nothing were it not for the presence among them of the three sonnets—"Tired with all these," (66), "Let not my love be call'd idolatry" (105), and "Let me not to the marriage of true minds" (116). The first gives the condition of apprehension, the second the numinous ritual, and the third the limits beyond us in hope and faith for the mighty effort, which in one of

A Poetics for Infatuation

our traditions is the highest of which we are capable from the *Symposium* and the *Vita Nuova* through these sonnets, the effort to make something last "fair, kind, and true" between one being and another. There is a trinity here. What wonder then, as we find ourselves short of these powers, if in vain hope we resort to infatuation?

And not once but again, with what we call the dark lady as our object, and this second (second or hundredth) time with a prophetic soul for abortion and no hope of children at all. One knows at once one is among the mistakes of life which, unless we can make something of them, are the terms of our central failure in human relation. Where with the young man it was a question of building something, if necessary with other means short, by the cultivated hysteria of infatuation, with the dark lady there is a kind of unbuilding going on, the deliberate exchange of pounds of flesh for pounds of spirit. It is like drinking too much; every morning the rewards show as losses, and the more they show so, the more one is bound to the system. One's private degradation is the grandest Sodom. If it were not for the seriousness of the language and its absolute jarring speed, a sonnet such as 129 ("The expense of spirit in a waste of shame") could have been written of any evening begun in liquor that did not come off well; but there is the language and its speed, and the apprehensions from the central lonely place that this lover must seek what he must shun. The two sonnets, number 133 ("Beshrew that heart that makes my heart to groan") and number 134 ("So, now I have confess'd that he is thine"), together with 129, make a dread commentary on *philia*. In this lover's triangle where each pair shares the third, mere sexual force—that treachery which moves like an army with banners—is superior to the mightiest effort *philia* can make alone. Once infatuation is simply sexual, it is the great swallower-up of friendship or love. Sonnet 134 does not exact Shylock's pound of flesh, which he was refused because it would have cost spirit, but is sexuality exacting—and receiving, since it does not harm the body—the pound of spirit.

> The statute of thy beauty thou wilt take,
> Thou usurer, that put'st forth all to use,
> And sue a friend came debtor for my sake;
> So him I lose through my unkind abuse.

The two sonnets are two maws for overinterpretation. Let us say that sexuality is indeterminate and undeterminable; a force that has too much left over to absorb into its immediate end; or a force of which the sexual is only a part, but which sex raises to its extortionate ability. In the impasse of these sonnets, it would help nothing that the dark lady can be thought a third man, but it would hinder only those who wish to improve Shakespeare's reputation. But I suggest this only to return to the possibility, with which I began this paper, that the poetics of infatuation move among the coils and recoils of the various selves that thrive and batten upon the Psyche. This is the sixth line of number 133:

> And my next self thou harder hast engross'd

Add to this only what evidence there may be in the two "Will" sonnets (135 and 136) where, other matters be-

A Poetics for Infatuation

ing present by chance, Shakespeare paid attention chiefly to the clenching of his wills in the general field of sexuality. Has no one suggested that this clenching of wills was Shakespeare's way of declaring his uncommitted anonymity? There is Thomas Mann's realm of the anonymous and the communal between us all. "Swear to thy blind soul that I was thy '*Will*.'"

Dark Lady, Third Man, Next Self, or the Anonymous One, there is no question of the sexuality and human infatuation pressing to find form within and under and among the words of the sonnets. In this second set, without the mighty effort to lift us that was in the first set, without Pygmalion and Narcissus and the Immortal Ink, the spirit wrestles in the flesh that engorges it, and the flesh—one's own flesh—is convulsed in the spirit that engulfs it. The two journeys are remarkably the same—as are the tower and the abyss—both in itinerary and target. Deceit, distrust, humiliation, jealousy, the plea for annihilation, and self-pity, with occasional glories in general disaster and with the world of the real senses—like the light and sweet air in Dante's Hell—always at hand; these are the common itinerary, with every other "tender feeling to base touches prone." The common target is repudiation—repudiation without an ounce of renunciation in it. "I am that I am." To say it once more, the sonnets illustrate the general or typical as the poetic, but there is a force under the words, and a force drawn from the words, which compels us to apprehend what had been generalized.

With that force in mind, let us look at two sonnets just before the end. Number 151 ("Love is too young to know what conscience is") has perhaps as one of its points that love asserts a special form of conscience by escaping its general form (as we use the word in English) into what we know now as consciousness. (The reader who delights in such matters should read the chapter on conscience and conscious in C. S. Lewis' *Studies in Words*; he does not touch on this sonnet's conscience, but he does discuss several other Shakespearean usages which help us to apprehend our present mystery.) I myself think that the two sets of meanings are deeply present here, on the simple rule of thumb that a poet can never know exactly which power or powers in his words he is drawing on, and the clearer the intention (what was to be *put* into words, not what was already there) the greater must be the uncertainty of his knowledge; and besides, the words may modify and even correct his intention, as well as ruin it—else there were no reality in words and no rush of meaning either from or to or among them. When I say the two sets of meanings are present, I do not intend to mark an ambiguity, but to urge that two voices are speaking at once which can be heard at once. This is the compacting power of poetry, which commands us so far as we hear it. Love is too young to know what true consciousness might be, Love is too young to know the pang of judgment as to the good and evil nature of an act or thought or condition, "Love is too young to know what conscience is." The second line, "Yet who knows not conscience is born of love?" suggests that intimate consciousness leads to the pang of judgment, just as the pang illuminates the knowledge one did not know that one had. Children and saints, said Dostoevsky, can believe two contrary things at once; poetry has also that

A Poetics for Infatuation

talent. Our common idiom, "I could (or couldn't) in all conscience," keeps the pair alive in what seems a single approach. The phrase "in all conscience" generalizes several sorts of behavior in a convenient singleness of form, so that none of them can be dismissed. I remember the anecdote a sociologist told me about an inmate in Trenton State Prison. When asked why he had stolen a car, he promptly answered that his conscience made him. "Yet who knows not that conscience is born of love?"

As we go further into this sonnet the voices thicken with tumescence, both of the body and of "the nobler part" as well. Priapus, rising, empties the rest of the body and drains something of the spirit ("tender feeling to base touches prone"); there is a physiological and spiritual disarray for the sake of a momentary concentration where it would be out of order to call for order.

This, then, is the priapic parallel, the comment of consciousness and conscience together, now that Pygmalion and Narcissus are in another limbo, for all the sonnets whether to the young man or to the dark lady. Pygmalion and Narcissus made human efforts, but Priapus is a god and undoes all efforts not his own. His comments are in his searching actions. We can see this in lines seven and eight.

> *My soul doth tell my body that he may*
> *Triumph in love; flesh stays no farther reason . . .*

The Greeks had a word for the bitterness of things too sweet, but Shakespeare has the verbal power for the sweetness of things too bitter. The soul in these lines cannot be taken as reason (the habit of ratio or proportion), and is unlikely to be the immortal soul which in the end must want another lodging and "desert the body it has used." I think rather of the "blind worm" in Yeats' very late poems, and of the stubbornness of dreams prompting, prompting, prompting—for lines forgotten and stage business impossible. The lines may return to mind and action ensue. Because I think of the blind worm I think the soul here is the Psyche, who is much older than the soul and is so much further back in the abysm that she is prepared to identify life with the blind stubbornness of the worm if necessary. It is the Psyche that gurgles in the words of this sonnet. When the Psyche speaks, and is heard, everything merely personal collapses—all that the Psyche must regard with the disdain owed to the mere artifact. One hunts for a grave that is not an artifact, not even the headstone. It is the Psyche's voice, then, in the couplet, where everything is known together and all is pang, all consciousness and conscience, but as a condition, not a commitment, of life.

> No want of conscience hold it that I call
> Her 'love' for whose dear love I rise and fall.

The labor of the Psyche is always toward the recovery of the animal life, since there can be none without.

But there is another voice than the Psyche's which makes another labor and another prayer. This is the labor and prayer of all we have made human in us, the prayer of the great lie—noble or ignoble—by which alone all that we create in ourselves or in society can survive. Consider Sonnet 152 ("In loving thee thou knows't I am forsworn); it is a repudiation, but also a reassertion.

A Poetics for Infatuation

> *I am perjur'd most;*
> *For all my vows are oaths but to misuse thee,*
> *And all my honest faith in thee is lost,*
> *For I have sworn deep oaths of thy deep kindness,*
> *Oaths of thy love, thy truth, thy constancy.*

Our oaths and promises are our best lies, if only because we know that the roughage of life will mar if not break them, but more because we know that they make our truth. We lie in search of truth: to build truth: and our great cities and monuments and poems are proof of our powers. They make us meaningful because they are that part of us which survives, what we admire in ourselves even to infatuation, whence our promises come.

> *Tired with all these, from these I would be gone,*
> *Save that, to die, I leave my love alone.*

OSCAR WILDE

The Portrait of Mr W. H.

When it was originally published in 1889, Oscar Wilde's "The Portrait of Mr W. H." was less than half the length of the complete text given here. Wilde rewrote and expanded the story after its first appearance, but that manuscript disappeared, under mysterious circumstances, in 1895. It turned up—in the United States—only after twenty-five years. Except for a limited edition of 1000 copies, distributed in 1921, this is the first American publication of the final version.

I

I HAD BEEN dining with Erskine in his pretty little house in Birdcage Walk, and we were sitting in the library over our coffee and cigarettes, when the question of literary forgeries happened to turn up in conversation. I cannot at present remember how it was that we struck upon this somewhat curious topic, as it was at that time, but I know we had a long discussion about Macpherson, Ireland, and Chatterton, and that with regard to the last I insisted that his so-called forgeries were merely the result of an artistic desire for perfect representation; that we had no right to quarrel with an artist for the conditions under which he chooses to present his work; and that all Art being to a certain degree a mode of acting, an attempt to realise one's own personality on some imaginative plane out of reach of the trammelling accidents and limitations of real life, to censure an artist for a forgery was to confuse an ethical with an æsthetical problem.

Erskine, who was a good deal older than I was, and had been listening to me with the amused deference of a man of forty, suddenly put his hand upon my shoulder and said to me, "What would you say about a young man who had a strange theory about a certain work of art, believed in his theory, and committed a forgery in order to prove it?"

"Ah! that is quite a different matter," I answered.

Erskine remained silent for a few moments, looking at the thin grey threads of smoke that were rising from his cigarette. "Yes," he said, after a pause, "quite different."

There was something in the tone of his voice, a slight touch of bitterness perhaps, that excited my curiosity. "Did you ever know anybody who did that?" I cried.

"Yes," he answered, throwing his cigarette into the fire—"a great friend of mine, Cyril Graham. He was very fascinating, and very foolish, and very heartless. However, he left me the only legacy I ever received in my life."

"What was that?" I exclaimed laughing. Erskine rose from his seat, and going over to a tall inlaid cabinet that stood between the two windows, unlocked it, and came back to where I was sitting, carrying a small panel picture set in an old and somewhat tarnished Elizabethan frame.

It was a full-length portrait of a young man in late sixteenth-century costume, standing by a table, with his right hand resting on an open book. He seemed about

The Portrait of Mr W. H.

seventeen years of age, and was of quite extraordinary personal beauty, though evidently somewhat effeminate. Indeed, had it not been for the dress and the closely cropped hair, one would have said that the face, with its dreamy, wistful eyes and its delicate scarlet lips, was the face of a girl. In manner, and especially in the treatment of the hands, the picture reminded one of François Clouet's later work. The black velvet doublet with its fantastically gilded points, and the peacock-blue background against which it showed up so pleasantly, and from which it gained such luminous value of colour, were quite in Clouet's style; and the two masks of Tragedy and Comedy that hung somewhat formally from the marble pedestal had that hard severity of touch—so different from the facile grace of the Italians—which even at the Court of France the great Flemish master never completely lost, and which in itself has always been a characteristic of the northern temper.

"It is a charming thing," I cried, "but who is this wonderful young man whose beauty Art has so happily preserved for us?"

"This is the portrait of Mr W. H.," said Erskine, with a sad smile. It might have been a chance effect of light, but it seemed to me that his eyes were swimming with tears.

"Mr W. H.!" I repeated; "who was Mr W. H.?"

"Don't you remember?" he answered; "look at the book on which his hand is resting."

"I see there is some writing there, but I cannot make it out," I replied.

"Take this magnifying-glass and try," said Erskine, with the same sad smile still playing about his mouth.

I took the glass, and moving the lamp a little nearer, I began to spell out the crabbed sixteenth-century handwriting. "To The Onlie Begetter Of These Insuing Sonnets." . . . "Good heavens!" I cried, "is this Shakespeare's Mr W. H.?"

"Cyril Graham used to say so," muttered Erskine.

"But it is not a bit like Lord Pembroke," I rejoined. "I know the Wilton portraits very well. I was staying near there a few weeks ago."

"Do you really believe then that the Sonnets are addressed to Lord Pembroke?" he asked.

"I am sure of it," I answered. "Pembroke, Shakespeare, and Mrs. Mary Fitton are the three personages of the Sonnets; there is no doubt at all about it."

"Well, I agree with you," said Erskine, "but I did not always think so. I used to believe—well, I suppose I used to believe in Cyril Graham and his theory."

"And what was that?" I asked, looking at the wonderful portrait, which had already begun to have a strange fascination for me.

"It is a long story," he murmured, taking the picture away from me—rather abruptly I thought at the time—"a very long story; but if you care to hear it, I will tell it to you."

"I love theories about the Sonnets," I cried; "but I don't think I am likely to be converted to any new idea. The matter has ceased to be a mystery to any one. Indeed, I wonder that it ever was a mystery."

"As I don't believe in the theory, I am not likely to convert you to it," said Erskine, laughing; "but it may interest you."

"Tell it to me, of course," I answered. "If it is half as

The Portrait of Mr W. H.

delightful as the picture, I shall be more than satisfied."

"Well," said Erskine, lighting a cigarette, "I must begin by telling you about Cyril Graham himself. He and I were at the same house at Eton. I was a year or two older than he was, but we were immense friends, and did all our work and all our play together. There was, of course, a good deal more play than work, but I cannot say that I am sorry for that. It is always an advantage not to have received a sound commercial education, and what I learned in the playing fields at Eton has been quite as useful to me as anything I was taught at Cambridge. I should tell you that Cyril's father and mother were both dead. They had been drowned in a horrible yachting accident off the Isle of Wight. His father had been in the diplomatic service, and had married a daughter, the only daughter, in fact, of old Lord Crediton, who became Cyril's guardian after the death of his parents. I don't think that Lord Crediton cared very much for Cyril. He had never really forgiven his daughter for marrying a man who had no title. He was an extraordinary old aristocrat who swore like a costermonger, and had the manners of a farmer. I remember seeing him once on Speech-day. He growled at me, gave me a sovereign, and told me not to grow up a 'damned Radical' like my father. Cyril had very little affection for him, and was only too glad to spend most of his holidays with us in Scotland. They never really got on together at all. Cyril thought him a bear, and he thought Cyril effeminate. He was effeminate, I suppose, in some things, though he was a capital rider and a capital fencer. In fact he got the foils before he left Eton. But he was very languid in his manner, and not a little vain of his good looks, and had a strong objection to football, which he used to say was a game only suitable for the sons of the middle classes. The two things that really gave him pleasure were poetry and acting. At Eton he was always dressing up and reciting Shakespeare, and when we went up to Trinity he became a member of the A.D.C. in his first term. I remember I was always very jealous of his acting. I was absurdly devoted to him; I suppose because we were so different in most things. I was a rather awkward, weakly lad, with huge feet, and horribly freckled. Freckles run in Scotch families just as gout does in English families. Cyril used to say that of the two he preferred the gout; but he always set an absurdly high value on personal appearance, and once read a paper before our Debating Society to prove that it was better to be good-looking than to be good. He certainly was wonderfully handsome. People who did not like him, philistines and college tutors, and young men reading for the Church, used to say that he was merely *pretty*; but there was a great deal more in his face than mere prettiness. I think he was the most splendid creature I ever saw, and nothing could exceed the grace of his movements, the charm of his manner. He fascinated everybody who was worth fascinating, and a great many people who were not. He was often wilful and petulant, and I used to think him dreadfully insincere. It was due, I think, chiefly to his inordinate desire to please. Poor Cyril! I told him once that he was contented with very cheap triumphs, but he only tossed his head, and smiled. He was horribly spoiled. All charming people, I fancy, are spoiled. It is the secret of their attraction.

"However, I must tell you about Cyril's acting. You

The Portrait of Mr W. H.

know that no women are allowed to play at the A.D.C. At least they were not in my time. I don't know how it is now. Well, of course Cyril was always cast for the girls' parts, and when 'As You Like It' was produced he played Rosalind. It was a marvellous performance. You will laugh at me, but I assure you that Cyril Graham was the only perfect Rosalind I have ever seen. It would be impossible to describe to you the beauty, the delicacy, the refinement of the whole thing. It made an immense sensation, and the horrid little theatre, as it was then, was crowded every night. Even now when I read the play I can't help thinking of Cyril; the part might have been written for him, he played it with such extraordinary grace and distinction. The next term he took his degree, and came to London to read for the Diplomatic. But he never did any work. He spent his days in reading Shakespeare's Sonnets, and his evenings at the theatre. He was, of course, wild to go on the stage. It was all that Lord Crediton and I could do to prevent him. Perhaps, if he had gone on the stage he would be alive now. It is always a silly thing to give advice, but to give good advice is absolutely fatal. I hope you will never fall into that error. If you do, you will be sorry for it.

"Well, to come to the real point of the story, one afternoon I got a letter from Cyril asking me to come round to his rooms that evening. He had charming chambers in Piccadilly overlooking the Green Park, and as I used to go to see him almost every day, I was rather surprised at his taking the trouble to write. Of course I went, and when I arrived I found him in a state of great excitement. He told me that he had at last discovered the true secret of Shakespeare's Sonnets; that all the scholars and critics had been entirely on the wrong track; and that he was the first who, working purely by internal evidence, had found out who Mr W. H. really was. He was perfectly wild with delight, and for a long time would not tell me his theory. Finally, he produced a bundle of notes, took his copy of the Sonnets off the mantelpiece, and sat down and gave me a long lecture on the whole subject.

"He began by pointing out that the young man to whom Shakespeare addressed these strangely passionate poems must have been somebody who was a really vital factor in the development of his dramatic art, and that this could not be said of either Lord Pembroke or Lord Southampton. Indeed, whoever he was, he could not have been anybody of high birth, as was shown very clearly by Sonnet 25, in which Shakespeare contrasts himself with men who are 'great princes' favourites'; says quite frankly—

> Let those who are in favour with their stars
> Of public honour and proud titles boast,
> Whilst I, whom fortune of such triumph bars,
> Unlooked for joy in that I honour most;

and ends the sonnet by congratulating himself on the mean state of him he so adored:

> Then happy I, that love and am beloved
> Where I may not remove nor be removed.

This sonnet Cyril declared would be quite unintelligible if we fancied that it was addressed to either the Earl of

The Portrait of Mr W. H.

Pembroke or the Earl of Southampton, both of whom were men of the highest position in England and fully entitled to be called 'great princes'; and he in corroboration of his view read me Sonnets 124 and 125, in which Shakespeare tells us that his love is not 'the child of state,' that it 'suffers not in smiling pomp,' but is 'builded far from accident.' I listened with a good deal of interest, for I don't think the point had ever been made before; but what followed was still more curious, and seemed to me at the time to dispose entirely of Pembroke's claim. We know from Meres that the Sonnets had been written before 1598, and Sonnet 104 informs us that Shakespeare's friendship for Mr W. H. had been already in existence for three years. Now Lord Pembroke, who was born in 1580, did not come to London till he was eighteen years of age, that is to say till 1598, and Shakespeare's acquaintance with Mr W. H. must have begun in 1594, or at the latest in 1595. Shakespeare, accordingly, could not have known Lord Pembroke until after the Sonnets had been written.

"Cyril pointed out also that Pembroke's father did not die until 1601; whereas it was evident from the line,

You had a father, let your son say so,

that the father of Mr W. H. was dead in 1598; and laid great stress on the evidence afforded by the Wilton portraits which represent Lord Pembroke as a swarthy dark-haired man, while Mr W. H. was one whose hair was like spun gold, and whose face the meeting-place for the 'lily's white' and the 'deep vermilion in the rose'; being himself 'fair,' and 'red,' and 'white and red,' and of beautiful aspect. Besides it was absurd to imagine that any publisher of the time, and the preface is from the publisher's hand, would have dreamed of addressing William Herbert, Earl of Pembroke, as Mr W. H.; the case of Lord Buckhurst being spoken of as Mr Sackville being not really a parallel instance, as Lord Buckhurst, the first of that title, was plain Mr Sackville when he contributed to the 'Mirror for Magistrates,' while Pembroke, during his father's lifetime, was always known as Lord Herbert. So far for Lord Pembroke, whose supposed claims Cyril easily demolished while I sat by in wonder. With Lord Southampton Cyril had even less difficulty. Southampton became at a very early age the lover of Elizabeth Vernon, so he needed no entreaties to marry; he was not beautiful; he did not resemble his mother, as Mr W. H. did—

> Thou art thy mother's glass, and she in thee
> Calls back the lovely April of her prime;

and, above all, his Christian name was Henry, whereas the punning sonnets (135 and 143) show that the Christian name of Shakespeare's friend was the same as his own—*Will*.

"As for the other suggestions of unfortunate commentators, that Mr W. H. is a misprint for Mr W. S., meaning Mr William Shakespeare; that 'Mr W. H. all' should be read 'Mr W. Hall'; that Mr W. H. is Mr William Hathaway; that Mr W. H. stands for Mr Henry Willobie, the young Oxford poet, with the initials of his name reversed; and that a full stop should be placed after 'wisheth,' making Mr W. H. the writer and not

The Portrait of Mr W. H.

the subject of the dedication,—Cyril got rid of them in a very short time; and it is not worth while to mention his reasons, though I remember he sent me off into a fit of laughter by reading to me, I am glad to say not in the original, some extracts from a German commentator called Barnstorff, who insisted that Mr W. H. was no less a person than 'Mr. William Himself.' Nor would he allow for a moment that the Sonnets are mere satires on the work of Drayton and John Davies of Hereford. To him, as indeed to me, they were poems of serious and tragic import, wrung out of the bitterness of Shakespeare's heart, and made sweet by the honey of his lips. Still less would he admit that they were merely philosophical allegory, and that in them Shakespeare is addressing his Ideal Self, or Ideal Manhood, or the Spirit of Beauty, or the Reason, or the Divine Logos, or the Catholic Church. He felt, as indeed I think we all must feel, that the Sonnets are addressed to an individual,—to a particular young man whose personality for some reason seems to have filled the soul of Shakespeare with terrible joy and no less terrible despair.

"Having in this manner cleared the way, as it were, Cyril asked me to dismiss from my mind any preconceived ideas I might have formed on the subject, and to give a fair and unbiased hearing to his own theory. The problem he pointed out was this: Who was that young man of Shakespeare's day who, without being of noble birth or even of noble nature, was addressed by him in terms of such passionate adoration that we can but wonder at the strange worship, and are almost afraid to turn the key that unlocks the mystery of the poet's heart? Who was he whose physical beauty was such that it became the very corner-stone of Shakespeare's art; the very source of Shakespeare's inspiration; the very incarnation of Shakespeare's dreams? To look upon him as simply the object of certain love-poems was to miss the whole meaning of the poems: for the art of which Shakespeare talks in the Sonnets is not the art of the Sonnets themselves, which indeed were to him but slight and secret things—it is the art of the dramatist to which he is always alluding; and he to whom Shakespeare said—

> Thou art all my art, and dost advance
> As high as learning my rude ignorance,—

he to whom he promised immortality,

> Where breath most breathes, even in the mouths of men,—

he who was to him the tenth 'muse' and

> Ten times more in worth
> Than those old nine which rhymers invocate,

was surely none other than the boy-actor for whom he created Viola and Imogen, Juliet and Rosalind, Portia and Desdemona, and Cleopatra herself."

"The boy-actor of Shakespeare's plays?" I cried.

"Yes," said Erskine. "This was Cyril Graham's theory, evolved as you see purely from the Sonnets themselves, and depending for its acceptance not so much on

The Portrait of Mr W. H.

demonstrable proof or formal evidence, but on a kind of spiritual and artistic sense, by which alone he claimed could the true meaning of the poems be discerned. I remember his reading to me that fine sonnet—

> How can my Muse want subject to invent,
> While thou dost breathe, that pour'st into my verse
> Thine own sweet argument, too excellent
> For every vulgar paper to rehearse
> O give thyself the thanks, if aught in me
> Worthy perusal stand against thy sight;
> For who's so dumb that cannot write to thee,
> When thou thyself dost give invention light?

—and pointing out how completely it corroborated his view; and indeed he went through all the Sonnets carefully, and showed, or fancied that he showed, that, according to his new explanation of their meaning, things that had seemed obscure, or evil, or exaggerated, became clear and rational, and of high artistic import, illustrating Shakespeare's conception of the true relations between the art of the actor and the art of the dramatist.

"It is of course evident that there must have been in Shakespeare's company some wonderful boy-actor of great beauty, to whom he intrusted the presentation of his noble heroines; for Shakespeare was a practical theatrical manager as well as an imaginative poet; and Cyril Graham had actually discovered the boy-actor's name. He was Will, or, as he preferred to call him, Willie Hughes. The Christian name he found of course in the punning sonnets, 135 and 143; the surname was, according to him, hidden in the seventh line of Sonnet 20, where Mr W. H. is described as—

A man in hew, all Hews in his controwling.

"In the original edition of the Sonnets 'Hews' is printed wih a capital letter and in italics, and this, he claimed, showed clearly that a play on words was intended, his view receiving a good deal of corroboration from those sonnets in which curious puns are made on the words 'use' and 'usury,' and from such lines as—

Thou art as fair in knowledge as in hew.

Of course I was converted at once, and Willie Hughes became to me as real a person as Shakespeare. The only objection I made to the theory was that the name of Willie Hughes does not occur in the list of the actors of Shakespeare's company as it is printed in the first folio. Cyril, however, pointed out that the absence of Willie Hughes' name from this list really corroborated the theory, as it was evident from Sonnet 86, that he had abandoned Shakespeare's company to play at a rival theatre, probably in some of Chapman's plays. It was in reference to this that in the great sonnet on Chapman Shakespeare said to Willie Hughes—

But when your countenance filled up his line,
Then lacked I matter; that enfeebled mine—

the expression 'when your countenance filled up his line' referring clearly to the beauty of the young actor giving

The Portrait of Mr W. H.

life and reality and added charm to Chapman's verse, the same idea being also put forward in Sonnet 79:

> Whilst I alone did call upon thy aid,
> My verse alone had all thy gentle grace,
> But now my gracious numbers are decayed,
> And my sick Muse doth give another place;

and in the immediately preceding sonnet, where Shakespeare says,

> every alien pen hath got my use
> And under thee their poesy disperse,

the play upon words (use = Hughes) being of course obvious, and the phrase, 'under thee their poesy disperse,' meaning 'by your assistance as an actor bring their plays before the people.'

"It was a wonderful evening, and we sat up almost till dawn reading and re-reading the Sonnets. After some time, however, I began to see that before the theory could be placed before the world in a really perfected form, it was necessary to get some independent evidence about the existence of this young actor, Willie Hughes. If this could be once established, there could be no possible doubt about his identity with Mr W. H.; but otherwise the theory would fall to the ground. I put this forward very strongly to Cyril, who was a good deal annoyed at what he called my philistine tone of mind, and indeed was rather bitter upon the subject. However, I made him promise that in his own interest he would not publish his discovery till he had put the whole matter beyond the reach of doubt; and for weeks and weeks we searched the registers of City churches, the Alleyn MSS. at Dulwich, the Record Office, the books of the Lord Chamberlain—everything, in fact, that we thought might contain some allusion to Willie Hughes. We discovered nothing, of course, and each day the existence of Willie Hughes seemed to me to become more problematical. Cyril was in a dreadful state, and used to go over the whole question again and again, entreating me to believe; but I saw the one flaw in the theory, and I refused to be convinced till the actual existence of Willie Hughes, a boy-actor of the Elizabethan stage, had been placed beyond the reach of doubt or cavil.

"One day Cyril left town to stay with his grandfather, I thought at the time, but I afterwards heard from Lord Crediton that this was not the case; and about a fortnight afterwards I received a telegram from him, handed in at Warwick, asking me to be sure to come and dine with him in his chambers, that evening at eight o'clock. When I arrived, he said to me, 'The only apostle who did not deserve proof was St Thomas, and St Thomas was the only apostle who got it.' I asked him what he meant. He answered that he had been able not merely to establish the existence in the sixteenth century of a boy-actor of the name of Willie Hughes, but to prove by the most conclusive evidence that he was the Mr W. H. of the Sonnets. He would not tell me anything more at the time; but after dinner he solemnly produced the picture I showed you, and told me that he had discovered it by the merest chance nailed to the side of an old chest that he had bought at a farmhouse in Warwickshire. The chest itself, which was a very fine ex-

The Portrait of Mr W. H.

ample of Elizabethan work, and thoroughly authentic, he had, of course, brought with him, and in the centre of the front panel the initials W. H. were undoubtedly carved. It was this monogram that had attracted his attention, and he told me that it was not till he had had the chest in his possession for several days that he had thought of making any careful examination of the inside. One morning, however, he saw that the right-hand side of the chest was much thicker than the other, and looking more closely, he discovered that a framed panel was clamped against it. On taking it out, he found it was the picture that is now lying on the sofa. It was very dirty, and covered with mould; but he managed to clean it, and, to his great joy, saw that he had fallen by mere chance on the one thing for which he had been looking. Here was an authentic portrait of Mr W. H. with his hand resting on the dedicatory page of the Sonnets, and on the corner of the picture could be faintly seen the name of the young man himself written in gold uncial letters on the faded *bleu de paon* ground, 'Master Will Hews.'

"Well, what was I to say? It is quite clear from Sonnet 47 that Shakespeare had a portrait of Mr W. H. in his possession, and it seemed to me more than probable that here we had the very 'painted banquet' on which he invited his eye to feast; the actual picture that awoke his heart 'to heart's and eye's delight.' It never occurred to me for a moment that Cyril Graham was playing a trick on me, or that he was trying to prove his theory by means of a forgery."

"But is it a forgery?" I asked.

"Of course it is," said Erskine. "It is a very good

forgery; but it is a forgery none the less. I thought at the time that Cyril was rather calm about the whole matter; but I remember he kept telling me that he himself required no proof of the kind, and that he thought the theory complete without it. I laughed at him, and told him that without it the entire theory would fall to the ground, and I warmly congratulated him on his marvellous discovery. We then arranged that the picture should be etched or facsimiled, and placed as the frontispiece to Cyril's edition of the Sonnets; and for three months we did nothing but go over each poem line by line, till we had settled every difficulty of text or meaning. One unlucky day I was in a print-shop in Holborn, when I saw upon the counter some extremely beautiful drawings in silver-point. I was so attracted by them that I bought them; and the proprietor of the place, a man called Rawlings, told me that they were done by a young painter of the name of Edward Merton, who was very clever, but as poor as a church mouse. I went to see Merton some days afterwards, having got his address from the print-seller, and found a pale, interesting young man, with a rather common-looking wife,—his model, as I subsequently learned. I told him how much I admired his drawings, at which he seemed very pleased, and I asked him if he would show me some of his other work. As we were looking over a portfolio, full of really very lovely things,—for Merton had a most delicate and delightful touch,—I suddenly caught sight of a drawing of the picture of Mr W. H. There was no doubt whatever about it. It was almost a facsimile,—the only difference being that the two masks of Tragedy and Comedy were not suspended from the marble table

The Portrait of Mr W. H.

as they are in the picture but were lying on the floor at the young man's feet. 'Where on earth did you get that?' I asked. He grew rather confused, and said,—'Oh, that is nothing. I did not know it was in this portfolio. It is not a thing of any value.' 'It is what you did for Mr Cyril Graham,' exclaimed his wife; 'and if this gentleman wishes to buy it, let him have it.' 'For Mr Cyril Graham?' I repeated. 'Did you paint the picture of Mr W. H.?' 'I don't understand what you mean,' he answered growing very red. Well, the whole thing was quite dreadful. The wife let it all out. I gave her five pounds when I was going away. I can't bear to think of it, now; but of course I was furious. I went off at once to Cyril's chambers, waited there for three hours before he came in, with that horrid lie staring me in the face, and told him I had discovered his forgery. He grew very pale, and said,—'I did it purely for your sake. You would not be convinced in any other way. It does not affect the truth of the theory.' 'The truth of the theory!' I exclaimed; 'the less we talk about that the better. You never even believed in it yourself. If you had, you would not have committed a forgery to prove it.' High words passed between us; we had a fearful quarrel. I daresay I was unjust, and the next morning he was dead.'

"Dead!" I cried.

"Yes, he shot himself with a revolver. By the time I arrived,—his servant had sent for me at once,—the police were already there. He had left a letter for me, evidently written in the greatest agitation and distress of mind."

"What was in it?" I asked.

"Oh, that he believed absolutely in Willie Hughes; that the forgery of the picture had been done simply as a concession to me, and did not in the slightest degree invalidate the truth of the theory; and that in order to show me how firm and flawless his faith in the whole thing was, he was going to offer his life as a sacrifice to the secret of the Sonnets. It was a foolish, mad letter. I remember he ended by saying that he intrusted to me the Willie Hughes theory, and that it was for me to present it to the world, and to unlock the secret of Shakespeare's heart."

"It is a most tragic story," I cried, "but why have you not carried out his wishes?"

Erskine shrugged his shoulders. "Because it is a perfectly unsound theory from beginning to end," he answered.

"My dear Erskine," I exclaimed, getting up from my seat, "you are entirely wrong about the whole matter. It is the only perfect key to Shakespeare's Sonnets that has ever been made. It is complete in every detail. I believe in Willie Hughes."

"Don't say that," said Erskine, gravely: "I believe there is something fatal about the idea, and intellectually there is nothing to be said for it. I have gone into the whole matter, and I assure you the theory is entirely fallacious. It is plausible up to a certain point. Then it stops. For heaven's sake, my dear boy, don't take up the subject of Willie Hughes. You will break your heart over it."

"Erskine," I answered, "it is your duty to give this theory to the world. If you will not do it, I will. By keeping it back you wrong the memory of Cyril Graham, the youngest and the most splendid of all the martyrs of literature. I entreat you to do him this bare act of jus-

The Portrait of Mr W. H.

tice. He died for this thing—don't let his death be in vain."

Erskine looked at me in amazement. "You are carried away by the sentiment of the whole story," he said. "You forget that a thing is not necessarily true because a man dies for it. I was devoted to Cyril Graham. His death was a horrible blow to me. I did not recover from it for years. I don't think I have ever recovered from it. But Willie Hughes! There is nothing in the idea of Willie Hughes. No such person ever existed. As for bringing the matter before the world,—the world thinks that Cyril Graham shot himself by accident. The only proof of his suicide was contained in the letter to me, and of this letter the public never heard anything. To the present day Lord Crediton is under the impression that the whole thing was accidental."

"Cyril Graham sacrificed his life to a great idea," I answered; "and if you will not tell of his martyrdom, tell at least of his faith."

"His faith," said Erskine, "was fixed in a thing that was false, in a thing that was unsound, in a thing that no Shakespearian scholar would accept for a moment. The theory would be laughed at. Don't make a fool of yourself, and don't follow a trail that leads nowhere. You start by assuming the existence of the very person whose existence is the thing to be proved. Besides, everybody knows that the Sonnets were addressed to Lord Pembroke. The matter is settled once for all."

"The matter is not settled," I exclaimed. "I will take up the theory where Cyril Graham left it, and I will prove to the world that he was right."

"Silly boy!" said Erskine. "Go home, it is after three,

and don't think about Willie Hughes any more. I am sorry I told you anything about it, and very sorry indeed that I should have converted you to a thing in which I don't believe."

"You have given me the key to the greatest mystery of modern literature," I answered; "and I will not rest till I have made you recognise, till I have made everybody recognise, that Cyril Graham was the most subtle Shakespearian critic of our day."

I was about to leave the room when Erskine called me back. "My dear fellow," he said, "let me advise you not to waste your time over the Sonnets. I am quite serious. After all, what do they tell us about Shakespeare? Simply that he was the slave of beauty."

"Well, that is the condition of being an artist!" I replied.

There was a strange silence for a few moments. Then Erskine got up, and looking at me with half closed eyes, said, "Ah! how you remind me of Cyril! He used to say just that sort of thing to me." He tried to smile, but there was a note of poignant pathos in his voice that I remember to the present day, as one remembers the tone of a particular violin that has charmed one, the touch of a particular woman's hand. The great events of life often leave one unmoved; they pass out of consciousness, and, when one thinks of them, become unreal. Even the scarlet flowers of passion seem to grow in the same meadow as the poppies of oblivion. We reject the burden of their memory, and have anodynes against them. But the little things, the things of no moment, remain with us. In some tiny ivory cell the brain stores the most delicate, and the most fleeting impressions.

As I walked home through St. James's Park, the dawn

The Portrait of Mr W. H.

was just breaking over London. The swans were lying asleep on the smooth surface of the polished lake, like white feathers fallen upon a mirror of black steel. The gaunt Palace looked purple against the pale green sky, and in the garden of Stafford House the birds were just beginning to sing. I thought of Cyril Graham, and my eyes filled with tears.

I I

It was past twelve o'clock when I awoke, and the sun was streaming in through the curtains of my room in long dusty beams of tremulous gold. I told my servant that I would not be at home to any one, and after I had discussed a cup of chocolate and a *petit-pain*, I took out of the library my copy of Shakespeare's Sonnets, and Mr Tyler's facsimile edition of the Quarto, and began to go carefully through them. Each poem seemed to me to corroborate Cyril Graham's theory. I felt as if I had my hand upon Shakespeare's heart, and was counting each separate throb and pulse of passion. I thought of the wonderful boy-actor, and saw his face in every line.

Previous to this, in my Lord Pembroke days, if I may so term them, I must admit that it had always seemed to me very difficult to understand how the creator of Hamlet and Lear and Othello could have addressed in such extravagant terms of praise and passion one who was merely an ordinary young nobleman of the day. Along with most students of Shakespeare, I had found myself compelled to set the Sonnets apart as things quite alien to Shakespeare's development as a dramatist, as things possibly unworthy of the intellectual side of his nature. But now that I began to realise the truth of Cyril Graham's theory, I saw that the moods and passions they mirrored were absolutely essential to Shakespeare's perfection as an artist writing for the Elizabethan stage, and that it was in the curious theatric conditions of that stage that the poems themselves had their origin. I remember what joy I had in feeling that these wonderful Sonnets,

> *Subtle as Sphinx; as sweet and musical*
> *As bright Apollo's lute, strung with his hair,*

were no longer isolated from the great æsthetic energies of Shakespeare's life, but were an essential part of his dramatic activity, and revealed to us something of the secret of his method. To have discovered the true name of Mr W. H. was comparatively nothing: others might have done that, had perhaps done it: but to have discovered his profession was a revolution in criticism.

Two sonnets, I remember, struck me particularly. In the first of these (53) Shakespeare, complimenting Willie Hughes on the versatility of his acting, on his wide range of parts, a range extending, as we know, from Rosalind to Juliet, and from Beatrice to Ophelia, says to him:—

> *What is your substance, whereof are you made,*
> *That millions of strange shadows on you tend?*
> *Since everyone hath, every one, one shade,*
> *And you, but one, can every shadow lend—*

lines that would be unintelligible if they were not addressed to an actor, for the word "shadow" had in Shake-

The Portrait of Mr W. H.

speare's day a technical meaning connected with the stage. "The best in this kind are but shadows," says Theseus of the actors in the "Midsummer Night's Dream";

> *Life's but a walking shadow, and poor player*
> *That struts and frets his hour upon the stage,*

cries Macbeth in the moment of his despair, and there are many similar allusions in the literature of the day. This sonnet evidently belonged to the series in which Shakespeare discusses the nature of the actor's art, and of the strange and rare temperament that is essential to the perfect stage-player. "How is it," says Shakespeare to Willie Hughes, "that you have so many personalities?" and then he goes on to point out that his beauty is such that it seems to realise every form and phase of fancy, to embody each dream of the creative imagination,—an idea that is still further expanded in the sonnet that immediately follows, where, beginning with the fine thought,

> *O, how much more doth beauty beauteous seem*
> *By that sweet ornament which truth doth give!*

Shakespeare invites us to notice how the truth of acting, the truth of visible presentation on the stage, adds to the wonder of poetry, giving life to its loveliness, and actual reality to its ideal form. And yet, in Sonnet 47, Shakespeare calls upon Willie Hughes to abandon the stage with its artificiality, its unreal life of painted face and mimic costume, its immoral influences and suggestions, its remoteness from the true world of noble action and sincere utterance.

> Ah, wherefore with infection should he live,
> And with his presence grace impiety,
> That sin by him advantage should receive,
> And lace itself with his society?
> Why should false painting imitate his cheek,
> And steal dead seeing of his living hue?
> Why should poor beauty indirectly seek
> Roses of shadow, since his rose is true?

It may seem strange that so great a dramatist as Shakespeare, who realised his own perfection as an artist and his full humanity as a man on the ideal plane of stage-writing and stage-playing, should have written in these terms about the theatre; but we must remember that in Sonnets 110 and 111, Shakespeare shows us that he too was wearied of the world of puppets, and full of shame at having made himself "a motley to the view." Sonnet 111 is especially bitter:—

> O, for my sake do you with Fortune chide,
> The guilty goddess of my harmful deeds,
> That did not better for my life provide
> Than public means which public manners breeds.
> Thence comes it that my name receives a brand,
> And almost thence my nature is subdued
> To what it works in, like the dyer's hand:
> Pity me, then, and wish I were renewed—

and there are many signs of the same feeling elsewhere, signs familiar to all real students of Shakespeare.

One point puzzled me immensely as I read the Sonnets, and it was days before I struck on the true inter-

The Portrait of Mr W. H.

pretation, which indeed Cyril Graham himself seemed to have missed. I could not understand how it was that Shakespeare set so high a value on his young friend marrying. He himself had married young and the result had been unhappiness, and it was not likely that he would have asked Willie Hughes to commit the same error. The boy-player of Rosalind had nothing to gain from marriage, or from the passions of real life. The early sonnets with their strange entreaties to love children seemed to be a jarring note.

The explanation of the mystery came on me quite suddenly and I found it in the curious dedication. It will be remembered that this dedication was as follows:—

"TO. THE. ONLIE. BEGETTER. OF.
THESE. INSUING. SONNETS.
MR. W. H. ALL. HAPPINESSE.
AND. THAT. ETERNITIE.
PROMISED. BY.
OUR. EVER-LIVING. POET.
WISHETH.
THE. WELL-WISHING.
ADVENTURER. IN.
SETTING.
FORTH.
T.T."

Some scholars have supposed that the word "begetter" here means simply the procurer of the Sonnets for Thomas Thorpe the publisher; but this view is now generally abandoned, and the highest authorities are quite agreed that it is to be taken in the sense of inspirer, the metaphor being drawn from the analogy of physical life. Now I saw that the same metaphor was used by Shakespeare himself all through the poems, and this set me on the right track. Finally I made my great discovery. The marriage that Shakespeare proposes for Willie Hughes is the "marriage with his Muse," an expression which is definitely put forward in Sonnet 82 where, in the bitterness of his heart at the defection of the boy-actor for whom he had written his greatest parts, and whose beauty had indeed suggested them, he opens his complaint by saying—

I grant thou wert not married to my Muse.

The children he begs him to beget are no children of flesh and blood, but more immortal children of undying fame. The whole cycle of the early sonnets is simply Shakespeare's invitations to Willie Hughes to go upon the stage and become a player. How barren and profitless a thing, he says, is this beauty of yours if it be not used:

*When forty winters shall besiege thy brow,
And dig deep trenches in thy beauty's field,
Thy youth's proud livery, so gazed on now,
Will be a tattered weed, of small worth held:
Then being asked where all thy beauty lies,
Where all the treasure of thy lusty days,
To say, within thine own deep-sunken eyes,
Were an all-eating shame and thriftless praise.*

The Portrait of Mr W. H.

You must create something in art: my verse "is thine and *born* of thee"; only listen to me, and I will

> bring forth eternal numbers to outlive long date,

and you shall people with forms of your own image the imaginary world of the stage. These children that you beget, he continues, will not wither away, as mortal children do, but you shall live in them and in my plays: do but—

> Make thee another self, for love of me,
> That beauty still may live in thine or thee!

Be not afraid to surrender your personality, to give your "semblance to some other":

> To give away yourself keeps yourself still,
> And you must live, drawn by your own sweet skill.

I may not be learned in astrology, and yet, in those "constant stars" your eyes,

> I read such art
> As truth and beauty shall together thrive,
> If from thyself to store thou wouldst convert.

What does it matter about others?

> Let those whom Nature hath not made for store,
> Harsh, featureless, and rude, barrenly perish:

With you it is different, Nature—

> carv'd thee for her seal, and meant thereby
> Thou shouldst print more, nor let that copy die.

Remember, too, how soon Beauty forsakes itself. Its action is no stronger than a flower, and like a flower it lives and dies. Think of "the stormy gusts of winter's day," of the "barren edge of Death's eternal cold," and—

>   ere thou be distilled,
> Make sweet some vial; treasure thou some place
> With beauty's treasure, ere it be self-killed.

Why, even flowers do not altogether die. When roses wither,

> Of their sweet deaths are sweetest odours made:

and you who are "my rose" should not pass away without leaving your form in Art. For Art has the very secret of joy.

> Ten times thyself were happier than thou art,
> If ten of thine ten times refigur'd thee.

You do not require the "bastard signs of fair," the painted face, the fantastic disguises of other actors:

> . . . the golden tresses of the dead,
> The right of sepulchers,

need not be shorn away for you. In you—

The Portrait of Mr W. H.

> . . . those holy antique hours are seen,
> Without all ornament, itself and true,
> Making no summer of another's green.

All that is necessary is to "copy what in you is writ"; to place you on the stage as you are in actual life. All those ancient poets who have written of "ladies dead and lovely knights" have been dreaming of such a one as you, and:

> All their praises are but prophecies
> Of this our time, all you prefiguring.

For your beauty seems to belong to all ages and to all lands. Your shade comes to visit me at night, but, I want to look upon your "shadow" in the living day, I want to see you upon the stage. Mere description of you will not suffice:

> If I could write the beauty of your eyes,
> And in fresh numbers number all your graces,
> The age to come would say, "This poet lies;
> Such heavenly touches ne'er touched earthly faces."

It is necessary that "some child of yours," some artistic creation that embodies you, and to which your imagination gives life, shall present you to the world's wondering eyes. Your own thoughts are your children, offspring of sense and spirit; give some expression to them, and you shall find—

> Those children nursed, delivered from thy brain.

My thoughts, also, are my "children." They are of your begetting and my brain is:

> the womb wherein they grew.

For this great friendship of ours is indeed a marriage, it is the "marriage of true minds."

   I collected together all the passages that seemed to me to corroborate this view, and they produced a strong impression on me, and showed me how complete Cyril Graham's theory really was. I also saw that it was quite easy to separate those lines in which Shakespeare speaks of the Sonnets themselves, from those in which he speaks of his great dramatic work. This was a point that had been entirely overlooked by all critics up to Cyril Graham's day. And yet it was one of the most important in the whole series of poems. To the Sonnets Shakespeare was more or less indifferent. He did not wish to rest his fame on them. They were to him his "slight Muse," as he calls them, and intended, as Meres tells us, for private circulation only among a few, a very few, friends. Upon the other hand he was extremely conscious of the high artistic value of his plays, and shows a noble self-reliance upon his dramatic genius. When he says to Willie Hughes:

> But thy eternal summer shall not fade,
> Nor lose possession of that fair thou owest;
> Nor shall Death brag thou wander'st in his shade,
> When in eternal lines to time thou growest:
>   So long as men can breathe or eyes can see,
>   So long lives this and this gives life to thee;—

The Portrait of Mr W. H.

the expression "eternal lines" clearly alludes to one of his plays that he was sending him at the time, just as the concluding couplet points to his confidence in the probability of his plays being always acted. In his address to the Dramatic Muse (Sonnets 100 and 101) we find the same feeling:

> Where art thou, Muse, that thou forget'st so long
> To speak of that which gives thee all thy might?
> Spend'st thou thy fury on some worthless song,
> Darkening thy power to lend base subjects light?

he cries, and he then proceeds to reproach the mistress of Tragedy and Comedy for her "neglect of truth in beauty dyed," and says:

> Because he needs no praise, wilt thou be dumb?
> Excuse not silence so; for't lies in thee
> To make him much outlive a gilded tomb,
> And to be praised of ages yet to be.
>   Then do thy office, Muse, I teach thee how,
>   To make him seem long hence as he shows now.

It is, however, perhaps in Sonnet 55 that Shakespeare gives to this idea its fullest expression. To imagine that the "powerful rhyme" of the second line refers to the sonnet itself was entirely to mistake Shakespeare's meaning. It seemed to me that it was extremely likely, from the general character of the sonnet, that a particular play was meant, and that the play was none other but "Romeo and Juliet."

Not marble, nor the gilded monuments
Of princes shall outlive this powerful rhyme;
But you shall shine more bright in these contents
Than unswept stone besmeared with sluttish time.
When wasteful war shall statues overturn,
And broils root out the work of masonry,
Not Mars his sword nor war's quick fire shall burn
The living record of your memory
'Gainst death and all-oblivious enmity
Shall you pace forth; your praise shall still find room
Even in the eyes of all posterity
That wear this world out to the ending doom.
    So, till the judgment that yourself arise,
    You live in this, and dwell in lovers' eyes.

It was also very suggestive to note how here as elsewhere Shakespeare promised Willie Hughes immortality in a form that appealed to men's eyes—that is to say, in a spectacular form, in a play that is to be looked at.

For two weeks I worked hard at the Sonnets, hardly ever going out, and refusing all invitations. Every day I seemed to be discovering something new, and Willie Hughes became to me a kind of spiritual presence, an ever-dominant personality. I could almost fancy that I saw him standing in the shadow of my room, so well had Shakespeare drawn him, with his golden hair, his tender flower-like grace, his dreamy deep-sunken eyes, his delicate mobile limbs, and his white lily hands. His very name fascinated me. Willie Hughes! Willie Hughes! How musically it sounded! Yes; who else but he could have been the master-mistress of Shakespeare's passion,[1]

---

[1] Sonnet 20, 2.

The Portrait of Mr W. H.

the lord of his love to whom he was bound in vassalage,[2] the delicate minion of pleasure,[3] the rose of the whole world,[4] the herald of the spring,[5] decked in the proud livery of youth,[6] the lovely boy whom it was sweet music to hear,[7] and whose beauty was the very raiment of Shakespeare's heart,[8] as it was the keystone of his dramatic power? How bitter now seemed the whole tragedy of his desertion and his shame!—shame that he made sweet and lovely[9] by the mere magic of his personality, but that was none the less shame. Yet as Shakespeare forgave him, should not we forgive him also? I did not care to pry into the mystery of his sin or of the sin, if such it was, of the great poet who had so dearly loved him. "I am that I am," said Shakespeare in a sonnet of noble scorn,—

I am that I am, and they that level
At my abuses reckon up their own;
I may be straight, though they themselves be bevel;
By their rank thoughts my deeds must not be shown.

Willie Hughes' abandonment of Shakespeare's theatre was a different matter, and I investigated it at great length. Finally I came to the conclusion that Cyril Graham had been wrong in regarding the rival dramatist of Sonnet 80 as Chapman. It was obviously Marlowe who was alluded to. At the time the Sonnets were writ-

---

[2] Sonnet 26, 1.   [3] Sonnet 126, 9.   [4] Sonnet 109, 14.
[5] Sonnet 1, 10.   [6] Sonnet 2, 3.   [7] Sonnet 8, 1.
[8] Sonnet 22, 6.   [9] Sonnet 95, 1.

ten, which must have been between 1590 and 1595, such an expression as "the proud full sail of his great verse" could not possibly have been used of Chapman's work, however applicable it might have been to the style of his later Jacobean plays. No; Marlowe was clearly the rival poet of whom Shakespeare spoke in such laudatory terms; the hymn he wrote in Willie Hughes' honour was the unfinished "Hero and Leander," and that

> affable familiar ghost
> Which nightly gulls him with intelligence,

was the Mephistophiles of his Doctor Faustus. No doubt, Marlowe was fascinated by the beauty and grace of the boy-actor, and lured him away from the Blackfriars Theatre, that he might play the Gaveston of his "Edward II." That Shakespeare had some legal right to retain Willie Hughes in his own company seems evident from Sonnet 87, where he says:

> Farewell! thou art too dear for my possessing,
> And like enough thou know'st thy estimate:
> The charter of thy worth gives thee releasing;
> My bonds in thee are all determinate.
> For how do I hold thee but by thy granting?
> And for that riches where is my deserving?
> The cause of this fair gift in me is wanting,
> And so my patent back again is swerving.
> Thyself thou gav'st, thy own worth then not knowing,
> Or me, to whom thou gav'st it, else mistaking;
> So thy great gift, upon misprision growing,

The Portrait of Mr W. H.

Comes home again, on better judgment making.
Thus have I had thee, as a dream doth flatter,
In sleep a king, but waking no such matter.

But him whom he could not hold by love, he would not hold by force. Willie Hughes became a member of Lord Pembroke's company, and perhaps in the open yard of the Red Bull Tavern, played the part of King Edward's delicate minion. On Marlowe's death, he seems to have returned to Shakespeare, who, whatever his fellow-partners may have thought of the matter, was not slow to forgive the wilfulness and treachery of the young actor.

How well, too, had Shakespeare drawn the temperament of the stage-player! Willie Hughes was one of those—

That do not do the thing they most do show,
Who, moving others, are themselves as stone.

He could act love, but could not feel it, could mimic passion without realising it.

In many's looks the false heart's history
Is writ in moods and frowns and wrinkles strange,

but with Willie Hughes it was not so. "Heaven," says Shakespeare, in a sonnet of mad idolatry—

Heaven in thy creation did decree
That in thy face sweet love should ever dwell;

> Whate'er thy thoughts or thy heart's workings be,
> Thy looks should nothing thence but sweetness tell.

In his "inconstant mind" and his "false heart" it was easy to recognise the insincerity that somehow seems inseparable from the artistic nature, as in his love of praise, that desire for immediate recognition that characterises all actors. And yet, more fortunate in this than other actors, Willie Hughes was to know something of immortality. Intimately connected with Shakespeare's plays, he was to live in them, and by their production.

> Your name from hence immortal life shall have,
> Though I, once gone, to all the world must die:
> The earth can yield me but a common grave,
> When you entombed in men's eyes shall lie.
> Your monument shall be my gentle verse,
> Which eyes not yet created shall o'er-read,
> And tongues to be your being shall rehearse,
> When all the breathers of this world are dead.

Nashe with his venomous tongue had railed against Shakespeare for "reposing eternity in the mouth of a player," the reference being obviously to the Sonnets.

But to Shakespeare, the actor was a deliberate and self-conscious fellow-worker who gave form and substance to a poet's fancy, and brought into Drama the elements of a noble realism. His silence could be as eloquent as words, and his gesture as expressive, and in those terrible moments of Titan agony or of god-like pain, when thought outstrips utterance, when the soul sick with excess of anguish stammers or is dumb, and

The Portrait of Mr W. H.

the very raiment of speech is rent and torn by passion in its storm, then the actor could become, though it were but for a moment, a creative artist, and touch by his mere presence and personality those springs of terror and of pity to which tragedy appeals. This full recognition of the actor's art, and of the actor's power, was one of the things that distinguished the Romantic from the Classical Drama, and one of the things, consequently, that we owed to Shakespeare, who, fortunate in much, was fortunate also in this, that he was able to find Richard Burbage and to fashion Willie Hughes.

With what pleasure he dwelt upon Willie Hughes' influence over his audience—the "gazers" as he calls them; with what charm of fancy did he analyse the whole art! Even in the "Lover's Complaint" he speaks of his acting, and tells us that he was a nature so impressionable to the quality of dramatic situations that he could assume all "strange forms"—

> Of burning blushes, or of weeping water,
> Or swooning paleness:

explaining his meaning more fully later on where he tells us how Willie Hughes was able to deceive others by his wonderful power to—

> Blush at speeches rank, to weep at woes,
> Or to turn white and swoon at tragic shows.

It had never been pointed out before that the shepherd of this lovely pastoral, whose "youth in art and art in youth" are described with such subtlety of phrase and passion, was none other than the Mr W. H. of the Sonnets. And yet there was no doubt that he was so. Not merely in personal appearance are the two lads the same, but their natures and temperaments are identical. When the false shepherd whispers to the fickle maid—

> All my offences that abroad you see
> Are errors of the blood, none of the mind;
> Love made them not:

when he says of his lovers,

> Harm have I done to them, but ne'er was harmed;
> Kept hearts in liveries, but mine own was free,
> And reigned, commanding in his monarchy:

when he tells us of the "deep-brained sonnets" that one of them had sent him, and cries out in boyish pride—

> The broken bosoms that to me belong
> Have emptied all their fountains in my well:

it is impossible not to feel that it is Willie Hughes who is speaking to us. "Deep-brained sonnets," indeed, had Shakespeare brought him, "jewels" that to his careless eyes were but as "trifles," though—

> each several stone,
> With wit well blazoned, smiled or made some moan;

and into the well of beauty he had emptied the sweet fountain of his song. That in both places it was an actor

The Portrait of Mr W. H.

who was alluded to, was also clear. The betrayed nymph tells us of the "false fire" in her lover's cheek, of the "forced thunder" of his sighs, and of his "borrowed motion": of whom, indeed, but of an actor could it be said that to him "thought, characters, and words" were "merely Art," or that—

> To make the weeper laugh, the laugher weep,
> He had the dialect and different skill,
> Catching all passions in his craft of will?

The play on words in the last line is the same as that used in the punning sonnets, and is continued in the following stanza of the poem, where we are told of the youth who—

> did in the general bosom reign
> Of young, of old; and sexes both enchanted,

that there were those who—

> . . dialogued for him what he would say,
> Asked their own wills, and made their Wills obey.

Yes: the "rose-cheeked Adonis" of the Venus poem, the false shepherd of the "Lover's Complaint," the "tender churl," the "beauteous niggard" of the Sonnets, was none other but a young actor; and as I read through the various descriptions given of him, I saw that the love that Shakespeare bore him was as the love of a musician for some delicate instrument on which he delights to play, as a sculptor's love for some rare and exquisite material that suggests a new form of plastic beauty, a new mode of plastic expression. For all Art has its medium, its material, be it that of rhythmical words, or of pleasurable colour, or of sweet and subtly-divided sound; and, as one of the most fascinating critics of our day has pointed out, it is to the qualities inherent in each material, and special to it, that we owe the sensuous element in Art, and with it all that in Art is essentially artistic. What then shall we say of the material that the Drama requires for its perfect presentation? What of the Actor, who is the medium through which alone the Drama can truly reveal itself? Surely, in that strange mimicry of life by the living which is the mode and method of theatric art, there are sensuous elements of beauty that none of the other arts possess. Looked at from one point of view, the common players of the saffron-strewn stage are Art's most complete, most satisfying instruments. There is no passion in bronze, nor motion in marble. The sculptor must surrender colour, and the painter fullness of form. The epos changes acts into words, and music changes words into tones. It is the Drama only that, to quote the fine saying of Gervinus, uses all means at once, and, appealing both to eye and ear, has at its disposal, and in its service, form and colour, tone, look, and word, the swiftness of motion, the intense realism of visible action.

It may be that in this very completeness of the instrument lies the secret of some weakness in the art. Those arts are happiest that employ a material remote from reality, and there is a danger in the absolute identity of medium and matter, the danger of ignoble realism and unimaginative imitation. Yet Shakespeare himself was a

The Portrait of Mr W. H.

player, and wrote for players. He saw the possibilities that lay hidden in an art that up to his time had expressed itself but in bombast or in clowning. He has left us the most perfect rules for acting that have ever been written. He created parts that can be only truly revealed to us on the stage, wrote plays that need the theatre for their full realisation, and we cannot marvel that he so worshipped one who was the interpreter of his vision, as he was the incarnation of his dreams.

There was, however, more in his friendship than the mere delight of a dramatist in one who helps him to achieve his end. This was indeed a subtle element of pleasure, if not of passion, and a noble basis for an artistic comradeship. But it was not all that the Sonnets revealed to us. There was something beyond. There was the soul, as well as the language, of neo-Platonism.

"The fear of the Lord is the beginning of wisdom," said the stern Hebrew prophet: "The beginning of wisdom is Love," was the gracious message of the Greek. And the spirit of the Renaissance, which already touched Hellenism at so many points, catching the inner meaning of this phrase and divining its secret, sought to elevate friendship to the high dignity of the antique ideal, to make it a vital factor in the new culture, and a mode of self-conscious intellectual development. In 1492 appeared Marsilio Ficino's translation of the "Symposium" of Plato, and this wonderful dialogue, of all the Platonic dialogues perhaps the most perfect, as it is the most poetical, began to exercise a strange influence over men, and to colour their words and thoughts, and manner of living. In its subtle suggestions of sex in soul, in the curious analogies it draws between intellectual enthusiasm and the physical passion of love, in its dream of the incarnation of the Idea in a beautiful and living form, and of a real spiritual conception with a travail and a bringing to birth, there was something that fascinated the poets and scholars of the sixteenth century. Shakespeare, certainly, was fascinated by it, and had read the dialogue, if not in Ficino's translation, of which many copies found their way to England, perhaps in that French translation by Leroy to which Joachim du Bellay contributed so many graceful metrical versions. When he says to Willie Hughes,

> he that calls on thee, let him bring forth
> Eternal numbers to outlive long date,

he is thinking of Diotima's theory that Beauty is the goddess who presides over birth, and draws into the light of day the dim conceptions of the soul: when he tells us of the "marriage of true minds," and exhorts his friend to beget children that time cannot destroy, he is but repeating the words in which the prophetess tells us that "friends are married by a far nearer tie than those who beget mortal children, for fairer and more immortal are the children who are their common offspring." So, also, Edward Blount in his dedication of "Hero and Leander" talks of Marlowe's works as his "right children," being the "issue of his brain"; and when Bacon claims that "the best works and of greatest merit for the public have proceeded from the unmarried and childless men, which both in affection and means have married and endowed the public," he is paraphrasing a passage in the "Symposium."

The Portrait of Mr W. H.

Friendship, indeed, could have desired no better warrant for its permanence or its ardours than the Platonic theory, or creed, as we might better call it, that the true world was the world of ideas, and that these ideas took visible form and became incarnate in man, and it is only when we realise the influence of neo-Platonism on the Renaissance that we can understand the true meaning of the amatory phrases and words with which friends were wont, at this time, to address each other. There was a kind of mystic transference of the expressions of the physical sphere to a sphere that was spiritual, that was removed from gross bodily appetite, and in which the soul was Lord. Love had, indeed, entered the olive garden of the new Academe, but he wore the same flame-coloured raiment, and had the same words of passion on his lips.

Michael Angelo, the "haughtiest spirit in Italy" as he has been called, addresses the young Tommaso Cavalieri in such fervent and passionate terms that some have thought that the sonnets in question must have been intended for that noble lady, the widow of the Marchese di Pescara, whose white hand, when she was dying, the great sculptor's lips had stooped to kiss. But that it was to Cavalieri that they were written, and that the literal interpretation is the right one, is evident not merely from the fact that Michael Angelo plays with his name, as Shakespeare plays with the name of Willie Hughes, but from the direct evidence of Varchi, who was well acquainted with the young man, and who, indeed, tells us that he possessed "besides imcomparable personal beauty, so much charm of nature, such excellent abilities, and such a graceful manner, that he deserved, and still deserves, to be the better loved the more he is known." Strange as these sonnets may seem to us now, when rightly interpreted they merely serve to show with what intense and religious fervour Michael Angelo addressed himself to the worship of intellectual beauty, and how, to borrow a fine phrase from Mr Symonds, he pierced through the veil of flesh and sought the divine idea it imprisoned. In the sonnet written for Luigi del Riccio on the death of his friend, Cecchino Bracci, we can also trace, as Mr Symonds points out, the Platonic conception of love as nothing if not spiritual, and of beauty as a form that finds its immortality within the lover's soul. Cecchino was a lad who died at the age of seventeen, and when Luigi asked Michael Angelo to make a portrait of him, Michael Angelo answered, "I can only do so by drawing you in whom he still lives."

> If the beloved in the lover shine,
> Since Art without him cannot work alone,
> Thee must I carve, to tell the world of him.

The same idea is also put forward in Montaigne's noble essay on Friendship, a passion which he ranks higher than the love of brother for brother, or the love of man for woman. He tells us—I quote from Florio's translation, one of the books with which Shakespeare was familiar—how "perfect amitie" is indivisible, how it "possesseth the soule, and swaies it in all soveraigntie," and how "by the interposition of a spiritual beauty the desire of a spiritual conception is engendered in the beloved." He writes of an "internall beauty, of difficile knowledge, and abtruse discovery" that is revealed unto

The Portrait of Mr W. H.

friends, and unto friends only. He mourns for the dead Etienne de la Boëtie, in accents of wild grief and inconsolable love. The learned Hubert Languet, the friend of Melanchthon and of the leaders of the reformed church, tells the young Philip Sidney how he kept his portrait by him some hours to feast his eyes upon it, and how his appetite was "rather increased than diminished by the sight," and Sidney writes to him, "the chief hope of my life, next to the everlasting blessedness of heaven, will always be the enjoyment of true friendship, and there you shall have the chiefest place." Later on there came to Sidney's house in London, one—some day to be burned at Rome, for the sin of seeing God in all things —Giordano Bruno, just fresh from his triumph before the University of Paris. "A filosofia à necessario amore" were the words ever upon his lips, and there was something in his strange ardent personality that made men feel that he had discovered the new secret of life. Ben Jonson writing to one of his friends subscribes himself "your true lover," and dedicates his noble eulogy on Shakespeare "To the memory of my Beloved." Richard Barnfield in his "Affectionate Shepherd" flutes on soft Virgilian reed the story of his attachment to some young Elizabethan of the day. Out of all the Eclogues, Abraham Fraunce selects the second for translation, and Fletcher's lines to Master W.C. show what fascination was hidden in the mere name of Alexis.

It was no wonder then that Shakespeare had been stirred by a spirit that so stirred his age. There had been critics, like Hallam, who had regretted that the Sonnets had ever been written, who had seen in them something dangerous, something unlawful even. To them it would have been sufficient to answer in Chapman's noble words:

> There is no danger to a man that knows
> What Life and Death is: there's not any law
> Exceeds his knowledge: neither is it lawful
> That he should stoop to any other law.

But it was evident that the Sonnets needed no such defence as this, and that those who had talked of "the folly of excessive and misplaced affection" had not been able to interpret either the language or the spirit of these great poems, so intimately connected with the philosophy and the art of their time. It is no doubt true that to be filled with an absorbing passion is to surrender the security of one's lover life, and yet in such surrender there may be gain; certainly there was for Shakespeare. When Pico della Mirandola crossed the threshold of the villa of Careggi, and stood before Marsilio Ficino in all the grace and comeliness of his wonderful youth, the aged scholar seemed to see in him the realisation of the Greek ideal, and determined to devote his remaining years to the translation of Plotinus, that new Plato, in whom, as Mr Pater reminds us, "the mystical element in the Platonic philosophy had been worked out to the utmost limit of vision and ecstasy." A romantic friendship with a young Roman of his day initiated Winckelmann into the secret of Greek art, taught him the mystery of its beauty and the meaning of its form. In Willie Hughes, Shakespeare found not merely a most delicate instrument for the presentation of his art, but the visible incarnation of his idea of beauty, and it is not too much

The Portrait of Mr W. H.

to say that to this young actor, whose very name the dull writers of his age forgot to chronicle, the Romantic Movement of English Literature is largely indebted.

I I I

One evening I thought that I had really discovered Willie Hughes in Elizabethan literature. In a wonderfully graphic account of the last days of the great Earl of Essex, his chaplain, Thomas Knell, tells us that the night before the Earl died, "he called William Hewes, which was his musician, to play upon the virginals and to sing. 'Play,' said he, 'my song, Will Hewes, and I will sing it myself.' So he did it most joyfully, not as the howling swan, which, still looking down, waileth her end, but as a sweet lark, lifting up his hands and casting up his eyes to his God, with this mounted the crystal skies, and reached with his unwearied tongue the top of highest heavens." Surely the boy who played on the virginals to the dying father of Sidney's Stella was none other than the Will Hews to whom Shakespeare dedicated the Sonnets, and who he tells us was himself sweet "music to hear." Yet Lord Essex died in 1576, when Shakespeare was but twelve years of age. It was impossible that his musician could have been the Mr W. H. of the Sonnets. Perhaps Shakespeare's young friend was the son of the player upon the virginals? It was at least something to have discovered that Will Hews was an Elizabethan name. Indeed the name Hews seemed to have been closely connected with music and the stage. The first English actress was the lovely Margaret Hews, whom Prince Rupert so madly adored. What more probable than that between her and Lord Essex' musician had come the boy-actor of Shakespeare's plays? In 1587 a certain Thomas Hews brought out at Gray's Inn a Euripidean tragedy entitled "The Misfortunes of Arthur," receiving much assistance in the arrangement of the dumb shows from one Francis Bacon, then a student of law. Surely he was some near kinsman of the lad to whom Shakespeare said—

Take all my loves, my love, yea, take them all;

the "profitless usurer" of "unused beauty," as he describes him. But the proofs, the links—where were they? Alas! I could not find them. It seemed to me that I was always on the brink of absolute verification, but that I could never really attain to it. I thought it strange that no one had ever written a history of the English boy-actors of the sixteenth and seventeenth centuries, and determined to undertake the task myself, and to try to ascertain their true relations to the drama. The subject was, certainly, full of artistic interest. These lads had been the delicate reeds through which our poets had sounded their sweetest strains, the gracious vessels of honour into which they had poured the purple wine of their song. Foremost, naturally, among them all had been the youth to whom Shakespeare had intrusted the realisation of his most exquisite creations. Beauty had been his, such as our age has never, or but rarely seen, a beauty that seemed to combine the charm of both sexes, and to have wedded, as the Sonnets tell us, the grace of Adonis and the loveliness of Helen. He had been quick-witted, too, and eloquent, and from those finely curved lips that the

The Portrait of Mr W. H.

satirist had mocked at had come the passionate cry of Juliet, and the bright laughter of Beatrice, Perdita's flower-like words, and Ophelia's wandering songs. Yet as Shakespeare himself had been but as a god among giants, so Willie Hughes had only been one out of many marvellous lads to whom our English Renaissance owed something of the secret of its joy, and it appeared to me that they also were worthy of some study and record.

In a little book with fine vellum leaves and damask silk cover—a fancy of mine in those fanciful days—I accordingly collected such information as I could about them, and even now there is something in the scanty record of their lives, in the mere mention of their names, that attracts me. I seemed to know them all: Robin Armin, the goldsmith's lad who was lured by Tarlton to go on the stage: Sandford, whose performance of the courtezan Flamantia Lord Burleigh witnessed at Gray's Inn: Cooke, who played Agrippina in the tragedy of "Sejanus": Nat. Field, whose young and beardless portrait is still preserved for us at Dulwich, and who in "Cynthia's Revels" played the "Queen and Huntress chaste and fair": Gil. Carie, who, attired as a mountain nymph, sang in the same lovely masque Echo's song of mourning for Narcissus: Parsons, the Salmacis of the strange pageant of "Tamburlaine": Will. Ostler, who was one of "The Children of the Queen's Chapel," and accompanied King James to Scotland: George Vernon, to whom the King sent a cloak of scarlet cloth, and a cape of crimson velvet: Alick Gough, who performed the part of Cænis, Vespasian's concubine, in Massingers' "Roman Actor," and three years later that of Acanthe, in the same dramatist's "Picture": Barrett, the heroine of Richards' tragedy of "Messalina": Dicky Robinson, "a very pretty fellow," Ben Jonson tells us, who was a member of Shakespeare's company, and was known for his exquisite taste in costume, as well as for his love of woman's apparel: Salathiel Pavy, whose early and tragic death Jonson mourned in one of the sweetest threnodies of our literature: Arthur Savile, who was one of "the players of Prince Charles," and took a girl's part in a comedy by Marmion: Stephen Hammerton, "a most noted and beautiful woman actor," whose pale oval face with its heavy-lidded eyes and somewhat sensuous mouth looks out at us from a curious miniature of the time: Hart, who made his first success by playing the Duchess in the tragedy of "The Cardinal," and who in a poem that is clearly modelled upon some of Shakespeare's Sonnets is described by one who had seen him as "beauty to the eye, and music to the ear": and Kynaston, of whom Betterton said that "it has been disputed among the judicious, whether any woman could have more sensibly touched the passions," and whose white hands and amber-coloured hair seem to have retarded by some years the introduction of actresses upon our stage.

The Puritans, with their uncouth morals and ignoble minds, had of course railed against them, and dwelt on the impropriety of boys disguising as women, and learning to affect the manners and passions of the female sex. Gosson, with his shrill voice, and Prynne, soon to be made earless for many shameful slanders, and others to whom the rare and subtle sense of abstract beauty was denied, had from pulpit and through pamphlet said foul or foolish things to their dishonour. To Francis Lenton, writing in 1629, what he speaks of as—

The Portrait of Mr W. H.

> loose action, mimic gesture
> By a poor boy clad in a princely vesture,

is but one of the many—

> tempting baits of hell
> Which draw more youth unto the damned cell
> Of furious lust, than all the devil could do
> Since he obtained his first overthrow.

Deuteronomy was quoted and the ill-digested learning of the period laid under contribution. Even our own time had not appreciated the artistic conditions of the Elizabethan and Jacobean drama. One of the most brilliant and intellectual actresses of this century had laughed at the idea of a lad of seventeen or eighteen playing Imogen, or Miranda, or Rosalind. "How could any youth, however gifted and specially trained, even faintly suggest these fair and noble women to an audience? . . . One quite pities Shakespeare, who had to put up with seeing his brightest creations marred, misrepresented, and spoiled." In his book on "Shakespeare's Predecessors" Mr John Addington Symonds also had talked of "hobbledehoys" trying to represent the pathos of Desdemona and Juliet's passion. Were they right? Are they right? I did not think so then. I do not think so now. Those who remember the Oxford production of the "Agamemnon," the fine utterance and marble dignity of the Clytemnestra, the romantic and imaginative rendering of the prophetic madness of Cassandra, will not agree with Lady Martin or Mr Symonds in their strictures on the conditions of the Elizabethan stage.

Oscar Wilde

Of all the motives of dramatic curiosity used by our great playwrights, there is none more subtle or more fascinating than the ambiguity of the sexes. This idea, invented, as far as an artistic idea can be said to be invented, by Lyly, perfected and made exquisite for us by Shakespeare, seems to me to owe its origin, as it certainly owes its possibility of lifelike presentation, to the circumstance that the Elizabethan stage, like the stage of the Greeks, admitted the appearance of no female performers. It is because Lyly was writing for the boy-actors of St Paul's that we have the confused sexes and complicated loves of Phillida and Gallathea: it is because Shakespeare was writing for Willie Hughes that Rosalind dons doublet and hose, and calls herself Ganymede, that Viola and Julia put on pages' dress, that Imogen steals away in male attire. To say that only a woman can portray the passions of a woman, and that therefore no boy can play Rosalind, is to rob the art of acting of all claim to objectivity, and to assign to the mere accident of sex what properly belongs to imaginative insight and creative energy. Indeed, if sex be an element in artistic creation, it might rather be urged that the delightful combination of wit and romance which characterises so many of Shakespeare's heroines was at least occasioned if it was not actually caused by the fact that the players of these parts were lads and young men, whose passionate purity, quick mobile fancy, and healthy freedom from sentimentality can hardly fail to have suggested a new and delightful type of girlhood or of womanhood. The very difference of sex between the player and the part he represented must also, as Professor Ward points out, have constituted "one more demand upon the imaginative

The Portrait of Mr W. H.

capacities of the spectators," and must have kept them from that over-realistic identification of the actor with his rôle, which is one of the weak points in modern theatrical criticism.

This, too, must be granted, that it was to these boy-actors that we owe the introduction of those lovely lyrics that star the plays of Shakespeare, Dekker, and so many of the dramatists of the period, those "snatches of bird-like or god-like song," as Mr Swinburne calls them. For it was out of the choirs of the cathedrals and royal chapels of England that most of these lads came, and from their earliest years they had been trained in the singing of anthems and madrigals, and in all that concerns the subtle art of music. Chosen at first for the beauty of their voices, as well as for a certain comeliness and freshness of appearance, they were then instructed in gesture, dancing, and elocution, and taught to play both tragedies and comedies in the English as well as in the Latin language. Indeed, acting seems to have formed part of the ordinary education of the time, and to have been much studied not merely by the scholars of Eton and Westminster, but also by the students at the Universities of Oxford and Cambridge, some of whom went afterwards upon the public stage, as is becoming not uncommon in our own day. The great actors, too, had their pupils and apprentices, who were formally bound over to them by legal warrant, to whom they imparted the secrets of their craft, and who were so much valued that we read of Henslowe, one of the managers of the Rose Theatre, buying a trained boy of the name of James Bristowe for eight pieces of gold. The relations that existed between the masters and their pupils seem to have been of the most cordial and affectionate character. Robin Armin was looked upon by Tarlton as his adopted son, and in a will dated "the fourth daie of Maie, anno Domini 1605," Augustine Phillips, Shakespeare's dear friend and fellow-actor, bequeathed to one of his apprentices his "purple cloke, sword, and dagger," his "base viall," and much rich apparel, and to another a sum of money and many beautiful instruments of music, "to be delivered unto him at the expiration of his terme of yeres in his indenture of apprenticehood." Now and then, when some daring actor kidnapped a boy for the stage, there was an outcry or an investigation. In 1600, for instance, a certain Norfolk gentleman of the name of Henry Clifton came to live in London in order that his son, then about thirteen years of age, might have the opportunity of attending the Bluecoat School, and from a petition which he presented to the Star Chamber, and which has been recently brought to light by Mr Greenstreet, we learn that as the boy was walking quietly to Christ Church cloister one winter morning he was waylaid by James Robinson, Henry Evans, and Nathaniel Giles, and carried off to the Blackfriars Theatre, "amongste a companie of lewde and dissolute mercenarie players," as his father calls them, in order that he might be trained "in acting of parts in base playes and enterludes." Hearing of his son's misadventure, Mr Clifton went down at once to the theatre, and demanded his surrender, but "the sayd Nathaniel Giles, James Robinson and Henry Evans most arrogantlie then and there answered that they had authoritie sufficient soe to take any noble man's sonne in this land," and handing the young schoolboy "a scrolle of paper, conteyning parte of one of their said playes and enterludes," commanded

The Portrait of Mr W. H.

him to learn it by heart. Through a warrant issued by Sir John Fortescue, however, the boy was restored to his father the next day, and the Court of Star Chamber seems to have suspended or cancelled Evans' privileges.

The fact is that, following a precedent set by Richard III, Elizabeth had issued a commission authorising certain persons to impress into her service all boys who had beautiful voices that they might sing for her in her Chapel Royal, and Nathaniel Giles, her Chief Commissioner, finding that he could deal profitably with the managers of the Globe Theatre, agreed to supply them with personable and graceful lads for the playing of female parts, under colour of taking them for the Queen's service. The actors, accordingly, had a certain amount of legal warrant on their side, and it is interesting to note that many of the boys whom they carried off from their schools or homes, such as Salathiel Pavy, Nat. Field, and Alvery Trussell, became so fascinated by their new art that they attached themselves permanently to the theatre, and would not leave it.

Once it seemed as if girls were to take the place of boys upon the stage, and among the christenings chronicled in the registers of St. Giles', Cripplegate, occurs the following strange and suggestive entry: "Comedia, baseborn, daughter of Alice Bowker and William Johnson, one of the Queen's plaiers, 10 Feb. 1589." But the child upon whom such high hopes had been built died at six years of age, and when, later on, some French actresses came over and played at Blackfriars, we learn that they were "hissed, hooted, and pippin-pelted from the stage." I think that, from what I have said above, we need not regret this in any way. The essentially male culture of the

English Renaissance found its fullest and most perfect expression by its own method, and in its own manner.

I remember I used to wonder, at this time, what had been the social position and early life of Willie Hughes before Shakespeare had met with him. My investigations into the history of the boy-actors had made me curious of every detail about him. Had he stood in the carved stall of some gilded choir, reading out of a great book painted with square scarlet notes and long black key-lines? We know from the Sonnets how clear and pure his voice was, and what skill he had in the art of music. Noble gentlemen, such as the Earl of Leicester and Lord Oxford, had companies of boy-players in their service as part of their household. When Leicester went to the Netherlands in 1585 he brought with him a certain "Will" described as a "plaier." Was this Willie Hughes? Had he acted for Leicester at Kenilworth, and was it there that Shakespeare had first known him? Or was he, like Robin Armin, simply a lad of low degree, but possessing some strange beauty and marvellous fascination? It was evident from the early sonnets that when Shakespeare first came across him he had no connection whatsoever with the stage, and that he was not of high birth has already been shewn. I began to think of him not as the delicate chorister of a Royal Chapel, not as a petted minion trained to sing and dance in Leicester's stately masque, but as some fair-haired English lad whom in one of London's hurrying streets, or on Windsor's green silent meadows, Shakespeare had seen and followed, recognising the artistic possibilities that lay hidden in so comely and gracious a form, and divining by a quick and subtle instinct what an actor the lad would make could

The Portrait of Mr W. H.

he be induced to go upon the stage. At this time Willie Hughes' father was dead, as we learn from Sonnet 13, and his mother, whose remarkable beauty he is said to have inherited, may have been induced to allow him to become Shakespeare's apprentice by the fact that boys who played female characters were paid extremely large salaries, larger salaries, indeed, than were given to grown-up actors. Shakespeare's apprentice, at any rate, we know that he became, and we know what a vital factor he was in the development of Shakespeare's art. As a rule, a boy-actor's capacity for representing girlish parts on the stage lasted but for a few years at most. Such characters as Lady Macbeth, Queen Constance and Volumnia, remained of course always within the reach of those who had true dramatic genius and noble presence. Absolute youth was not necessary here, not desirable even. But with Imogen, and Perdita, and Juliet, it was different. "Your beard has begun to grow, and I pray God your voice be not cracked," says Hamlet mockingly to the boy-actor of the strolling company that came to visit him at Elsinore; and certainly when chins grew rough and voices harsh much of the charm and grace of the performance must have gone. Hence comes Shakespeare's passionate preoccupation with the youth of Willie Hughes, his terror of old age and wasting years, his wild appeal to time to spare the beauty of his friend:

> Make glad and sorry seasons as thou fleet'st,
> And do whate'er thou wilt, swift-footed time,
> To the wide world and all her fading sweets;
> But I forbid thee one most heinous crime:
> O carve not with thy hours my Love's fair brow

> Nor draw no lines there with thine antique pen;
> Him in thy course untainted do allow
> For beauty's pattern to succeeding men.

Time seems to have listened to Shakespeare's prayers, or perhaps Willie Hughes had the secret of perpetual youth. After three years he is quite unchanged:

> To me, fair friend, you never can be old,
> For as you were when first your eye I eyed,
> Such seems your beauty still. Three winters' cold
> Have from the forests shook three summers' pride,
> Three beauteous springs to yellow autumn turned,
> In process of the seasons have I seen,
> Three April perfumes in three hot Junes burned,
> Since first I saw you fresh which yet are green.

More years pass over, and the bloom of his boyhood seems to be still with him. When, in "The Tempest," Shakespeare, through the lips of Prospero, flung away the wand of his imagination and gave his poetic sovereignty into the weak, graceful hands of Fletcher, it may be that the Miranda who stood wondering by was none other than Willie Hughes himself, and in the last sonnet that his friend addressed to him, the enemy that is feared is not Time but Death.

> O thou, my lovely boy, who in thy power
> Dost hold time's fickle glass, his sickle hour;
> Who hast by waning grown, and therein show'st
> Thy lovers withering as thy sweet self grow'st;
> If Nature, sovereign mistress over wrack,

The Portrait of Mr W. H.

As thou goest onwards, still will pluck thee back,
She keeps thee to this purpose, that her skill
May Time disgrace and wretched minutes kill.
Yet fear her, O thou minion of her pleasure!
She may detain, but not still keep, her treasure.
Her audit, though delay'd, answer'd must be,
And her quietus is to render thee.

IV

It was not for some weeks after I had begun my study of the subject that I ventured to approach the curious group of Sonnets (127-152) that deal with the dark woman who, like a shadow or thing of evil omen, came across Shakespeare's great romance, and for a season stood between him and Willie Hughes. They were obviously printed out of their proper place and should have been inserted between Sonnets 33 and 40. Psychological and artistic reasons necessitated this change, a change which I hope will be adopted by all future editors, as without it an entirely false impression is conveyed of the nature and final issue of this noble friendship.

Who was she, this black-browed, olive-skinned woman, with her amorous mouth "that Love's own hand did make," her "cruel eye," and her "foul pride," her strange skill on the virginals and her false, fascinating nature? An over-curious scholar of our day had seen in her a symbol of the Catholic Church, of that Bride of Christ who is "black but comely." Professor Minto, following in the footsteps of Henry Brown, had regarded the whole group of Sonnets as simply "exercises of skill undertaken in a spirit of wanton defiance and derision of the commonplace." Mr Gerald Massey, without any historical proof or probability, had insisted that they were addressed to the celebrated Lady Rich, the Stella of Sir Philip Sidney's sonnets, the Philoclea of his "Arcadia," and that they contained no personal revelation of Shakespeare's life and love, having been written in Lord Pembroke's name and at his request. Mr Tyler had suggested that they referred to one of Queen Elizabeth's maids-of-honour, by name Mary Fitton. But none of these explanations satisfied the conditions of the problem. The woman that came between Shakespeare and Willie Hughes was a real woman, black-haired, and married, and of evil repute. Lady Rich's fame was evil enough, it is true, but her hair was of—

> fine threads of finest gold,
> In curled knots man's thought to hold,

and her shoulders like "white doves perching." She was, as King James said to her lover, Lord Mountjoy, "a fair woman with a black soul." As for Mary Fitton, we know that she was unmarried in 1601, the time when her amour with Lord Pembroke was discovered, and besides, any theories that connected Lord Pembroke with the Sonnets were, as Cyril Graham had shewn, put entirely out of court by the fact that Lord Pembroke did not come to London till they had been actually written and read by Shakespeare to his friends.

It was not, however, her name that interested me. I was content to hold with Professor Dowden that "To the eyes of no diver among the wrecks of time will that curious

The Portrait of Mr W. H.

talisman gleam." What I wanted to discover was the nature of her influence over Shakespeare, as well as the characteristics of her personality. Two things were certain: she was much older than the poet, and the fascination that she exercised over him was at first purely intellectual. He began by feeling no physical passion for her. "I do not love thee with mine eyes," he says:

> Nor are mine ears with thy tongue's tune delighted;
> Nor tender feeling to base touches prone,
> Nor taste, nor smell, desire to be invited
> To any senual feast with thee alone.

He did not even think her beautiful:

> My mistress' eyes are nothing like the sun;
> Coral is far more red than her lips' red:
> If snow be white, why then her breasts are dun;
> If hairs be wires, black wires grow on her head.

He had his moments of loathing for her, for, not content with enslaving the soul of Shakespeare, she seems to have sought to snare the senses of Willie Hughes. Then Shakespeare cries aloud,—

> Two loves I have of comfort and despair,
> Which like two spirits do suggest me still:
> The better angel is a man right fair,
> The worser spirit a woman colour'd ill.
> To win me soon to hell, my female evil
> Tempteth my better angel from my side,
> And would corrupt my saint to be a devil,
> Wooing his purity with her foul pride.

Then he sees her as she really is, the "bay where all men ride," the "wide world's common place," the woman who is in the "very refuse" of her evil deeds, and who is "as black as hell, as dark as night." Then it is that he pens that great sonnet upon Lust ("Th' expense of spirit in a waste of shame"), of which Mr Theodore Watts says rightly that it is the greatest sonnet ever written. And it is then, also, that he offers to mortgage his very life and genius to her if she will but restore to him that "sweetest friend" of whom she had robbed him.

To compass this end he abandons himself to her, feigns to be full of an absorbing and sensuous passion of possession, forges false words of love, lies to her, and tells her that he lies.

My thoughts and my discourse as madmen's are,
At random from the truth vainly express'd;
  For I have sworn thee fair, and thought thee bright,
  Who art as black as hell, as dark as night.

Rather than suffer his friend to be treacherous to him, he will himself be treacherous to his friend. To shield his purity, he will himself be vile. He knew the weakness of the boy-actor's nature, his susceptibility to praise, his inordinate love of admiration, and deliberately set himself to fascinate the woman who had come between them.

It is never with impunity that one's lips say Love's Litany. Words have their mystical power over the soul, and form can create the feeling from which it should have sprung. Sincerity itself, the ardent, momentary sincerity of the artist, is often the unconscious result of style, and in the case of those rare temperaments that are

The Portrait of Mr W. H.

exquisitely susceptible to the influences of language, the use of certain phrases and modes of expression can stir the very pulse of passion, can send the red blood coursing through the veins, and can transform into a strange sensuous energy what in its origin had been mere æsthetic impulse, and desire of art. So, at least, it seems to have been with Shakespeare. He begins by pretending to love, wears a lover's apparel and has a lover's words upon his lips. What does it matter? It is only acting, only a comedy in real life. Suddenly he finds that what his tongue had spoken his soul had listened to, and that the raiment that he had put on for disguise is a plague-stricken and poisonous thing that eats into his flesh, and that he cannot throw away. Then comes Desire, with its many maladies, and Lust that makes one love all that one loathes, and Shame, with its ashen face and secret smile. He is enthralled by this dark woman, is for a season separated from his friend, and becomes the "vassal-wretch" of one whom he knows to be evil and perverse and unworthy of his love, as of the love of Willie Hughes. "O, from what power," he says,—

> hast thou this powerful might,
> With insufficiency my heart to sway?
> To make me give the lie to my true sight,
> And swear that brightness does not grace the day?
> Whence has thou this becoming of things ill,
> That in the very refuse of thy deeds
> There is such strength and warrantise of skill
> That, in my mind, thy worst all best exceeds?

He is keenly conscious of his own degradation, and finally, realising that his genius is nothing to her compared to the physical beauty of the young actor, he cuts with a quick knife the bond that binds him to her, and in this bitter sonnet bids her farewell:—

> In loving thee thou know'st I am forsworn,
> But thou art twice forsworn, to me love swearing;
> In act thy bed-vow broke, and new faith torn,
> In vowing new hate after new love bearing.
> But why of two oaths' breach do I accuse thee,
> When I break twenty? I am perjur'd most;
> For all my vows are oaths but to misuse thee,
> And all my honest faith in thee is lost:
> For I have sworn deep oaths of thy deep kindness,
> Oaths of thy love, thy truth, thy constancy;
> And, to enlighten thee, gave eyes to blindness,
> Or made them swear against the thing they see;
>   For I have sworn thee fair; more perjur'd I,
>   To swear against the truth so foul a lie!

His attitude towards Willie Hughes in the whole matter shews at once the fervour and the self-abnegation of the great love he bore him. There is a poignant touch of pathos in the close of this sonnet:

> Those pretty wrongs that liberty commits,
> When I am sometime absent from thy heart,
> Thy beauty and thy years full well befits,
> For still temptation follows where thou art.
> Gentle thou art, and therefore to be won,
> Beauteous thou art, therefore to be assailed;
> And when a woman woos, what woman's son
> Will sourly leave her till she have prevailed?
> Ay me! but yet thou mightst my seat forbear,

The Portrait of Mr W. H.

> And chide thy beauty and thy straying youth,
> Who lead thee in their riot even there
> Where thou art forc'd to break a two-fold truth,—
> > Hers, by thy beauty tempting her to thee,
> > Thine, by thy beauty being false to me.

But here he makes it manifest that his forgiveness was full and complete:

> No more be griev'd at that which thou hast done:
> Roses have thorns, and silver fountains mud;
> Clouds and eclipses stain both moon and sun,
> And loathsome canker lives in sweetest bud.
> All men make faults, and even I in this,
> Authorising thy trespass with compare,
> Myself corrupting, salving thy amiss,
> Excusing thy sins more than thy sins are;
> For to thy sensual fault I bring in sense,—
> Thy adverse party is thy advocate,—
> And 'gainst myself a lawful plea commence:
> Such civil war is in my love and hate,
> > That I an accessary needs must be
> > To that sweet thief which sourly robs from me.

Shortly afterwards Shakespeare left London for Stratford (Sonnets 43-52), and when he returned Willie Hughes seems to have grown tired of the woman who for a little time had fascinated him. Her name is never mentioned again in the Sonnets, nor is there any allusion made to her. She had passed out of their lives.

But who was she? And, even if her name has not come down to us, were there any allusions to her in contemporary literature? It seems to me that although better educated than most of the women of her time, she was not nobly born, but was probably the profligate wife of some old and wealthy citizen. We know that women of this class, which was then first rising into social prominence, were strangely fascinated by the new art of stage playing. They were to be found almost every afternoon at the theatre, when dramatic performances were being given, and "The Actors' Remonstrance" is eloquent on the subject of their amours with the young actors.

Cranley in his "Amanda" tells us of one who loved to mimic the actor's disguises, appearing one day "embroidered, laced, perfumed, in glittering show . . . as brave as any Countess," and the next day, "all in mourning, black and sad," now in the grey cloak of a country wench, and now "in the neat habit of a citizen." She was a curious woman, "more changeable and wavering than the moon," and the books that she loved to read were Shakespeare's "Venus and Adonis," Beaumont's "Salmacis and Hermaphroditus," amorous pamphlets, and "songs of love and sonnets exquisite." These sonnets, that were to her the "bookes of her devotion," were surely none other but Shakespeare's own, for the whole description reads like the portrait of the woman who fell in love with Willie Hughes, and, lest we should have any doubt on the subject, Cranley, borrowing Shakespeare's play on words, tells us that, in her "proteus-like strange shapes," she is one who—

Changes hews with the chameleon.

Manningham's Table-book, also, contains a clear allusion to the same story. Manningham was a student at

The Portrait of Mr W. H.

the Middle Temple with Sir Thomas Overbury and Edmund Curle, whose chambers he seems to have shared; and his Diary is still preserved among the Harleian MSS. at the British Museum, a small duodecimo book written in a fair and tolerably legible hand, and containing many unpublished anecdotes about Shakespeare, Sir Walter Raleigh, Spenser, Ben Jonson and others. The dates, which are inserted with much care, extend from January 1600-1 to April 1603, and under the heading "March 13, 1601," Manningham tells us that he heard from a member of Shakespeare's company that a certain citizen's wife being at the Globe Theatre one afternoon, fell in love with one of the actors, and "grew so farre in liking with him, that before shee went from the play shee appointed him to come that night unto hir," but that Shakespeare "overhearing their conclusion" anticipated his friend and came first to the lady's house, "went before and was entertained," as Manningham puts it, with some added looseness of speech which it is unnecessary to quote.

It seemed to me that we had here a common and distorted version of the story that is revealed to us in the Sonnets, the story of the dark woman's love for Willie Hughes, and Shakespeare's mad attempt to make her love him in his friend's stead. It was not, of course, necessary to accept it as absolutely true in every detail. According to Manningham's informant, for instance, the name of the actor in question was not Willie Hughes, but Richard Burbage. Tavern gossip, however, is proverbially inaccurate, and Burbage was, no doubt, dragged into the story to give point to the foolish jest about William the Conqueror and Richard the Third, with which the entry in Manningham's Diary ends. Burbage was our first great tragic actor, but it needed all his genius to counterbalance the physical defects of low stature and corpulent figure under which he laboured, and he was not the sort of man who would have fascinated the dark woman of the Sonnets, or would have cared to be fascinated by her. There was no doubt that Willie Hughes was referred to, and the private diary of a young law student of the time thus curiously corroborated Cyril Graham's wonderful guess at the secret of Shakespeare's great romance. Indeed, when taken in conjunction with "Amanda," Manningham's Table-book seemed to me to be an extremely strong link in the chain of evidence, and to place the new interpretation of the Sonnets on something like a secure historic basis, the fact that Cranley's poem was not published till after Shakespeare's death being really rather in favour of this view, as it was not likely that he would have ventured during the lifetime of the great dramatist to revive the memory of this tragic and bitter story.

This passion for the dark lady also enabled me to fix with still greater certainty the date of the Sonnets. From internal evidence, from the characteristics of language, style, and the like, it was evident that they belonged to Shakespeare's early period, the period of "Love's Labour's Lost" and "Venus and Adonis." With the play, indeed, they are intimately connected. They display the same delicate euphuism, the same delight in fanciful phrase and curious expression, the artistic wilfulness and studied graces of the same "fair tongue, conceit's expositor," Rosaline, the—

> whitely wanton with a velvet brow,
> With two pitch balls stuck in her face for eyes,

The Portrait of Mr W. H.

who is born "to make black fair," and whose "favour turns the fashion of the days," is the dark lady of the Sonnets who makes black "beauty's successive heir." In the comedy as well as in the poems we have that half-sensuous philosophy that exalts the judgment of the senses "above all slower, more toilsome means of knowledge," and Berowne is perhaps, as Walter Pater suggests, a reflex of Shakespeare himself "when he has just become able to stand aside from and estimate the first period of his poetry."

Now though "Love's Labour's Lost" was not published till 1598, when it was brought out "newlie corrected and augmented" by Cuthbert Burby, there is no doubt that it was written and produced on the stage at a much earlier date, probably, as Professor Dowden points out, in 1588-9. If this be so, it is clear that Shakespeare's first meeting with Willie Hughes must have been in 1585, and it is just possible that this young actor may, after all, have been in his boyhood the musician of Lord Essex.

It is clear, at any rate, that Shakespeare's love for the dark lady must have passed away before 1594. In this year there appeared, under the editorship of Hadrian Dorell, that fascinating poem, or series of poems, "Willobie his Avisa," which is described by Mr Swinburne as the one contemporary book which has been supposed to throw any direct or indirect light on the mystic matter of the Sonnets. In it we learn how a young gentleman of St. John's College, Oxford, by name Henry Willobie, fell in love with a woman so "fair and chaste" that he called her Avisa, either because such beauty as hers had never been seen, or because she fled like a bird from the snare of his passion, and spread her wings for flight when he ventured but to touch her hand. Anxious to win his mistress, he consults his familiar friend W. S., "who not long before had tried the curtesy of the like passion, and was now newly recovered of the like infection." Shakespeare encouraged him in the siege that he is laying to the Castle of Beauty, telling him that every woman is to be wooed, and every woman to be won; views this "loving comedy" from far off, in order to see "whether it would sort to a happier end for this new actor than it did for the old player," and "enlargeth the wound with the sharpe razor of a willing conceit," feeling the purely æsthetic interest of the artist in the moods and emotions of others. It is unnecessary, however, to enter more fully into this curious passage in Shakespeare's life, as all that I wanted to point out was that in 1594 he had been cured of his infatuation for the dark lady, and had already been acquainted for at least three years with Willie Hughes.

My whole scheme of the Sonnets was now complete, and, by placing those that refer to the dark lady in their proper order and position, I saw the perfect unity and completeness of the whole. The drama—for indeed they formed a drama and a soul's tragedy of fiery passion and of noble thought—is divided into four scenes or acts. In the first of these (Sonnets 1-32) Shakespeare invites Willie Hughes to go upon the stage as an actor, and to put to the service of Art his wonderful physical beauty, and his exquisite grace of youth, before passion has robbed him of the one, and time taken from him the other. Willie Hughes, after a time, consents to be a player in Shakespeare's company, and soon becomes the very centre and keynote of his inspiration. Suddenly, in one red-rose July (Sonnets 33-52, 61, and 127-152) there comes to the Globe Theatre a dark woman with won-

The Portrait of Mr W. H.

derful eyes, who falls passionately in love with Willie Hughes. Shakespeare, sick with the malady of jealousy, and made mad by many doubts and fears, tries to fascinate the woman who had come between him and his friend. The love, that is at first feigned, becomes real, and he finds himself enthralled and dominated by a woman whom he knows to be evil and unworthy. To her the genius of a man is as nothing compared to a boy's beauty. Willie Hughes becomes for a time her slave and the toy of her fancy, and the second act ends with Shakespeare's departure from London. In the third act her influence has passed away. Shakespeare returns to London, and renews his friendship with Willie Hughes, to whom he promises immortality in his plays. Marlowe, hearing of the wonder and grace of the young actor, lures him away from the Globe Theatre to play Gaveston in the tragedy of "Edward II," and for the second time Shakespeare is separated from his friend. The last act (Sonnets 100-126) tells us of the return of Willie Hughes to Shakespeare's company. Evil rumour has now stained the white purity of his name, but Shakespeare's love still endures and is perfect. Of the mystery of this love, and of the mystery of passion, we are told strange and marvellous things, and the Sonnets conclude with an envoi of twelve lines, whose motive is the triumph of Beauty over Time, and of Death over Beauty.

And what had been the end of him who had been so dear to the soul of Shakespeare, and who by his presence and passion had given reality to Shakespeare's art? When the Civil War broke out, the English actors took the side of their king, and many of them, like Robinson foully slain by Major Harrison at the taking of Basing House, laid down their lives in the king's service. Perhaps on the trampled heath of Marston, or on the bleak hills of Naseby, the dead body of Willie Hughes had been found by some of the rough peasants of the district, his gold hair "dabbled with blood," and his breast pierced with many wounds. Or it may be that the Plague, which was very frequent in London at the beginning of the seventeenth century, and was indeed regarded by many of the Christians as a judgment sent on the city for its love of "vaine plaies and idolatrous shewes," had touched the lad while he was acting, and he had crept home to his lodging to die there alone, Shakespeare being far away at Stratford, and those who had flocked in such numbers to see him, the "gazers" whom, as the Sonnets tell us, he had "led astray," being too much afraid of contagion to come near him. A story of this kind was current at the time about a young actor, and was made much use of by the Puritans in their attempts to stifle the free development of the English Renaissance. Yet, surely, had this actor been Willie Hughes, tidings of his tragic death would have been speedily brought to Shakespeare as he lay dreaming under the mulberry tree in his garden at New Place, and in an elegy as sweet as that written by Milton on Edward King, he would have mourned for the lad who had brought such joy and sorrow into his life, and whose connection with his art had been of so vital and intimate a character. Something made me feel certain that Willie Hughes had survived Shakespeare, and had fulfilled in some measure the high prophecies the poet had made about him, and one evening the true secret of his end flashed across me.

He had been one of those English actors who in 1611,

The Portrait of Mr W. H.

the year of Shakespeare's retirement from the stage, went across sea to Germany and played before the great Duke Henry Julius of Brunswick, himself a dramatist of no mean order, and at the Court of that strange Elector of Brandenburg, who was so enamoured of beauty that he was said to have bought for his weight in amber the young son of a travelling Greek merchant, and to have given pageants in honour of his slave, all through that dreadful famine year of 1606-7, when the people died of hunger in the very streets of the town, and for the space of seven months there was no rain. The Library at Cassel contains to the present day a copy of the first edition of Marlowe's "Edward II," the only copy in existence, Mr Bullen tells us. Who could have brought it to that town, but he who had created the part of the king's minion, and for whom indeed it had been written? Those stained and yellow pages had once been touched by his white hands. We also know that "Romeo and Juliet," a play specially connected with Willie Hughes, was brought out at Dresden, in 1613, along with "Hamlet" and "King Lear," and certain of Marlowe's plays, and it was surely to none other than Willie Hughes himself that in 1617 the death-mask of Shakespeare was brought by one of the suite of the English ambassador, pale token of the passing away of the great poet who had so dearly loved him. Indeed there was something peculiarly fitting in the idea that the boy-actor, whose beauty had been so vital an element in the realism and romance of Shakespeare's art, had been the first to have brought to Germany the seed of the new culture, and was in his way the precursor of the *Aufklärung* or Illumination of the eighteenth century, that splendid movement which, though begun by

Lessing and Herder, and brought to its full and perfect issue by Goethe was in no small part helped on by a young actor—Friedrich Schroeder—who awoke the popular consciousness, and by means of the feigned passions and mimetic methods of the stage showed the intimate, the vital, connection between life and literature. If this was so,—and there was certainly no evidence against it, —it was not improbable that Willie Hughes was one of those English comedians (*mimi quidam ex Britannia*, as the old chronicle calls them), who were slain at Nuremberg in a sudden uprising of the people, and were secretly buried in a little vineyard outside the city by some young men "who had found pleasure in their performances, and of whom some had sought to be instructed in the mysteries of the new art." Certainly no more fitting place could there be for him to whom Shakespeare said "thou art all my art," than this little vineyard outside the city walls. For was it not from the sorrows of Dionysos that Tragedy sprang? Was not the light laughter of Comedy, with its careless merriment and quick replies, first heard on the lips of the Sicilian vine-dressers? Nay, did not the purple and red stain of the wine-froth on face and limbs give the first suggestion of the charm and fascination of disguise?—the desire for self-concealment, the sense of the value of objectivity, thus showing itself in the rude beginnings of the art. At any rate, wherever he lay—whether in the little vineyard at the gate of the Gothic town, or in some dim London churchyard amidst the roar and bustle of our great city—no gorgeous monument marked his resting place. His true tomb, as Shakespeare saw, was the poet's verse, his true monument the permanence of the drama. So had it been with

The Portrait of Mr W. H.

others whose beauty had given a new creative impulse to their age. The ivory body of the Bithynian slave rots in the green ooze of the Nile, and on the yellow hills of the Cerameicus is strewn the dust of the young Athenian; but Antinous lives in sculpture, and Charmides in philosophy.

V

A young Elizabethan, who was enamoured of a girl so white that he named her Alba, has left on record the impression produced on him by one of the first performances of "Love's Labour's Lost." Admirable though the actors were, and they played "in cunning wise," he tells us, especially those who took the lovers' parts, he was conscious that everything was "feigned," that nothing came "from the heart," that though they appeared to grieve they "felt no care," and were merely presenting "a show in jest." Yet, suddenly, this fanciful comedy of unreal romance became to him, as he sat in the audience, the real tragedy of his life. The moods of his own soul seemed to have taken shape and substance, and to be moving before him. His grief had a mask that smiled, and his sorrow wore gay raiment. Behind the bright and quickly-changing pageant of the stage, he saw himself, as one sees one's image in a fantastic glass. The very words that came to the actors' lips were wrung out of his pain. Their false tears were of his shedding.

There are few of us who have not felt something akin to this. We become lovers when we see Romeo and Juliet, and Hamlet makes us students. The blood of Duncan is upon our hands, with Timon we rage against the world, and when Lear wanders out upon the heath the terror of madness touches us. Ours is the white sinlessness of Desdemona, and ours, also, the sin of Iago. Art, even the art of fullest scope and widest vision, can never really show us the external world. All that it shows us is our own soul, the one world of which we have any real cognizance. And the soul itself, the soul of each one of us, is to each one of us a mystery. It hides in the dark and broods, and consciousness cannot tell us of its workings. Consciousness, indeed, is quite inadequate to explain the contents of personality. It is Art, and Art only, that reveals us to ourselves.

We sit at the play with the woman we love, or listen to the music in some Oxford garden, or stroll with our friend through the cool galleries of the Pope's house at Rome, and suddenly we become aware that we have passions of which we have never dreamed, thoughts that make us afraid, pleasures whose secret has been denied to us, sorrows that have been hidden from our tears. The actor is unconscious of our presence: the musician is thinking of the subtlety of the fugue, of the tone of his instrument; the marble gods that smile so curiously at us are made of insensate stone. But they have given form and substance to what was within us; they have enabled us to realise our personality; and a sense of perilous joy, or some touch or thrill of pain, or that strange self-pity that man so often feels for himself, comes over us and leaves us different.

Some such impression the Sonnets of Shakespeare had certainly produced on me. As from opal dawns to sunsets

The Portrait of Mr W. H.

of withered rose I read and re-read them in garden or chamber, it seemed to me that I was deciphering the story of a life that had once been mine, unrolling the record of a romance that, without my knowing it, had coloured the very texture of my nature, had dyed it with strange and subtle dyes. Art, as so often happens, had taken the place of personal experience. I felt as if I had been initiated into the secret of that passionate friendship, that love of beauty and beauty of love, of which Marsilio Ficino tells us, and of which the Sonnets, in their noblest and purest significance, may be held to be the perfect expression.

Yes: I had lived it all. I had stood in the round theatre with its open roof and fluttering banners, had seen the stage draped with black for a tragedy, or set with gay garlands for some brighter show. The young gallants came out with their pages, and took their seats in front of the tawny curtain that hung from the satyr-carved pillars of the inner scene. They were insolent and debonair in their fantastic dresses. Some of them wore French love-locks, and white doublets stiff with Italian embroidery of gold thread, and long hose of blue or pale yellow silk. Others were all in black, and carried huge plumed hats. These affected the Spanish fashion. As they played at cards, and blew thin wreaths of smoke from the tiny pipes that the pages lit for them, the truant prentices and idle schoolboys that thronged the yard mocked them. But they only smiled at each other. In the side boxes some masked women were sitting. One of them was waiting with hungry eyes and bitten lips for the drawing back of the curtain. As the trumpet sounded for the third time she leant forward, and I saw her olive skin and raven's-wing hair. I knew her. She had marred for a season the great friendship of my life. Yet there was something about her that fascinated me.

The play changed according to my mood. Sometimes it was "Hamlet." Taylor acted the Prince, and there were many who wept when Ophelia went mad. Sometimes it was "Romeo and Juliet." Burbage was Romeo. He hardly looked the part of the young Italian, but there was a rich music in his voice, and passionate beauty in every gesture. I saw "As You Like It," and "Cymbeline," and "Twelfth Night," and in each play there was some one whose life was bound up into mine, who realised for me every dream, and gave shape to every fancy. How gracefully he moved! The eyes of the audience were fixed on him.

And yet it was in this century that it had all happened. I had never seen my friend, but he had been with me for many years, and it was to his influence that I had owed my passion for Greek thought and art, and indeed all my sympathy with the Hellenic spirit. ($\Phi\iota\lambda o\sigma o\phi\epsilon\tilde{\iota}\nu\ \mu\epsilon\tau'\ \dot{\epsilon}\rho\tilde{\omega}\tau o\varsigma$!) How that phrase had stirred me in my Oxford days! I did not understand then why it was so. But I knew now. There had been a presence beside me always. Its silver feet had trod night's shadowy meadows, and the white hands had moved aside the trembling curtains of the dawn. It had walked with me through the grey cloisters, and when I sat reading in my room, it was there also. What though I had been unconscious of it? The soul had a life of its own, and the brain its own sphere of action. There was something within us that knew nothing of sequence or extension, and yet, like the philosopher of the Ideal City, was the spectator of all time and

The Portrait of Mr W. H.

of all existence. It had senses that quickened, passions that came to birth, spiritual ecstasies of contemplation, ardours of fiery-coloured love. It was we who were unreal, and our conscious life was the least important part of our development. The soul, the secret soul, was the only reality.

How curiously it had all been revealed to me! A book of Sonnets, published nearly three hundred years ago, written by a dead hand and in honour of a dead youth, had suddenly explained to me the whole story of my soul's romance. I remembered how once in Egypt I had been present at the opening of a frescoed coffin that had been found in one of the basalt tombs at Thebes. Inside there was the body of a young girl swathed in tight bands of linen, and with a gilt mask over her face. As I stooped down to look at it, I had seen that one of the little withered hands held a scroll of yellow papyrus covered with strange characters. How I wished now that I had had it read to me! It might have told me something more about the soul that hid within me, and had its mysteries of passion of which I was kept in ignorance. Strange, that we knew so little about ourselves, and that our most intimate personality was concealed from us! Were we to look in tombs for our real life, and in art for the legend of our days?

Week after week, I pored over these poems, and each new form of knowledge seemed to me a mode of reminiscence. Finally, after two months had elapsed, I determined to make a strong appeal to Erskine to do justice to the memory of Cyril Graham, and to give to the world his marvellous interpretation of the Sonnets—the only interpretation that thoroughly explained the problem. I have not any copy of my letter, I regret to say, nor have I been able to lay my hand upon the original; but I remember that I went over the whole ground, and covered sheets of paper with passionate reiteration of the arguments and proofs that my study had suggested to me.

It seemed to me that I was not merely restoring Cyril Graham to his proper place in literary history, but rescuing the honour of Shakespeare himself from the tedious memory of a commonplace intrigue. I put into the letter all my enthusiasm. I put into the letter all my faith.

No sooner, in fact, had I sent it off than a curious reaction came over me. It seemed to me that I had given away my capacity for belief in the Willie Hughes theory of the Sonnets, that something had gone out of me, as it were, and that I was perfectly indifferent to the whole subject. What was it that had happened? It is difficult to say. Perhaps, by finding perfect expression for a passion, I had exhausted the passion itself. Emotional forces, like the forces of physical life, have their positive limitations. Perhaps the mere effort to convert any one to a theory involves some form of renunciation of the power of credence. Influence is simply a transference of personality, a mode of giving away what is most precious to one's self, and its exercise produces a sense, and, it may be, a reality of loss. Every disciple takes away something from his master. Or perhaps I had become tired of the whole thing, wearied of its fascination, and, my enthusiasm having burnt out, my reason was left to its own unimpassioned judgment. However it came about, and I cannot pretend to explain it, there was no doubt that Willie Hughes suddenly became to me a mere myth, an idle dream, the boyish fancy of a young man who, like most

The Portrait of Mr W. H.

ardent spirits, was more anxious to convince others than to be himself convinced.

I must admit that this was a bitter disappointment to me. I had gone through every phase of this great romance. I had lived with it, and it had become part of my nature. How was it that it had left me? Had I touched upon some secret that my soul desired to conceal? Or was there no permanence in personality? Did things come and go through the brain, silently, swiftly, and without footprints, like shadows through a mirror? Were we at the mercy of such impressions as Art or Life chose to give us? It seemed to me to be so.

It was at night-time that this feeling first came to me. I had sent my servant out to post the letter to Erskine, and was seated at the window looking out at the blue and gold city. The moon had not yet risen, and there was only one star in the sky, but the streets were full of quick-moving and flashing lights, and the windows of Devonshire House were illuminated for a great dinner to be given to some of the foreign princes then visiting London. I saw the scarlet liveries of the royal carriages, and the crowd hustling about the sombre gates of the courtyard.

Suddenly, I said to myself: "I have been dreaming, and all my life for these two months has been unreal. There was no such person as Willie Hughes." Something like a faint cry of pain came to my lips as I began to realise how I had deceived myself, and I buried my face in my hands, struck with a sorrow greater than any I had felt since boyhood. After a few moments I rose, and going into the library took up the Sonnets, and began to read them. But it was all to no avail. They gave me back nothing of the feeling that I had brought to them; they revealed to me nothing of what I had found hidden in their lines. Had I merely been influenced by the beauty of the forged portrait, charmed by that Shelley-like face into faith and credence? Or, as Erskine had suggested, was it the pathetic tragedy of Cyril Graham's death that had so deeply stirred me? I could not tell. To the present day I cannot understand the beginning or the end of the strange passage in my life.

However, as I had said some very unjust and bitter things to Erskine in my letter, I determined to go and see him as soon as possible, and make my apologies to him for my behaviour. Accordingly, the next morning I drove down to Birdcage Walk, where I found him sitting in his library, with the forged picture of Willie Hughes in front of him.

"My dear Erskine!" I cried, "I have come to apologise to you."

"To apologise to me?" he said. "What for?"

"For my letter," I answered.

"You have nothing to regret in your letter," he said. "On the contrary, you have done me the greatest service in your power. You have shown me that Cyril Graham's theory is perfectly sound."

I stared at him in blank wonder.

"You don't mean to say that you believe in Willie Hughes?" I exclaimed.

"Why not?" he rejoined. "You have proved the thing to me. Do you think I cannot estimate the value of evidence?"

"But there is no evidence at all," I groaned, sinking into a chair. "When I wrote to you I was under the influence of a perfectly silly enthusiasm. I had been

The Portrait of Mr W. H.

touched by the story of Cyril Graham's death, fascinated by his artistic theory, enthralled by the wonder and novelty of the whole idea. I see now that the theory is based on a delusion. The only evidence for the existence of Willie Hughes is that picture in front of you, and that picture is a forgery. Don't be carried away by mere sentiment in this matter. Whatever romance may have to say about the Willie Hughes theory, reason is dead against it."

"I don't understand you," said Erskine, looking at me in amazement. "You have convinced me by your letter that Willie Hughes is an absolute reality. Why have you changed your mind? Or is all that you have been saying to me merely a joke?"

"I cannot explain it to you," I rejoined, "but I see now that there is really nothing to be said in favour of Cyril Graham's interpretation. The Sonnets may not be addressed to Lord Pembroke. They probably are not. But for heaven's sake don't waste your time in a foolish attempt to discover a young Elizabethan actor who never existed, and to make a phantom puppet the centre of the great cycle of Shakespeare's Sonnets."

"I see that you don't understand the theory," he replied.

"My dear Erskine," I cried, "not understand it! Why, I feel as if I had invented it. Surely my letter shows you that I not merely went into the whole matter, but that I contributed proofs of every kind. The one flaw in the theory is that it presupposes the existence of the person whose existence is the subject of dispute. If we grant that there was in Shakespeare's company a young actor of the name of Willie Hughes, it is not difficult to make him the object of the Sonnets. But as we know that there was no actor of this name in the company of the Globe Theatre, it is idle to pursue the investigation further."

"But that is exactly what we don't know," said Erskine. "It is quite true that his name does not occur in the list given in the first folio; but, as Cyril pointed out, that is rather a proof in favour of the existence of Willie Hughes than against it, if we remember his treacherous desertion of Shakespeare for a rival dramatist. Besides," and here I must admit that Erskine made what seems to me now a rather good point, though, at the time, I laughed at it, "there is no reason at all why Willie Hughes should not have gone upon the stage under an assumed name. In fact it is extremely probable that he did so. We know that there was a very strong prejudice against the theatre in his day, and nothing is more likely than that his family insisted upon his adopting some *nom de plume*. The editors of the first folio would naturally put him down under his stage name, the name by which he was best known to the public, but the Sonnets were of course an entirely different matter, and in the dedication to them the publisher very properly addresses him under his real initials. If this be so, and it seems to me the most simple and rational explanation of the matter, I regard Cyril Graham's theory as absolutely proved."

"But what evidence have you?" I exclaimed, laying my hand on his. "You have no evidence at all. It is a mere hypothesis. And which of Shakespeare's actors do you think that Willie Hughes was? The 'pretty fellow' Ben Jonson tells us of, who was so fond of dressing up in girls' clothes?"

The Portrait of Mr W. H.

"I don't know," he answered rather irritably. "I have not had time to investigate the point yet. But I feel quite sure that my theory is the true one. Of course it is a hypothesis, but then it is a hypothesis that explains everything, and if you had been sent to Cambridge to study science, instead of to Oxford to dawdle over literature, you would know that a hypothesis that explains everything is a certainty."

"Yes, I am aware that Cambridge is a sort of educational institute," I murmured. "I am glad I was not there."

"My dear fellow," said Erskine, suddenly turning his keen grey eyes on me, "you believe in Cyril Graham's theory, you believe in Willie Hughes, you know that the Sonnets are addressed to an actor, but for some reason or other you won't acknowledge it."

"I wish I could believe it," I rejoined. "I would give anything to be able to do so. But I can't. It is a sort of moonbeam theory, very lovely, very fascinating, but intangible. When one thinks that one has got hold of it, it escapes one. No: Shakespeare's heart is still to us 'a closet never pierc'd with crystal eyes,' as he calls it in one of the sonnets. We shall never know the true secret of the passion of his life."

Erskine sprang from the sofa, and paced up and down the room. "We know it already," he cried, "and the world shall know it some day."

I had never seen him so excited. He would not hear of my leaving him, and insisted on my stopping for the rest of the day.

We argued the matter over for hours, but nothing that I could say could make him surrender his faith in Cyril

Graham's interpretation. He told me that he intended to devote his life to proving the theory, and that he was determined to do justice to Cyril Graham's memory. I entreated him, laughed at him, begged of him, but it was to no use. Finally we parted, not exactly in anger, but certainly with a shadow between us. He thought me shallow, I thought him foolish. When I called on him again, his servant told me that he had gone to Germany. The letters that I wrote to him remained unanswered.

Two years afterwards, as I was going into my club, the hall porter handed me a letter with a foreign postmark. It was from Erskine, and written at the Hôtel d'Angleterre, Cannes. When I had read it, I was filled with horror, though I did not quite believe that he would be so mad as to carry his resolve into execution. The gist of the letter was that he had tried in every way to verify the Willie Hughes theory, and had failed, and that as Cyril Graham had given his life for this theory, he himself had determined to give his own life also to the same cause. The concluding words of the letter were these: "I still believe in Willie Hughes; and by the time you receive this I shall have died by my own hand for Willie Hughes' sake: for his sake, and for the sake of Cyril Graham, whom I drove to his death by my shallow scepticism and ignorant lack of faith. The truth was once revealed to you, and you rejected it. It comes to you now, stained with the blood of two lives.—Do not turn away from it."

It was a horrible moment. I felt sick with misery, and yet I could not believe that he would really carry out his intention. To die for one's theological opinions is the worst use a man can make of his life; but to die for a literary theory! It seemed impossible.

The Portrait of Mr W. H.

I looked at the date. The letter was a week old. Some unfortunate chance had prevented my going to the club for several days, or I might have got it in time to save him. Perhaps it was not too late. I drove off to my rooms, packed up my things, and started by the night mail from Charing Cross. The journey was intolerable. I thought I would never arrive.

As soon as I did, I drove to the Hôtel d'Angleterre. It was quite true. Erskine was dead. They told me that he had been buried two days before in the English cemetery. There was something horribly grotesque about the whole tragedy. I said all kinds of wild things, and the people in the hall looked curiously at me.

Suddenly Lady Erskine, in deep mourning, passed across the vestibule. When she saw me she came up to me, murmured something about her poor son, and burst into tears. I led her into her sitting room. An elderly gentleman was there, reading a newspaper. It was the English doctor.

We talked a great deal about Erskine, but I said nothing about his motive for committing suicide. It was evident that he had not told his mother anything about the reason that had driven him to so fatal, so mad an act. Finally Lady Erskine rose and said, "George left you something as a memento. It was a thing he prized very much. I will get it for you."

As soon as she had left the room I turned to the doctor and said, "What a dreadful shock it must have been for Lady Erskine! I wonder that she bears it as well as she does."

"Oh, she knew for months past that it was coming," he answered.

"Knew it for months past!" I cried. "But why didn't

she stop him? Why didn't she have him watched? He must have been out of his mind."

The doctor stared at me. "I don't know what you mean," he said.

"Well," I cried, "if a mother knows that her son is going to commit suicide—"

"Suicide!" he answered. "Poor Erskine did not commit suicide. He died of consumption. He came here to die. The moment I saw him I knew that there was no chance. One lung was almost gone, and the other was very much affected. Three days before he died he asked me was there any hope. I told him frankly that there was none, and that he had only a few days to live. He wrote some letters, and was quite resigned, retaining his senses to the last."

I got up from my seat, and going over to the open window I looked out on the crowded promenade. I remember that the brightly-coloured umbrellas and gay parasols seemed to me like huge fantastic butterflies fluttering by the shore of a blue-metal sea, and that the heavy odour of violets that came across the garden made me think of that wonderful sonnet in which Shakespeare tells us that the scent of these flowers always reminded him of his friend. What did it all mean? Why had Erskine written me that extraordinary letter? Why when standing at the very gate of death had he turned back to tell me what was not true? Was Hugo right? Is affectation the only thing that accompanies a man up the steps of the scaffold? Did Erskine merely want to produce a dramatic effect? That was not like him. It was more like something I might have done myself. No: he was simply actuated by a desire to reconvert me to Cyril Graham's

The Portrait of Mr W. H.

theory, and he thought that if I could be made to believe that he too had given his life for it, I would be deceived by the pathetic fallacy of martyrdom. Poor Erskine! I had grown wiser since I had seen him. Martyrdom was to me merely a tragic form of scepticism, an attempt to realise by fire what one had failed to do by faith. No man dies for what he knows to be true. Men die for what they want to be true, for what some terror in their hearts tells them is not true. The very uselessness of Erskine's letter made me doubly sorry for him. I watched the people strolling in and out of the cafés, and wondered if any of them had known him. The white dust blew down the scorched sunlit road, and the feathery palms moved restlessly in the shaken air.

At that moment Lady Erskine returned to the room carrying the fatal portrait of Willie Hughes. "When George was dying, he begged me to give you this," she said. As I took it from her, her tears fell on my hand.

This curious work of art hangs now in my library, where it is very much admired by my artistic friends, one of whom has etched it for me. They have decided that it is not a Clouet, but an Ouvry. I have never cared to tell them its true history, but sometimes, when I look at it, I think there is really a great deal to be said for the Willie Hughes theory of Shakespeare's Sonnets.

The Sonnets

TO. THE. ONLIE. BEGETTER. OF.

THESE. INSUING. SONNETS.

MR. W. H. ALL. HAPPINESSE.

AND. THAT. ETERNITIE.

PROMISED. BY.

OUR. EVER-LIVING. POET.

WISHETH.

THE. WELL-WISHING.

ADVENTURER. IN.

SETTING.

FORTH.

                              T. T.

ONE

FROM fairest creatures we desire increase,
That thereby beauty's rose might never die,
But as the riper should by time decease,
His tender heir might bear his memory:
But thou, contracted to thine own bright eyes,
Feed'st thy light's flame with self-substantial fuel,
Making a famine where abundance lies,
Thyself thy foe, to thy sweet self too cruel.
Thou that art now the world's fresh ornament
And only herald to the gaudy spring,
Within thine own bud buriest thy content
And, tender churl, makest waste in niggarding.
 Pity the world, or else this glutton be,
 To eat the world's due, by the grave and thee.

TWO

WHEN forty winters shall besiege thy brow,
And dig deep trenches in thy beauty's field,
Thy youth's proud livery, so gazed on now,
Will be a tatter'd weed, of small worth held:
Then being ask'd where all thy beauty lies,
Where all the treasure of thy lusty days,
To say, within thine own deep-sunken eyes,
Were an all-eating shame and thriftless praise.
How much more praise deserved thy beauty's use,
If thou couldst answer 'This fair child of mine
Shall sum my count and make my old excuse,'
Proving his beauty by succession thine!
    This were to be new made when thou art old,
    And see thy blood warm when thou feel'st it cold.

THREE

LOOK in thy glass and tell the face thou viewest
Now is the time that face should form another;
Whose fresh repair if now thou not renewest,
Thou dost beguile the world, unbless some mother.
For where is she so fair whose unear'd womb
Disdains the tillage of thy husbandry?
Or who is he so fond will be the tomb
Of his self-love, to stop posterity?
Thou art thy mother's glass, and she in thee
Calls back the lovely April of her prime:
So thou through windows of thine age shalt see
Despite of wrinkles this thy golden time.
    But if thou live, remember'd not to be,
    Die single, and thine image dies with thee.

FOUR

UNTHRIFTY loveliness, why dost thou spend
Upon thyself thy beauty's legacy?
Nature's bequest gives nothing but doth lend,
And being frank she lends to those are free.
Then, beauteous niggard, why dost thou abuse
The bounteous largess given thee to give?
Profitless usurer, why dost thou use
So great a sum of sums, yet canst not live?
For having traffic with thyself alone,
Thou of thyself thy sweet self dost deceive.
Then how, when nature calls thee to be gone,
What acceptable audit canst thou leave?
    Thy unused beauty must be tomb'd with thee,
    Which, used, lives th' executor to be.

FIVE

THOSE hours, that with gentle work did frame
The lovely gaze where every eye doth dwell,
Will play the tyrants to the very same
And that unfair which fairly doth excel;
For never-resting time leads summer on
To hideous winter and confounds him there;
Sap check'd with frost and lusty leaves quite gone,
Beauty o'ersnow'd and bareness every where:
Then, were not summer's distillation left,
A liquid prisoner pent in walls of glass,
Beauty's effect with beauty were bereft,
Nor it nor no remembrance what it was:
    But flowers distill'd, though they with winter meet,
    Leese but their show; their substance still lives sweet.

SIX

THEN let not winter's ragged hand deface
In thee thy summer, ere thou be distill'd:
Make sweet some vial; treasure thou some place
With beauty's treasure, ere it be self-kill'd.
That use is not forbidden usury
Which happies those that pay the willing loan;
That's for thyself to breed another thee,
Or ten times happier, be it ten for one;
Ten times thyself were happier than thou art,
If ten of thine ten times refigured thee:
Then what could death do, if thou shouldst depart,
Leaving thee living in posterity?
  Be not self-will'd, for thou art much too fair
  To be death's conquest and make worms thine heir.

SEVEN

LO! in the orient when the gracious light
Lifts up his burning head, each under eye
Doth homage to his new-appearing sight,
Serving with looks his sacred majesty;
And having climb'd the steep-up heavenly hill,
Resembling strong youth in his middle age,
Yet mortal looks adore his beauty still,
Attending on his golden pilgrimage;
But when from highmost pitch, with weary car,
Like feeble age, he reeleth from the day,
The eyes, 'fore duteous, now converted are
From his low tract and look another way:
  So thou, thyself out-going in thy noon,
  Unlook'd on diest, unless thou get a son.

EIGHT

MUSIC to hear, why hear'st thou music sadly?
Sweets with sweets war not, joy delights in joy.
Why lovest thou that which thou receivest not gladly,
Or else receivest with pleasure thine annoy?
If the true concord of well-tuned sounds,
By unions married, do offend thine ear,
They do but sweetly chide thee, who confounds
In singleness the parts that thou shouldst bear.
Mark how one string, sweet husband to another,
Strikes each in each by mutual ordering,
Resembling sire and child and happy mother
Who all in one, one pleasing note do sing:
    Whose speechless song, being many, seeming one,
    Sings this to thee: 'thou single wilt prove none.'

NINE

IS it for fear to wet a widow's eye
That thou consumest thyself in single life?
Ah! if thou issueless shall hap to die,
The world will wail thee, like a makeless wife;
The world will be thy widow and still weep
That thou no form of thee hast left behind,
When every private widow well may keep
By children's eyes her husband's shape in mind.
Look, what an unthrift in the world doth spend
Shifts but his place, for still the world enjoys it;
But beauty's waste hath in the world an end,
And kept unused, the user so destroys it.
    No love toward others in that bosom sits
    That on himself such murderous shame commits.

TEN

FOR shame! deny that thou bear'st love to any,
Who for thyself art so unprovident.
Grant, if thou wilt, thou art beloved of many,
But that thou none lovest is most evident;
For thou art so possess'd with murderous hate
That 'gainst thyself thou stick'st not to conspire,
Seeking that beauteous roof to ruinate
Which to repair should be thy chief desire.
O, change thy thought, that I may change my mind!
Shall hate be fairer lodged than gentle love?
Be, as thy presence is, gracious and kind,
Or to thyself at least kind-hearted prove:
 Make thee another self, for love of me,
 That beauty still may live in thine or thee.

ELEVEN

AS fast as thou shalt wane, so fast thou growest
In one of thine, from that which thou departest;
And that fresh blood which youngly thou bestowest
Thou mayst call thine when thou from youth convertest.
Herein lies wisdom, beauty and increase;
Without this, folly, age and cold decay:
If all were minded so the times should cease
And threescore year would make the world away.
Let those whom Nature hath not made for store,
Harsh, featureless and rude, barrenly perish:
Look, whom she best endow'd she gave the more;
Which bounteous gift thou shouldst in bounty cherish:
 She carved thee for her seal, and meant thereby
 Thou shouldst print more, not let that copy die.

TWELVE

WHEN I do count the clock that tells the time,
And see the brave day sunk in hideous night;
When I behold the violet past prime,
And sable curls all silver'd o'er with white;
When lofty trees I see barren of leaves
Which erst from heat did canopy the herd,
And summer's green all girded up in sheaves
Borne on the bier with white and bristly beard,
Then of thy beauty do I question make,
That thou among the wastes of time must go,
Since sweets and beauties do themselves forsake
And die as fast as they see others grow;
    And nothing 'gainst Time's scythe can make defence
    Save breed, to brave him when he takes thee hence.

THIRTEEN

O, that you were yourself! but love, you are
No longer yours than you yourself here live:
Against this coming end you should prepare,
And your sweet semblance to some other give.
So should that beauty which you hold in lease
Find no determination; then you were
Yourself again after yourself's decease,
When your sweet issue your sweet form should bear.
Who lets so fair a house fall to decay,
Which husbandry in honour might uphold
Against the stormy gusts of winter's day
And barren rage of death's eternal cold?
    O, none but unthrifts! Dear my love, you know
    You had a father: let your son say so.

FOURTEEN

NOT from the stars do I my judgement pluck;
And yet methinks I have astronomy,
But not to tell of good or evil luck,
Of plagues, of dearths, or season's quality;
Nor can I fortune to brief minutes tell,
Pointing to each his thunder, rain and wind,
Or say with princes if it shall go well,
By oft predict that I in heaven find:
But from thine eyes my knowledge I derive,
And, constant stars, in them I read such art
As truth and beauty shall together thrive,
If from thyself to store thou wouldst convert;
    Or else of thee this I prognosticate:
    Thy end is truth's and beauty's doom and date.

FIFTEEN

WHEN I consider every thing that grows
Holds in perfection but a little moment,
That this huge stage presenteth nought but shows
Whereon the stars in secret influence comment;
When I perceive that men as plants increase,
Cheered and check'd even by the self-same sky,
Vaunt in their youthful sap, at height decrease,
And wear their brave state out of memory;
Then the conceit of this inconstant stay
Sets you most rich in youth before my sight,
Where wasteful Time debateth with Decay,
To change your day of youth to sullied night;
    And all in war with Time for love of you,
    As he takes from you, I engraft you new.

SIXTEEN

BUT wherefore do not you a mightier way
Make war upon this bloody tyrant, Time?
And fortify yourself in your decay
With means more blessed than my barren rhyme?
Now stand you on the top of happy hours,
And many maiden gardens yet unset
With virtuous wish would bear your living flowers,
Much liker than your painted counterfeit:
So should the lines of life that life repair,
Which this, Time's pencil, or my pupil pen,
Neither in inward worth nor outward fair,
Can make you live yourself in eyes of men.
    To give away yourself keeps yourself still,
    And you must live, drawn by your own sweet skill.

SEVENTEEN

WHO will believe my verse in time to come,
If it were fill'd with your most high deserts?
Though yet, heaven knows, it is but as a tomb
Which hides your life and shows not half your parts.
If I could write the beauty of your eyes
And in fresh numbers number all your graces,
The age to come would say 'This poet lies;
Such heavenly touches ne'er touched earthly faces.'
So should my papers yellow'd with their age
Be scorn'd like old men of less truth than tongue,
And your true rights be term'd a poet's rage
And stretched metre of an antique song:
    But were some child of yours alive that time,
    You should live twice; in it and in my rhyme.

EIGHTEEN

SHALL I compare thee to a summer's day?
Thou art more lovely and more temperate:
Rough winds do shake the darling buds of May,
And summer's lease hath all too short a date:
Sometime too hot the eye of heaven shines,
And often is his gold complexion dimm'd;
And every fair from fair sometimes declines,
By chance or nature's changing course untrimm'd;
But thy eternal summer shall not fade
Nor lose possession of that fair thou owest;
Nor shall Death brag thou wander'st in his shade,
When in eternal lines to time thou growest:
 So long as men can breathe or eyes can see,
 So long lives this, and this gives life to thee.

NINETEEN

DEVOURING Time, blunt thou the lion's paws,
And make the earth devour her own sweet brood;
Pluck the keen teeth from the fierce tiger's jaws,
And burn the long-lived phoenix in her blood;
Make glad and sorry seasons as thou fleets,
And do whate'er thou wilt, swift-footed Time,
To the wide world and all her fading sweets,
But I forbid thee one most heinous crime:
O, carve not with thy hours my love's fair brow,
Nor draw no lines there with thine antique pen:
Him in thy course untainted do allow
For beauty's pattern to succeeding men.
 Yet, do thy worst, old Time: despite thy wrong,
 My love shall in my verse ever live young.

TWENTY

A woman's face with Nature's own hand painted,
Hast thou, the master-mistress of my passion;
A woman's gentle heart, but not acquainted
With shifting change, as is false women's fashion;
An eye more bright than theirs, less false in rolling,
Gilding the object whereupon it gazeth;
A man in hue, all 'hues' in his controlling,
Which steals men's eyes and women's souls amazeth.
And for a woman wert thou first created;
Till Nature, as she wrought thee, fell a-doting,
And by addition me of thee defeated,
By adding one thing to my purpose nothing.
  But since she prick'd thee out for women's pleasure,
  Mine be thy love and thy love's use their treasure.

TWENTY-ONE

SO is it not with me as with that Muse
Stirr'd by a painted beauty to his verse,
Who heaven itself for ornament doth use
And every fair with his fair doth rehearse;
Making a couplement of proud compare,
With sun and moon, with earth and sea's rich gems,
With April's first-born flowers, and all things rare
That heaven's air in this huge rondure hems.
O, let me, true in love, but truly write,
And then believe me, my love is as fair
As any mother's child, though not so bright
As those gold candles fix'd in heaven's air:
  Let them say more that like of hearsay well;
  I will not praise that purpose not to sell.

TWENTY-TWO

MY glass shall not persuade me I am old,
So long as youth and thou are of one date;
But when in thee time's furrows I behold,
Then look I death my days should expiate.
For all that beauty that doth cover thee
Is but the seemly raiment of my heart,
Which in thy breast doth live, as thine in me:
How can I then be elder than thou art?
O, therefore, love, be of thyself so wary
As I, not for myself, but for thee will;
Bearing thy heart, which I will keep so chary
As tender nurse her babe from faring ill.
 Presume not on thy heart when mine is slain;
 Thou gavest me thine, not to give back again.

TWENTY-THREE

AS an imperfect actor on the stage
Who with his fear is put besides his part,
Or some fierce thing replete with too much rage,
Whose strength's abundance weakens his own heart,
So I, for fear of trust, forget to say
The perfect ceremony of love's rite,
And in mine own love's strength seem to decay,
O'ercharged with burden of mine own love's might.
O, let my books be then the eloquence
And dumb presagers of my speaking breast,
Who plead for love and loom for recompense
More than that tongue that more hath more express'd.
 O, learn to read what silent love hath writ:
 To hear with eyes belongs to love's fine wit.

TWENTY-FOUR

MINE eye hath play'd the painter and hath stell'd
Thy beauty's form in table of my heart;
My body is the frame wherein 'tis held,
And perspective it is best painter's art.
For through the painter must you see his skill,
To find where your true image pictured lies;
Which in my bosom's shop is hanging still,
That hath his windows glazed with thine eyes.
Now see what good turns eyes for eyes have done:
Mine eyes have drawn thy shape, and thine for me
Are windows to my breast, where-through the sun
Delights to peep, to gaze therein on thee:
    Yet eyes this cunning want to grace their art;
    They draw but what they see, know not the heart.

TWENTY-FIVE

LET those who are in favour with their stars
Of public honour and proud titles boast
Whilst I, whom fortune of such triumphs bars,
Unlook'd for joy in that I honour most.
Great princes' favourites their fair leaves spread
But as the marigold at the sun's eye,
And in themselves their pride lies buried,
For at a frown they in their glory die.
The painful warrior famoused for fight,
After a thousand victories once foil'd,
Is from the book of honour razed quite,
And all the rest forgot for which he toil'd:
    Then happy I, that love and am beloved
    Where I may not remove or be removed.

TWENTY-SIX

LORD of my love, to whom in vassalage
Thy merit hath my duty strongly knit,
To thee I send this written embassage,
To witness duty, not to show my wit:
Duty so great, which wit so poor as mine
May make seem bare, in wanting words to show it,
But that I hope some good conceit of thine
In thy soul's thought, all naked, will bestow it;
Till whatsoever star that guides my moving
Points on me graciously with fair aspect
And puts apparel on my tatter'd loving,
To show me worthy of thy sweet respect:
    Then may I dare to boast how I do love thee:
    Till then not show my head where thou mayst
        prove me.

TWENTY-SEVEN

WEARY with toil, I haste me to my bed,
The dear repose for limbs with travel tired;
But then begins a journey in my head,
To work my mind, when body's work's expired:
For then my thoughts, from far where I abide,
Intend a zealous pilgrimage to thee,
And keep my drooping eyelids open wide,
Looking on darkness which the blind do see:
Save that my soul's imaginary sight
Presents thy shadow to my sightless view,
Which, like a jewel hung in ghastly night,
Makes black night beauteous and her old face new.
    Lo! thus, by day my limbs, by night my mind,
    For thee and for myself no quiet find.

TWENTY-EIGHT

HOW can I then return in happy plight,
That am debarr'd the benefit of rest?
When day's oppression is not eased by night,
But day by night, and night by day, oppress'd?
And each, though enemies to either's reign,
Do in consent shake hands to torture me;
The one by toil, the other to complain
How far I toil, still farther off from thee.
I tell the day, to please him thou art bright
And dost him grace when clouds do blot the heaven:
So flatter I the swart-complexion'd night,
When sparkling stars twire not thou gild'st the even.
    But day doth daily draw my sorrows longer
    And night doth nightly make grief's strength seem stronger.

TWENTY-NINE

WHEN, in disgrace with fortune and men's eyes,
I all alone beweep my outcast state
And trouble deaf heaven with my bootless cries
And look upon myself and curse my fate,
Wishing me like to one more rich in hope,
Featured like him, like him with friends possess'd,
Desiring this man's art and that man's scope,
With what I most enjoy contented least;
Yet in these thoughts myself almost despising,
Haply I think on thee, and then my state,
Like to the lark at break of day arising
From sullen earth, sings hymns at heaven's gate;
    For thy sweet love remember'd such wealth brings
    That then I scorn to change my state with kings.

THIRTY

WHEN to the sessions of sweet silent thought
I summon up remembrance of things past,
I sigh the lack of many a thing I sought,
And with old woes new wail my dear time's waste:
Then can I drown an eye, unused to flow,
For precious friends hid in death's dateless night,
And weep afresh love's long since cancell'd woe,
And moan the expense of many a vanish'd sight:
Then can I grieve at grievances foregone,
And heavily from woe to woe tell o'er
The sad account of fore-bemoaned moan,
Which I now pay as if not paid before.
    But if the while I think on thee, dear friend,
    All losses are restored and sorrows end.

THIRTY-ONE

THY bosom is endeared with all hearts,
Which I by lacking have supposed dead,
And there reigns love and all love's loving parts,
And all those friends which I thought buried.
How many a holy and obsequious tear
Hath dear religious love stol'n from mine eye
As interest of the dead, which now appear
But things removed that hidden in thee lie!
Thou art the grave where buried love doth live,
Hung with the trophies of my lovers gone,
Who all their parts of me to thee did give;
That due of many now is thine alone:
    Their images I loved I view in thee,
    And thou, all they, hast all the all of me.

THIRTY-TWO

IF thou survive my well-contented day,
When that churl Death my bones with dust shall cover,
And shalt by fortune once more re-survey
These poor rude lines of thy deceased lover,
Compare them with the bettering of the time,
And though they be outstripp'd by every pen,
Reserve them for my love, not for their rhyme,
Exceeded by the height of happier men.
O, then vouchsafe me but this loving thought:
'Had my friend's Muse grown with this growing age,
A dearer birth than this his love had brought,
To march in ranks of better equipage:
    But since he died and poets better prove,
    Theirs for the style I'll read, his for his love.'

THIRTY-THREE

FULL many a glorious morning have I seen
Flatter the mountain-tops with sovereign eye,
Kissing with golden face the meadows green,
Gilding pale streams with heavenly alchemy;
Anon permit the basest clouds to ride
With ugly rack on his celestial face,
And from the forlorn world his visage hide,
Stealing unseen to west with this disgrace:
Even so my sun one early morn did shine
With all-triumphant splendour on my brow;
But out, alack! he was but one hour mine;
The region cloud hath mask'd him from me now.
    Yet him for this my love no whit disdaineth;
    Suns of the world may stain when heaven's sun
        staineth.

THIRTY-FOUR

WHY didst thou promise such a beauteous day
And make me travel forth without my cloak,
To let base clouds o'ertake me in my way,
Hiding thy bravery in their rotten smoke?
'Tis not enough that through the cloud thou break,
To dry the rain on my storm-beaten face,
For no man well of such a salve can speak
That heals the wound and cures not the disgrace:
Nor can thy shame give physic to my grief;
Though thou repent, yet I have still the loss:
The offender's sorrow lends but weak relief
To him that bears the strong offence's cross.
    Ah! but those tears are pearl which thy love sheds,
    And they are rich and ransom all ill deeds.

THIRTY-FIVE

NO more be grieved at that which thou hast done:
Roses have thorns, and silver fountains mud;
Clouds and eclipses stain both moon and sun,
And loathsome canker lives in sweetest bud.
All men make faults, and even I in this,
Authorizing thy trespass with compare,
Myself corrupting, salving thy amiss,
Excusing thy sins more than thy sins are;
For to thy sensual fault I bring in sense—
Thy adverse party is thy advocate—
And 'gainst myself a lawful plea commence:
Such civil war is in my love and hate
    That I an accessary needs must be
    To that sweet thief which sourly robs from me.

THIRTY-SIX

LET me confess that we two must be twain,
Although our undivided loves are one:
So shall those blots that do with me remain
Without thy help by me be borne alone.
In our two loves there is but one respect,
Though in our lives a separable spite,
Which though it alter not love's sole effect,
Yet doth it steal sweet hours from love's delight.
I may not evermore acknowledge thee,
Lest my bewailed guilt should do thee shame,
Nor thou with public kindness honour me,
Unless thou take that honour from thy name:
    But do not so; I love thee in such sort
    As, thou being mine, mine is thy good report.

THIRTY-SEVEN

AS a decrepit father takes delight
To see his active child do deeds of youth,
So I, made lame by fortune's dearest spite,
Take all my comfort of thy worth and truth.
For whether beauty, birth, or wealth, or wit,
Or any of these all, or all, or more,
Entitled in thy parts do crowned sit,
I make my love engrafted to this store:
So then I am not lame, poor, nor despised,
Whilst that this shadow doth such substance give
That I in thy abundance am sufficed
And by a part of all thy glory live.
    Look, what is best, that best I wish in thee:
    This wish I have; then ten times happy me!

THIRTY-EIGHT

HOW can my Muse want subject to invent,
While thou dost breathe, that pour'st into my verse
Thine own sweet argument, too excellent
For every vulgar paper to rehearse?
O, give thyself the thanks, if aught in me
Worthy perusal stand against thy sight;
For who's so dumb that cannot write to thee,
When thou thyself dost give invention light?
Be thou the tenth Muse, ten times more in worth
Than those old nine which rhymers invocate;
And he that calls on thee, let him bring forth
Eternal numbers to outlive long date.
 If my slight Muse do please these curious days,
 The pain be mine, but thine shall be the praise.

THIRTY-NINE

O, how thy worth with manners may I sing,
When thou art all the better part of me?
What can mine own praise to mine own self bring?
And what is't but mine own when I praise thee?
Even for this let us divided live,
And our dear love lose name of single one,
That by this separation I may give
That due to thee which thou deservest alone.
O absence, what a torment wouldst thou prove,
Were it not thy sour leisure gave sweet leave
To entertain the time with thoughts of love,
Which time and thoughts so sweetly doth deceive,
 And that thou teachest how to make one twain,
 By praising him here who doth hence remain!

FORTY

TAKE all my loves, my love, yea, take them all;
What hast thou then more than thou hadst before?
No love, my love, that thou mayst true love call;
All mine was thine before thou hadst this more.
Then if for my love thou my love receivest,
I cannot blame thee for my love thou usest;
But yet be blamed, if thou thyself deceivest
By wilful taste of what thyself refusest.
I do forgive thy robbery, gentle thief,
Although thou steal thee all my poverty;
And yet, love knows, it is a greater grief
To bear love's wrong than hate's known injury.
    Lascivious grace, in whom all ill well shows,
    Kill me with spites; yet we must not be foes.

FORTY-ONE

THOSE pretty wrongs that liberty commits,
When I am sometime absent from thy heart,
Thy beauty and thy years full well befits,
For still temptation follows where thou art.
Gentle thou art and therefore to be won,
Beauteous thou art, therefore to be assailed;
And when a woman woos, what woman's son
Will sourly leave her till she have prevailed?
Ay me! but yet thou mightst my seat forbear,
And chide thy beauty and thy straying youth,
Who lead thee in their riot even there
Where thou art forced to break a twofold truth,
    Hers, by thy beauty tempting her to thee,
    Thine, by thy beauty being false to me.

FORTY-TWO

THAT thou hast her, it is not all my grief,
And yet it may be said I loved her dearly;
That she hath thee, is of my wailing chief,
A loss in love that touches me more nearly.
Loving offenders, thus I will excuse ye:
Thou dost love her, because thou know'st I love her;
And for my sake even so doth she abuse me,
Suffering my friend for my sake to approve her.
If I lose thee, my loss is my love's gain,
And losing her, my friend hath found that loss;
Both find each other, and I lose both twain,
And both for my sake lay on me this cross:
    But here's the joy; my friend and I are one;
    Sweet flattery! then she loves but me alone.

FORTY-THREE

WHEN most I wink, then do mine eyes best see,
For all the day they view things unrespected;
But when I sleep, in dreams they look on thee,
And darkly bright are bright in dark directed.
Then thou, whose shadow shadows doth make bright,
How would thy shadow's form form happy show
To the clear day with thy much clearer light,
When to unseeing eyes thy shade shines so!
How would, I say, mine eyes be blessed made
By looking on thee in the living day,
When in dead night thy fair imperfect shade
Through heavy sleep on sightless eyes doth stay!
    All days are nights to see till I see thee,
    And nights bright days when dreams do show thee me.

FORTY-FOUR

IF the dull substance of my flesh were thought,
Injurious distance should not stop my way;
For then despite of space I would be brought,
From limits far remote, where thou dost stay.
No matter then although my foot did stand
Upon the farthest earth removed from thee;
For nimble thought can jump both sea and land
As soon as think the place where he would be.
But, ah! thought kills me that I am not thought,
To leap large lengths of miles when thou art gone,
But that so much of earth and water wrought
I must attend time's leisure with my moan,
    Receiving nought by elements so slow
    But heavy tears, badges of either's woe.

FORTY-FIVE

THE other two, slight air and purging fire,
Are both with thee, wherever I abide;
The first my thought, the other my desire,
These present-absent with swift motion slide.
For when these quicker elements are gone
In tender embassy of love to thee,
My life, being made of four, with two alone
Sinks down the death, oppress'd with melancholy;
Until life's composition be recurred
By those swift messengers return'd from thee,
Who even but now come back again, assured
Of thy fair health, recounting it to me:
    This told, I joy; but then no longer glad,
    I send them back again and straight grow sad.

FORTY-SIX

MINE eye and heart are at a mortal war
How to divide the conquest of thy sight;
Mine eye my heart thy picture's sight would bar,
My heart mine eye the freedom of that right.
My heart doth plead that thou in him dost lie,—
A closet never pierced with crystal eyes—
But the defendant doth that plea deny
And says in him thy fair appearance lies.
To 'cide this title is impanneled
A quest of thoughts, all tenants to the heart,
And by their verdict is determined
The clear eye's moiety and the dear heart's part:
 As thus; mine eye's due is the outward part,
 And my heart's right thy inward love of heart.

FORTY-SEVEN

BETWIXT mine eye and heart a league is took,
And each doth good turns now unto the other:
When that mine eye is famish'd for a look,
Or heart in love with sighs himself doth smother,
With my love's picture then my eye doth feast
And to the painted banquet bids my heart;
Another time mine eye is my heart's guest
And in his thoughts of love doth share a part;
So, either by thy picture or my love,
Thyself away art present still with me;
For thou not farther than my thoughts canst move,
And I am still with them and they with thee;
 Or, if they sleep, thy picture in my sight
 Awakes my heart to heart's and eye's delight.

FORTY-EIGHT

HOW careful was I, when I took my way,
Each trifle under truest bars to thrust,
That to my use it might unused stay
From hands of falsehood, in sure wards of trust!
But thou, to whom my jewels trifles are,
Most worthy of comfort, now my greatest grief,
Thou, best of dearest and mine only care,
Art left the prey of every vulgar thief.
Thee have I not lock'd up in any chest,
Save where thou art not, though I feel thou art,
Within the gentle closure of my breast,
From whence at pleasure thou mayst come and part;
    And even thence thou wilt be stol'n, I fear,
    For truth proves thievish for a prize so dear.

FORTY-NINE

AGAINST that time, if ever that time come,
When I shall see thee frown on my defects,
When as thy love hath cast his utmost sum,
Call'd to that audit by advised respects;
Against that time when thou shalt strangely pass
And scarcely greet me with that sun, thine eye,
When love, converted from the thing it was,
Shall reasons find of settled gravity,—
Against that time do I ensconce me here
Within the knowledge of mine own desert,
And this my hand against myself uprear,
To guard the lawful reasons on thy part:
    To leave poor me thou hast the strength of laws,
    Since why to love I can allege no cause.

FIFTY

HOW heavy do I journey on the way,
When what I seek, my weary travel's end,
Doth teach that ease and that repose to say
'Thus far the miles are measured from thy friend!'
The beast that bears me, tired with my woe,
Plods dully on, to bear that weight in me,
As if by some instinct the wretch did know
His rider loved not speed, being made from thee:
The bloody spur cannot provoke him on
That sometimes anger thrusts into his hide;
Which heavily he answers with a groan,
More sharp to me than spurring to his side;
> For that same groan doth put this in my mind;
> My grief lies onward and my joy behind.

FIFTY-ONE

THUS can my love excuse the slow offence
Of my dull bearer when from thee I speed:
From where thou art why should I haste me thence?
Till I return, of posting is no need.
O, what excuse will my poor beast then find,
When swift extremity can seem but slow?
Then should I spur, though mounted on the wind;
In winged speed no motion shall I know:
Then can no horse with my desire keep pace;
Therefore desire, of perfect'st love being made,
Shall neigh—no dull flesh—in his fiery race;
But love, for love, thus shall excuse my jade;
> Since from thee going he went wilful-slow,
> Towards thee I'll run, and give him leave to go.

FIFTY-TWO

SO am I as the rich, whose blessed key
Can bring him to his sweet up-locked treasure,
The which he will not every hour survey,
For blunting the fine point of seldom pleasure.
Therefore are feasts so solemn and so rare,
Since, seldom coming, in the long year set,
Like stones of worth they thinly placed are,
Or captain jewels in the carcanet.
So is the time that keeps you as my chest,
Or as the wardrobe which the robe doth hide,
To make some special instant special blest,
By new unfolding his imprison'd pride.
    Blessed are you, whose worthiness gives scope,
    Being had, to triumph, being lack'd, to hope.

FIFTY-THREE

WHAT is your substance, whereof are you made,
That millions of strange shadows on you tend?
Since every one hath, every one, one shade,
And you, but one, can every shadow lend.
Describe Adonis, and the counterfeit
Is poorly imitated after you;
On Helen's cheek all art of beauty set,
And you in Grecian tires are painted new:
Speak of the spring and foison of the year;
The one doth shadow of your beauty show,
The other as your bounty doth appear;
And you in every blessed shape we know.
    In all eternal grace you have some part,
    But you like none, none you, for constant heart.

FIFTY-FOUR

O, how much more doth beauty beauteous seem
By that sweet ornament which truth doth give!
The rose looks fair, but fairer it we deem
For that sweet odour which doth in it live.
The canker-blooms have full as deep a dye
As the perfumed tincture of the roses,
Hang on such thorns and play as wantonly
When summer's breath their masked buds discloses:
But, for their virtue only is their show,
They live unwoo'd and unrespected fade,
Die to themselves. Sweet roses do not so;
Of their sweet deaths are sweetest odours made:
    And so of you, beauteous and lovely youth,
    When that shall fade, my verse distills your truth.

FIFTY-FIVE

NOT marble, nor the gilded monuments
Of princes, shall outlive this powerful rhyme;
But you shall shine more bright in these contents
Than unswept stone besmear'd with sluttish time.
When wasteful war shall statues overturn,
And broils root out the work of masonry,
Nor Mars his sword nor war's quick fire shall burn
The living record of your memory.
'Gainst death and all-oblivious enmity
Shall you pace forth; your praise shall still find room
Even in the eyes of all posterity
That wear this world out to the ending doom.
    So, till the judgement that yourself arise,
    You live in this, and dwell in lovers' eyes.

FIFTY-SIX

SWEET love, renew thy force; be it not said
Thy edge should blunter be than appetite,
Which but to-day by feeding is allay'd,
To-morrow sharpen'd in his former might:
So, love, be thou; although to-day thou fill
Thy hungry eyes even till they wink with fullness,
To-morrow see again, and do not kill
The spirit of love with a perpetual dullness.
Let this sad interim like the ocean be
Which parts the shore, where two contracted new
Come daily to the banks, that, when they see
Return of love, more blest may be the view;
    Else call it winter, which being full of care
    Makes summer's welcome thrice more wish'd, more
        rare.

FIFTY-SEVEN

BEING your slave, what should I do but tend
Upon the hours and times of your desire?
I have no precious time at all to spend,
Nor services to do, till you require.
Nor dare I chide the world-without-end hour
Whilst I, my sovereign, watch the clock for you,
Nor think the bitterness of absence sour
When you have bid your servant once adieu;
Nor dare I question with my jealous thought
Where you may be, or your affairs suppose,
But, like a sad slave, stay and think of nought
Save, where you are how happy you make those.
    So true a fool is love that in your will,
    Though you do anything, he thinks no ill.

FIFTY-EIGHT

THAT god forbid that made me first your slave,
I should in thought control your times of pleasure,
Or at your hand the account of hours to crave,
Being your vassal, bound to stay your leisure!
O, let me suffer, being at your beck,
The imprison'd absence of your liberty;
And patience, tame to sufferance, bide each check,
Without accusing you of injury.
Be where you list, your charter is so strong
That you yourself may privilege your time
To what you will; to you it doth belong
Yourself to pardon of self-doing crime.
    I am to wait, though waiting so be hell;
    Not blame your pleasure, be it will or well.

FIFTY-NINE

IF there be nothing new, but that which is
Hath been before, how are our brains beguiled,
Which, labouring for invention, bear amiss
The second burthen of a former child!
O, that record could with backward look,
Even of five hundred courses of the sun,
Show me your image in some antique book,
Since mind at first in character was done!
That I might see what the old world could say
To this composed wonder of your frame;
Whether we are mended, or whether better they,
Or whether revolution be the same.
    O, sure I am, the wits of former days
    To subjects worse have given admiring praise.

SIXTY

LIKE as the waves make towards the pebbled shore,
So do our minutes hasten to their end;
Each changing place with that which goes before,
In sequent toil all forwards do contend.
Nativity, once in the main of light,
Crawls to maturity, wherewith being crown'd,
Crooked eclipses 'gainst his glory fight,
And Time that gave doth now his gift confound.
Time doth transfix the flourish set on youth
And delves the parallels in beauty's brow,
Feeds on the rarities of nature's truth,
And nothing stands but for his scythe to mow:
    And yet to times in hope my verse shall stand,
    Praising thy worth, despite his cruel hand.

SIXTY-ONE

IS it thy will thy image should keep open
My heavy eyelids to the weary night?
Dost thou desire my slumbers should be broken,
While shadows like to thee do mock my sight?
Is it thy spirit that thou send'st from thee
So far from home into my deeds to pry,
To find out shames and idle hours in me,
The scope and tenour of thy jealousy?
O, no! thy love, though much, is not so great:
It is my love that keeps mine eye awake;
Mine own true love that doth my rest defeat,
To play the watchman ever for thy sake:
    For thee watch I whilst thou dost wake elsewhere,
    From me far off, with others all too near.

SIXTY-TWO

SIN of self-love possesseth all mine eye
And all my soul and all my every part;
And for this sin there is no remedy,
It is so grounded inward in my heart.
Methinks no face so gracious is as mine,
No shape so true, no truth of such account,
And for myself mine own worth do define,
As I all other in all worths surmount.
But when my glass shows me myself indeed,
Beated and chopp'd with tann'd antiquity,
Mine own self-love quite contrary I read;
Self so self-loving were iniquity.
    'Tis thee, myself, that for myself I praise,
    Painting my age with beauty of thy days.

SIXTY-THREE

AGAINST my love shall be, as I am now,
With Time's injurious hand crush'd and o'erworn;
When hours have drain'd his blood and fill'd his brow
With lines and wrinkles; when his youthful morn
Hath travell'd on to age's steepy night,
And all those beauties whereof now he's king
Are vanishing or vanish'd out of sight,
Stealing away the treasure of his spring;
For such a time do I now fortify
Against confounding age's cruel knife,
That he shall never cut from memory
My sweet love's beauty, though my lover's life:
    His beauty shall in these black lines be seen,
    And they shall live, and he in them still green.

SIXTY-FOUR

WHEN I have seen by Time's fell hand defaced
The rich proud cost of outworn buried age;
When sometime lofty towers I see down-razed
And brass eternal slave to mortal rage;
When I have seen the hungry ocean gain
Advantage on the kingdom of the shore,
And the firm soil win of the watery main,
Increasing store with loss and loss with store;
When I have seen such interchange of state,
Or state itself confounded to decay;
Ruin hath taught me thus to ruminate,
That Time will come and take my love away.
    This thought is as a death, which cannot choose
    But weep to have that which it fears to lose.

SIXTY-FIVE

SINCE brass, nor stone, nor earth, nor boundless sea,
But sad mortality o'er-sways their power,
How with this rage shall beauty hold a plea,
Whose action is no stronger than a flower?
O, how shall summer's honey breath hold out
Against the wreckful siege of battering days,
When rocks impregnable are not so stout,
Nor gates of steel so strong, but Time decays?
O fearful meditation! where, alack,
Shall Time's best jewel from Time's chest lie hid?
Or what strong hand can hold his swift foot back?
Or who his spoil of beauty can forbid?
    O, none, unless this miracle have might,
    That in black ink my love may still shine bright.

SIXTY-SIX

TIRED with all these, for restful death I cry,
As, to behold desert a beggar born,
And needy nothing trimm'd in jollity,
And purest faith unhappily forsworn,
And gilded honour shamefully misplaced,
And maiden virtue rudely strumpeted,
And right perfection wrongfully disgraced,
And strength by limping sway disabled,
And art made tongue-tied by authority,
And folly doctor-like controlling skill,
And simple truth miscall'd simplicity,
And captive good attending captain ill:
    Tired with all these, from these would I be gone,
    Save that, to die, I leave my love alone.

SIXTY-SEVEN

AH! wherefore with infection should he live,
And with his presence grace impiety,
That sin by him advantage should achieve
And lace itself with his society?
Why should false painting imitate his cheek
And steal dead seeing of his living hue?
Why should poor beauty indirectly seek
Roses of shadow, since his rose is true?
Why should he live, now Nature bankrupt is,
Beggar'd of blood to blush through lively veins?
For she hath no exchequer now but his,
And, proud of many, lives upon his gains.
    O, him she stores, to show what wealth she had
    In days long since, before these last so bad.

SIXTY-EIGHT

THUS is his cheek the map of days outworn,
When beauty lived and died as flowers do now,
Before these bastard signs of fair were born,
Or durst inhabit on a living brow;
Before the golden tresses of the dead,
The right of sepulchres, were shorn away,
To live a second life on second head;
Ere beauty's dead fleece made another gay:
In him those holy antique hours are seen,
Without all ornament, itself and true,
Making no summer of another's green,
Robbing no old to dress his beauty new;
    And him as for a map doth Nature store,
    To show false Art what beauty was of yore.

SIXTY-NINE

THOSE parts of thee that the world's eye doth view
Want nothing that the thought of hearts can mend;
All tongues, the voice of souls, give thee that due,
Uttering bare truth, even so as foes commend.
Thy outward thus with outward praise is crown'd;
But those same tongues that give thee so thine own
In other accents do this praise confound
By seeing farther than the eye hath shown.
They look into the beauty of thy mind,
And that, in guess, they measure by thy deeds;
Then, churls, their thoughts, although their eyes were
    kind,
To thy fair flower add the rank smell of weeds:
    But why thy odour matcheth not thy show,
    The solve is this, that thou dost common grow.

SEVENTY

THAT thou art blamed shall not be thy defect,
For slander's mark was ever yet the fair;
The ornament of beauty is suspect,
A crow that flies in heaven's sweetest air.
So thou be good, slander doth but approve
Thy worth the greater, being woo'd of time;
For canker vice the sweetest buds doth love,
And thou present'st a pure unstained prime.
Thou hast pass'd by the ambush of young days,
Either not assail'd or victor being charged;
Yet this thy praise cannot be so thy praise,
To tie up envy evermore enlarged:
    If some suspect of ill mask'd not thy show,
    Then thou alone kingdoms of hearts shouldst owe.

SEVENTY-ONE

NO longer mourn for me when I am dead
Than you shall hear the surly sullen bell
Give warning to the world that I am fled
From this vile world, with vilest worms to dwell:
Nay, if you read this line, remember not
The hand that writ it; for I love you so
That I in your sweet thoughts would be forgot
If thinking on me then should make you woe.
O, if, I say, you look upon this verse
When I perhaps compounded am with clay,
Do not so much as my poor name rehearse,
But let your love even with my life decay,
    Lest the wise world should look into your moan
    And mock you with me after I am gone.

SEVENTY-TWO

O, lest the world should task you to recite
What merit lived in me, that you should love
After my death, dear love, forget me quite,
For you in me can nothing worthy prove;
Unless you would devise some virtuous lie,
To do more for me than mine own desert,
And hang more praise upon deceased I
Than niggard truth would willingly impart:
O, lest your true love may seem false in this,
That you for love speak well of me untrue,
My name be buried where my body is,
And live no more to shame nor me nor you.
    For I am shamed by that which I bring forth,
    And so should you, to love things nothing worth.

SEVENTY-THREE

THAT time of year thou mayst in me behold
When yellow leaves, or none, or few, do hang
Upon those boughs which shake against the cold,
Bare ruin'd choirs, where late the sweet birds sang.
In me thou see'st the twilight of such day
As after sunset fadeth in the west,
Which by and by black night doth take away,
Death's second self, that seals up all in rest.
In me thou see'st the glowing of such fire
That on the ashes of his youth doth lie,
As the death-bed whereon it must expire
Consumed with that which it was nourish'd by.
    This thou perceivest, which makes thy love more strong,
    To love that well which thou must leave ere long.

SEVENTY-FOUR

BUT be contented: when that fell arrest
Without all bail shall carry me away,
My life hath in this line some interest,
Which for memorial still with thee shall stay.
When thou reviewest this, thou dost review
The very part was consecrate to thee:
The earth can have but earth, which is his due;
My spirit is thine, the better part of me:
So then thou hast but lost the dregs of life,
The prey of worms, my body being dead,
The coward conquest of a wretch's knife,
Too base of thee to be remembered.
    The worth of that is that which it contains,
    And that is this, and this with thee remains.

SEVENTY-FIVE

SO are you to my thoughts as food to life,
Or as sweet-season'd showers are to the ground;
And for the peace of you I hold such strife
As 'twixt a miser and his wealth is found;
Now proud as an enjoyer and anon
Doubting the filching age will steal his treasure,
Now counting best to be with you alone,
Then better'd that the world may see my pleasure;
Sometime all full with feasting on your sight
And by and by clean starved for a look;
Possessing or pursuing no delight,
Save what is had or must from you be took.
    Thus do I pine and surfeit day by day,
    Or gluttoning on all, or all away.

SEVENTY-SIX

WHY is my verse so barren of new pride,
So far from variation or quick changes?
Why with the time do I not glance aside
To new-found methods and to compounds strange?
Why write I still all one, ever the same,
And keep invention in a noted weed,
That every word doth almost tell my name,
Showing their birth and where they did proceed?
O, know, sweet love, I always write of you,
And you and love are still my argument;
So all my best is dressing old words new,
Spending again what is already spent:
    For as the sun is daily new and old,
    So is my love still telling what is told.

SEVENTY-SEVEN

THY glass will show thee how thy beauties wear,
Thy dial how thy precious minutes waste;
The vacant leaves thy mind's imprint will bear,
And of this book this learning mayst thou taste.
The wrinkles which thy glass will truly show
Of mouthed graves will give thee memory;
Thou by thy dial's shady stealth mayst know
Time's thievish progress to eternity.
Look, what thy memory can not contain
Commit to these waste blanks, and thou shalt find
Those children nursed, deliver'd from thy brain,
To take a new acquaintance of thy mind.
    These offices, so oft as thou wilt look,
    Shall profit thee and much enrich thy book.

SEVENTY-EIGHT

SO oft have I invoked thee for my Muse
And found such fair assistance in my verse
As every alien pen hath got my use
And under thee their poesy disperse.
Thine eyes that taught the dumb on high to sing
And heavy ignorance aloft to fly
Have added feathers to the learned's wing
And given grace a double majesty.
Yet be most proud of that which I compile,
Whose influence is thine and born of thee:
In others' works thou dost but mend the style,
And arts with thy sweet graces graced be;
> But thou art all my art and dost advance
> As high as learning my rude ignorance.

SEVENTY-NINE

WHILST I alone did call upon thy aid,
My verse alone had all thy gentle grace,
But now my gracious numbers are decay'd
And my sick Muse doth give another place.
I grant, sweet love, thy lovely argument
Deserves the travail of a worthier pen,
Yet what of thee thy poet doth invent
He robs thee of and pays it thee again.
He lends thee virtue and he stole that word
From thy behaviour; beauty doth he give
And found it in thy cheek; he can afford
No praise to thee but what in thee doth live.
> Then thank him not for that which he doth say,
> Since what he owes thee thou thyself dost pay.

EIGHTY

O, how I faint when I of you do write,
Knowing a better spirit doth use your name,
And in the praise thereof spends all his might,
To make me tongue-tied, speaking of your fame!
But since your worth, wide as the ocean is,
The humble as the proudest sail doth bear,
My saucy bark inferior far to his
On your broad main doth wilfully appear.
Your shallowest help will hold me up afloat,
Whilst he upon your soundless deep doth ride;
Or, being wreck'd, I am a worthless boat,
He of tall building and of goodly pride:
    Then if he thrive and I be cast away,
    The worst was this; my love was my decay.

EIGHTY-ONE

OR I shall live your epitaph to make,
Or you survive when I in earth am rotten;
From hence your memory death cannot take,
Although in me each part will be forgotten.
Your name from hence immortal life shall have,
Though I, once gone, to all the world must die:
The earth can yield me but a common grave,
When you entombed in men's eyes shall lie.
Your monument shall be my gentle verse,
Which eyes not yet created shall o'er-read,
And tongues to be your being shall rehearse
When all the breathers of this world are dead;
    You still shall live—such virtue hath my pen—
    Where breath most breathes, even in the mouths of men.

EIGHTY-TWO

I grant thou wert not married to my Muse
And therefore mayst without attaint o'erlook
The dedicated words which writers use
Of their fair subject, blessing every book.
Thou art as fair in knowledge as in hue,
Finding thy worth a limit past my praise,
And therefore art enforced to seek anew
Some fresher stamp of the time-bettering days.
And do so, love; yet when they have devised
What strained touches rhetoric can lend,
Thou truly fair wert truly sympathized
In true plain words by thy true-telling friend;
    And their gross painting might be better used
    Where cheeks need blood; in thee it is abused.

EIGHTY-THREE

I never saw that you did painting need
And therefore to your fair no painting set;
I found, or thought I found, you did exceed
The barren tender of a poet's debt;
And therefore have I slept in your report,
That you yourself being extant well might show
How far a modern quill doth come too short,
Speaking of worth, what worth in you doth grow.
This silence for my sin you did impute,
Which shall be most my glory, being dumb;
For I impair not beauty being mute,
When others would give life and bring a tomb.
    There lives more life in one of your fair eyes
    Than both your poets can in praise devise.

EIGHTY-FOUR

WHO is it that says most? which can say more
Than this rich praise, that you alone are you?
In whose confine immured is the store
Which should example where your equal grew.
Lean penury within that pen doth dwell
That to his subject lends not some small glory;
But he that writes of you, if he can tell
That you are you, so dignifies his story,
Let him but copy what in you is writ,
Not making worse what nature made so clear,
And such a counterpart shall fame his wit,
Making his style admired every where.
    You to your beauteous blessings add a curse,
    Being fond on praise, which makes your praises
        worse.

EIGHTY-FIVE

MY tongue-tied Muse in manners holds her still,
While comments of your praise, richly compiled,
Reserve their character with golden quill
And precious phrase by all the Muses filed.
I think good thoughts whilst others write good words,
And like unletter'd clerk still cry 'Amen'
To every hymn that able spirit affords
In polish'd form of well-refined pen.
Hearing you praised, I say ' 'Tis so, 'tis true,'
And to the most of praise add something more;
But that is in my thought, whose love to you,
Though words come hindmost, holds his rank before.
    Then others for the breath of words respect,
    Me for my dumb thoughts, speaking in effect.

EIGHTY-SIX

WAS it the proud full sail of his great verse,
Bound for the prize of all too precious you,
That did my ripe thoughts in my brain inhearse,
Making their tomb the womb wherein they grew?
Was it his spirit, by spirits taught to write
Above a mortal pitch, that struck me dead?
No, neither he, nor his compeers by night
Giving him aid, my verse astonished.
He, nor that affable familiar ghost
Which nightly gulls him with intelligence,
As victors of my silence cannot boast;
I was not sick of any fear from thence:
> But when your countenance fill'd up his line,
> Then lack'd I matter; that enfeebled mine.

EIGHTY-SEVEN

FAREWELL! thou art too dear for my possessing,
And like enough thou know'st thy estimate:
The charter of thy worth gives thee releasing;
My bonds in thee are all determinate.
For how do I hold thee but by thy granting?
And for that riches where is my deserving?
The cause of this fair gift in me is wanting,
And so my patent back again is swerving.
Thyself thou gavest, thy own worth then not knowing,
Or me, to whom thou gavest it, else mistaking;
So thy great gift, upon misprision growing,
Comes home again, on better judgement making.
> Thus have I had thee, as a dream doth flatter,
> In sleep a king, but waking no such matter.

EIGHTY-EIGHT

WHEN thou shalt be disposed to set me light
And place my merit in the eye of scorn,
Upon thy side against myself I'll fight
And prove thee virtuous, though thou art forsworn.
With mine own weakness being best acquainted,
Upon thy part I can set down a story
Of faults conceal'd, wherein I am attainted,
That thou in losing me shalt win much glory:
And I by this will be a gainer too;
For bending all my loving thoughts on thee,
The injuries that to myself I do,
Doing thee vantage, double-vantage me.
    Such is my love, to thee I so belong,
    That for thy right myself will bear all wrong.

EIGHTY-NINE

SAY that thou didst forsake me for some fault,
And I will comment upon that offence;
Speak of my lameness, and I straight will halt,
Against thy reasons making no defence.
Thou canst not, love, disgrace me half so ill,
To set a form upon desired change,
As I'll myself disgrace: knowing thy will,
I will acquaintance strangle and look strange,
Be absent from thy walks, and in my tongue
Thy sweet beloved name no more shall dwell,
Lest I, too much profane, should do it wrong
And haply of our old acquaintance tell.
    For thee against myself I'll vow debate,
    For I must ne'er love him whom thou dost hate.

NINETY

THEN hate me when thou wilt; if ever, now;
Now, while the world is bent my deeds to cross,
Join with the spite of fortune, make me bow,
And do not drop in for an after-loss:
Ah, do not, when my heart hath 'scaped this sorrow,
Come in the rearward of a conquer'd woe;
Give not a windy night a rainy morrow,
To linger out a purposed overthrow.
If thou wilt leave me, do not leave me last,
When other petty griefs have done their spite,
But in the onset come; so shall I taste
At first the very worst of fortune's might,
    And other strains of woe, which now seem woe,
    Compared with loss of thee will not seem so.

NINETY-ONE

SOME glory in their birth, some in their skill,
Some in their wealth, some in their bodies' force,
Some in their garments, though new-fangled ill,
Some in their hawks and hounds, some in their horse;
And every humour hath his adjunct pleasure,
Wherein it finds a joy above the rest:
But these particulars are not my measure;
All these I better in one general best.
Thy love is better than high birth to me,
Richer than wealth, prouder than garments' cost,
Of more delight than hawks or horses be;
And having thee, of all men's pride I boast:
    Wretched in this alone, that thou mayst take
    All this away and me most wretched make.

NINETY-TWO

BUT do thy worst to steal thyself away,
For term of life thou art assured mine,
And life no longer than thy love will stay,
For it depends upon that love of thine.
Then need I not to fear the worst of wrongs,
When in the least of them my life hath end.
I see a better state to me belongs
Than that which on thy humour doth depend;
Thou canst not vex me with inconstant mind,
Since that my life on thy revolt doth lie.
O, what a happy title do I find,
Happy to have thy love, happy to die!
    But what's so blessed-fair that fears no blot?
    Thou mayst be false, and yet I know it not.

NINETY-THREE

SO shall I live, supposing thou art true,
Like a deceived husband; so love's face
May still seem love to me, though alter'd new;
Thy looks with me, thy heart in other place:
For there can live no hatred in thine eye,
Therefore in that I cannot know thy change.
In many's looks the false heart's history
Is writ in moods and frowns and wrinkles strange,
But heaven in thy creation did decree
That in thy face sweet love should ever dwell;
Whate'er thy thoughts or thy heart's workings be,
Thy looks should nothing thence but sweetness tell.
    How like Eve's apple doth thy beauty grow,
    If thy sweet virtue answer not thy show!

NINETY-FOUR

THEY that have power to hurt and will do none,
That do not do the thing they most do show,
Who, moving others, are themselves as stone,
Unmoved, cold, and to temptation slow,
They rightly do inherit heaven's graces
And husband nature's riches from expense;
They are the lords and owners of their faces,
Others but stewards of their excellence.
The summer's flower is to the summer sweet,
Though to itself it only live and die,
But if that flower with base infection meet,
The basest weed outbraves his dignity:
    For sweetest things turn sourest by their deeds;
    Lilies that fester smell far worse than weeds.

NINETY-FIVE

HOW sweet and lovely dost thou make the shame
Which, like a canker in the fragrant rose,
Doth spot the beauty of thy budding name!
O, in what sweets dost thou thy sins enclose!
That tongue that tells the story of thy days,
Making lascivious comments on thy sport,
Cannot dispraise but in a kind of praise;
Naming thy name blesses an ill report.
O, what a mansion have those vices got
Which for their habitation chose out thee,
Where beauty's veil doth cover every blot,
And all things turn to fair that eyes can see!
    Take heed, dear heart, of this large privilege;
    The hardest knife ill-used doth lose his edge.

NINETY-SIX

SOME say thy fault is youth, some wantonness;
Some say thy grace is youth and gentle sport;
Both grace and faults are loved of more and less;
Thou makest faults graces that to thee resort.
As on the finger of a throned queen
The basest jewel will be well esteem'd,
So are those errors that in thee are seen
To truths translated and for true things deem'd.
How many lambs might the stern wolf betray,
If like a lamb he could his looks translate!
How many gazers mightst thou lead away,
If thou wouldst use the strength of all thy state!
  But do not so; I love thee in such sort
  As, thou being mine, mine is thy good report.

NINETY-SEVEN

HOW like a winter hath my absence been
From thee, the pleasure of the fleeting year!
What freezings have I felt, what dark days seen!
What old December's bareness every where!
And yet this time removed was summer's time,
The teeming autumn, big with rich increase,
Bearing the wanton burthen of the prime,
Like widow'd wombs after their lords' decease:
Yet this abundant issue seem'd to me
But hope of orphans and unfather'd fruit;
For summer and his pleasures wait on thee,
And, thou away, the very birds are mute;
  Or, if they sing, 'tis with so dull a cheer
  That leaves look pale, dreading the winter's near.

NINETY-EIGHT

FROM you have I been absent in the spring,
When proud-pied April dress'd in all his trim
Hath put a spirit of youth in every thing,
That heavy Saturn laugh'd and leap'd with him.
Yet nor the lays of birds nor the sweet smell
Of different flowers in odour and in hue
Could make me any summer's story tell,
Or from their proud lap pluck them where they grew;
Nor did I wonder at the lily's white,
Nor praise the deep vermilion in the rose;
They were but sweet, but figures of delight,
Drawn after you, you pattern of all those.
    Yet seem'd it winter still, and, you away,
    As with your shadow I with these did play:

NINETY-NINE

THE forward violet thus did I chide:
Sweet thief, whence didst thou steal thy sweet that smells,
If not from my love's breath? The purple pride
Which on thy soft cheek for complexion dwells
In my love's veins thou hast too grossly dyed.
The lily I condemned for thy hand,
And buds of marjoram had stol'n thy hair:
The roses fearfully on thorns did stand,
One blushing shame, another white despair;
A third, nor red nor white, had stol'n of both
And to his robbery had annex'd thy breath;
But, for his theft, in pride of all his growth
A vengeful canker eat him up to death.
    More flowers I noted, yet I none could see
    But sweet or colour it had stol'n from thee.

ONE HUNDRED

WHERE art thou, Muse, that thou forget'st so long
To speak of that which gives thee all thy might?
Spend'st thou thy fury on some worthless song,
Darkening thy power to lend base subjects light?
Return, forgetful Muse, and straight redeem
In gentle numbers time so idly spent;
Sing to the ear that doth thy lays esteem
And gives thy pen both skill and argument.
Rise, resty Muse, my love's sweet face survey,
If Time have any wrinkle graven there;
If any, be a satire to decay,
And make Time's spoils despised every where.
    Give my love fame faster than Time wastes life;
    So thou prevent'st his scythe and crooked knife.

ONE HUNDRED ONE

O truant Muse, what shall be thy amends
For thy neglect of truth in beauty dyed?
Both truth and beauty on my love depends;
So dost thou too, and therein dignified.
Make answer, Muse: wilt thou not haply say
'Truth needs no colour, with his colour fix'd;
Beauty no pencil, beauty's truth to lay;
But best is best, if never intermix'd'?
Because he needs no praise, wilt thou be dumb?
Excuse not silence so; for't lies in thee
To make him much outlive a gilded tomb,
And to be praised of ages yet to be.
    Then do thy office, Muse; I teach thee how
    To make him seem long hence as he shows now.

ONE HUNDRED TWO

MY love is strengthen'd, though more weak in seeming;
I love not less, though less the show appear:
That love is merchandized whose rich esteeming
The owner's tongue doth publish every where.
Our love was new and then but in the spring
When I was wont to greet it with my lays,
As Philomel in summer's front doth sing
And stops her pipe in growth of riper days:
Not that the summer is less pleasant now
Than when her mournful hymns did hush the night,
But that wild music burthens every bough
And sweets grown common lose their dear delight.
    Therefore like her I sometime hold my tongue,
    Because I would not dull you with my song.

ONE HUNDRED THREE

ALACK, what poverty my Muse brings forth,
That having such a scope to show her pride,
The argument all bare is of more worth
Than when it hath my added praise beside!
O, blame me not, if I no more can write!
Look in your glass, and there appears a face
That over-goes my blunt invention quite,
Dulling my lines and doing me disgrace.
Were it not sinful then, striving to mend,
To mar the subject that before was well?
For to no other pass my verses tend
Than of your graces and your gifts to tell;
    And more, much more, than in my verse can sit
    Your own glass shows you when you look in it.

ONE HUNDRED FOUR

TO me, fair friend, you never can be old,
For as you were when first your eye I eyed,
Such seems your beauty still. Three winters cold
Have from the forests shook three summers' pride,
Three beauteous springs to yellow autumn turn'd
In process of the seasons have I seen,
Three April perfumes in three hot Junes burn'd,
Since first I saw you fresh, which yet are green.
Ah! yet doth beauty, like a dial-hand,
Steal from his figure and no pace perceived;
So your sweet hue, which methinks still doth stand,
Hath motion and mine eye may be deceived:
    For fear of which, hear this, thou age unbred;
    Ere you were born was beauty's summer dead.

ONE HUNDRED FIVE

LET not my love be call'd idolatry,
Nor my beloved as an idol show,
Since all alike my songs and praises be
To one, of one, still such, and ever so.
Kind is my love to-day, to-morrow kind,
Still constant in a wondrous excellence;
Therefore my verse to constancy confined,
One thing expressing, leaves out difference.
'Fair, kind, and true' is all my argument,
'Fair, kind, and true' varying to other words;
And in this change is my invention spent,
Three themes in one, which wondrous scope affords.
    'Fair, kind, and true,' have often lived alone,
    Which three till now never kept seat in one.

ONE HUNDRED SIX

WHEN in the chronicle of wasted time
I see descriptions of the fairest wights,
And beauty making beautiful old rhyme
In praise of ladies dead and lovely knights,
Then, in the blazon of sweet beauty's best,
Of hand, of foot, of lip, of eye, of brow,
I see their antique pen would have express'd
Even such a beauty as you master now.
So all their praises are but prophecies
Of this our time, all you prefiguring;
And, for they look'd but with divining eyes,
They had not skill enough your worth to sing:
    For we, which now behold these present days,
    Have eyes to wonder, but lack tongues to praise.

ONE HUNDRED SEVEN

NOT mine own fears, nor the prophetic soul
Of the wide world dreaming on things to come,
Can yet the lease of my true love control,
Supposed as forfeit to a confined doom.
The mortal moon hath her eclipse endured
And the sad augers mock their own presage;
Incertainties now crown themselves assured
And peace proclaims olives of endless age.
Now with the drops of this most balmy time
My love looks fresh, and Death to me subscribes,
Since, spite of him, I'll love in this poor rhyme,
While he insults o'er dull and speechless tribes:
    And thou in this shalt find thy monument,
    When tyrants' crests and tombs of brass are spent.

ONE HUNDRED EIGHT

WHAT'S in the brain that ink may character
Which hath not figured to thee my true spirit?
What's new to speak, what new to register,
That may express my love or thy dear merit?
Nothing, sweet boy; but yet, like prayers divine,
I must each day say o'er the very same,
Counting no old thing old, thou mine, I thine,
Even as when first I hallow'd thy fair name.
So that eternal love in love's fresh case
Weighs not the dust and injury of age,
Nor gives to necessary wrinkles place,
But makes antiquity for aye his page,
    Finding the first conceit of love there bred
    Where time and outward form would show it dead.

ONE HUNDRED NINE

O, never say that I was false of heart,
Though absence seem'd my flame to qualify.
As easy might I from myself depart
As from my soul, which in thy breast doth lie:
That is my home of love: if I have ranged,
Like him that travels I return again,
Just to the time, not with the time exchanged,
So that myself bring water for my stain.
Never believe, though in my nature reign'd
All frailties that beseige all kinds of blood,
That it could so preposterously be stain'd,
To leave for nothing all thy sum of good;
    For nothing this wide universe I call,
    Save thou, my rose; in it thou art my all.

ONE HUNDRED TEN

ALAS, 'tis true I have gone here and there
And made myself a motley to the view,
Gored mine own thoughts, sold cheap what is most dear,
Made old offences of affections new;
Most true it is that I have look'd on truth
Askance and strangely: but, by all above,
These blenches gave my heart another youth,
And worse essays proved thee my best of love.
Now all is done, have what shall have no end:
Mine appetite I never more will grind
On newer proof, to try an older friend,
A god in love, to whom I am confined.
    Then give me welcome, next my heaven the best,
    Even to thy pure and most most loving breast.

ONE HUNDRED ELEVEN

O, for my sake do you with Fortune chide,
The guilty goddess of my harmful deeds,
That did not better for my life provide
Than public means which public manners breeds.
Thence comes it that my name receives a brand,
And almost thence my nature is subdued
To what it works in, like the dyer's hand:
Pity me then and wish I were renew'd:
Whilst, like a willing patient, I will drink
Potions of eisel 'gainst my strong infection;
No bitterness that I will bitter think,
Nor double penance, to correct correction.
    Pity me then, dear friend, and I assure ye
    Even that your pity is enough to cure me.

ONE HUNDRED FOURTEEN

OR whether doth my mind, being crown'd with you,
Drink up the monarch's plague, this flattery?
Or whether shall I say, mine eyes saith true,
And that your love taught it this alchemy,
To make of monsters and things indigest
Such cherubins as your sweet self resemble,
Creating every bad a perfect best,
As fast as objects to his beams assemble?
O, 'tis the first; 'tis flattery in my seeing,
And my great mind most kingly drinks it up
Mine eye well knows what with his gust is 'greeing,
And to his palate doth prepare the cup:
    If it be poison'd, 'tis the lesser sin
    That mine eye loves it and doth first begin.

ONE HUNDRED FIFTEEN

THOSE lines that I before have writ do lie,
Even those that said I could not love you dearer:
Yet then my judgement knew no reason why
My most full flame should afterwards burn clearer.
But reckoning time, whose million'd accidents
Creep in 'twixt vows and change decrees of kings,
Tan sacred beauty, blunt the sharp'st intents,
Divert strong minds to the course of altering things;
Alas, why, fearing of time's tyranny,
Might I not then say 'Now I love you best,'
When I was certain o'er incertainty,
Crowning the present, doubting of the rest?
    Love is a babe; then might I not say so,
    To give full growth to that which still doth grow?

ONE HUNDRED TWELVE

YOUR love and pity doth the impression fill
Which vulgar scandal stamp'd upon my brow;
For what care I who calls me well or ill,
So you o'er-green my bad, my good allow?
You are my all the world, and I must strive
To know my shames and praises from your tongue
None else to me, nor I to none alive,
That my steel'd sense or changes right or wrong.
In so profound abysm I throw all care
Of others' voices, that my adder's sense
To critic and to flatterer stopped are.
Mark how with my neglect I do dispense:
    You are so strongly in my purpose bred
    That all the world besides methinks are dead.

ONE HUNDRED THIRTEEN

SINCE I left you, mine eye is in my mind;
And that which governs me to go about
Doth part his function and is partly blind,
Seems seeing, but effectually is out;
For it no form delivers to the heart
Of bird, of flower, or shape, which it doth latch:
Of his quick objects hath the mind no part,
Nor his own vision holds what it doth catch;
For if it see the rudest or gentlest sight,
The most sweet favour or deformed'st creature,
The mountain or the sea, the day or night,
The crow or dove, it shapes them to your feature:
    Incapable of more, replete with you,
    My most true mind thus makes mine eye untrue.

ONE HUNDRED SIXTEEN

LET me not to the marriage of true minds
Admit impediments. Love is not love
Which alters when it alteration finds,
Or bends with the remover to remove:
O, no! it is an ever-fixed mark
That looks on tempests and is never shaken;
It is the star to every wandering bark,
Whose worth's unknown, although his height be taken.
Love's not Time's fool, though rosy lips and cheeks
Within his bending sickle's compass come;
Love alters not with his brief hours and weeks,
But bears it out even to the edge of doom.
    If this be error and upon me proved,
    I never writ, nor no man ever loved.

ONE HUNDRED SEVENTEEN

ACCUSE me thus: that I have scanted all
Wherein I should your great deserts repay,
Forgot upon your dearest love to call,
Whereto all bonds do tie me day by day;
That I have frequent been with unknown minds
And given to time your own dear-purchased right;
That I have hoisted sail to all the winds
Which should transport me farthest from your sight.
Book both my wilfulness and errors down
And on just proof surmise accumulate;
Bring me within the level of your frown,
But shoot not at me in your waken'd hate;
    Since my appeal says I did strive to prove
    The constancy and virtue of your love.

ONE HUNDRED EIGHTEEN

LIKE as, to make our appetites more keen,
With eager compounds we our palate urge,
As, to prevent our maladies unseen,
We sicken to shun sickness when we purge,
Even so, being full of your ne'er-cloying sweetness,
To bitter sauces did I frame my feeding
And, sick of welfare, found a kind of meetness
To be diseased ere that there was true needing.
Thus policy in love, to anticipate
The ills that were not, grew to faults assured
And brought to medicine a healthful state
Which, rank of goodness, would by ill be cured:
    But thence I learn, and find the lesson true,
    Drugs poison him that so fell sick of you.

ONE HUNDRED NINETEEN

WHAT potions have I drunk of Siren tears,
Distill'd from limbecks foul as hell within,
Applying fears to hopes and hopes to fears,
Still losing when I saw myself to win!
What wretched errors hath my heart committed,
Whilst it hath thought itself so blessed never!
How have mine eyes out of their spheres been fitted
In the distraction of this madding fever!
O benefit of ill! now I find true
That better is by evil still made better;
And ruin'd love, when it is built anew,
Grows fairer than at first, more strong, far greater.
    So I return rebuked to my content
    And gain by ill thrice more than I have spent.

ONE HUNDRED TWENTY

THAT you were once unkind befriends me now,
And for that sorrow which I then did feel
Needs must I under my transgression bow,
Unless my nerves were brass or hammer'd steel.
For if you were by my unkindness shaken
As I by yours, you've pass'd a hell of time,
And I, a tyrant, have no leisure taken
To weigh how once I suffer'd in your crime.
O, that our night of woe might have remember'd
My deepest sense, how hard true sorrow hits,
And soon to you, as you to me, then tender'd
The humble salve which wounded bosoms fits!
    But that your trespass now becomes a fee;
    Mine ransoms yours, and yours must ransom me.

ONE HUNDRED TWENTY-ONE

'TIS better to be vile than vile esteem'd,
When not to be receives reproach of being,
And the just pleasure lost which is so deem'd
Not by our feeling but by others' seeing:
For why should others' false adulterate eyes
Give salutation to my sportive blood?
Or on my frailties why are frailer spies,
Which in their wills count bad what I think good?
No, I am that I am, and they that level
At my abuses reckon up their own:
I may be straight, though they themselves be bevel;
By their rank thoughts my deeds must not be shown;
    Unless this general evil they maintain,
    All men are bad, and in their badness reign.

ONE HUNDRED TWENTY-TWO

THY gift, thy tables, are within my brain
Full character'd with lasting memory,
Which shall above that idle rank remain
Beyond all date, even to eternity;
Or at the least, so long as brain and heart
Have faculty by nature to subsist;
Till each to razed oblivion yield his part
Of thee, thy record never can be miss'd.
That poor retention could not so much hold,
Nor need I tallies thy dear love to score;
Therefore to give them from me was I bold,
To trust those tables that receive thee more:
    To keep an adjunct to remember thee
    Were to import forgetfulness in me.

ONE HUNDRED TWENTY-THREE

NO, Time, thou shalt not boast that I do change:
Thy pyramids built up with newer might
To me are nothing novel, nothing strange;
They are but dressings of a former sight.
Our dates are brief, and therefore we admire
What thou dost foist upon us that is old,
And rather make them born to our desire
Than think that we before have heard them told.
Thy registers and thee I both defy,
Not wondering at the present nor the past,
For thy records and what we see doth lie,
Made more or less by thy continual haste.
    This I do vow and this shall ever be;
    I will be true, despite thy scythe and thee.

ONE HUNDRED TWENTY-FOUR

IF my dear love were but the child of state,
It might for Fortune's bastard be unfather'd,
As subject to Time's love or to Time's hate,
Weeds among weeds, or flowers with flowers gather'd.
No, it was builded far from accident;
It suffers not in smiling pomp, nor falls
Under the blow of thralled discontent,
Whereto the inviting time our fashion calls:
It fears not policy, that heretic,
Which works on leases of short-number'd hours,
But all alone stands hugely politic,
That it nor grows with heat nor drowns with showers.
    To this I witness call the fools of time,
    Which die for goodness, who have lived for crime.

ONE HUNDRED TWENTY-FIVE

WERE'T aught to me I bore the canopy,
With my extern the outward honouring,
Or laid great bases for eternity,
Which prove more short than waste or ruining?
Have I not seen dwellers on form and favour
Lose all, and more, by paying too much rent,
For compound sweet forgoing simple savour,
Pitiful thrivers, in their gazing spent?
No, let me be obsequious in thy heart,
And take thou my oblation, poor but free,
Which is not mix'd with seconds, knows no art,
But mutual render, only me for thee.
    Hence, thou suborn'd informer! a true soul
    When most impeach'd stands least in thy control.

ONE HUNDRED TWENTY-SIX

O thou, my lovely boy, who in thy power
Dost hold Time's fickle glass, his sickle, hour;
Who hast by waning grown, and therein show'st
Thy lovers withering as thy sweet self grow'st;
If Nature, sovereign mistress over wrack,
As thou goest onwards, still will pluck thee back,
She keeps thee to this purpose, that her skill
May time disgrace and wretched minutes kill.
Yet fear her, O thou minion of her pleasure!
She may detain, but not still keep, her treasure:
    Her audit, though delay'd, answer'd must be,
    And her quietus is to render thee.

ONE HUNDRED TWENTY-SEVEN

IN the old age black was not counted fair,
Or if it were, it bore not beauty's name;
But now is black beauty's successive heir,
And beauty slander'd with a bastard shame:
For since each hand hath put on nature's power,
Fairing the foul with art's false borrow'd face,
Sweet beauty hath no name, no holy bower,
But is profaned, if not lives in disgrace.
Therefore my mistress' brows are raven black,
Her eyes so suited, and they mourners seem
At such who, not born fair, no beauty lack,
Slandering creation with a false esteem:
    Yet so they mourn, becoming of their woe,
    That every tongue says beauty should look so.

ONE HUNDRED TWENTY-EIGHT

HOW oft, when thou, my music, music play'st,
Upon that blessed wood whose motion sounds
With thy sweet fingers, when thou gently sway'st
The wiry concord that mine ear confounds,
Do I envy those jacks that nimble leap
To kiss the tender inward of thy hand,
Whilst my poor lips, which should that harvest reap,
At the wood's boldness by thee blushing stand!
To be so tickled, they would change their state
And situation with those dancing chips,
O'er whom thy fingers walk with gentle gait,
Making dead wood more blest than living lips.
    Since saucy jacks so happy are in this,
    Give them thy fingers, me thy lips to kiss.

ONE HUNDRED TWENTY-NINE

THE expense of spirit in a waste of shame
Is lust in action; and till action, lust
Is perjured, murderous, bloody, full of blame,
Savage, extreme, rude, cruel, not to trust,
Enjoy'd no sooner but despised straight,
Past reason hunted, and no sooner had
Past reason hated, as a swallow'd bait
On purpose laid to make the taker mad;
Mad in pursuit and in possession so;
Had, having, and in quest to have, extreme;
A bliss in proof, and proved, a very woe;
Before, a joy proposed; behind, a dream.
    All this the world well knows; yet none knows well
    To shun the heaven that leads men to this hell.

ONE HUNDRED THIRTY

MY mistress' eyes are nothing like the sun;
Coral is far more red than her lips' red;
If snow be white, why then her breasts are dun;
If hairs be wires, black wires grow on her head.
I have seen roses damask'd, red and white,
But no such roses see I in her cheeks;
And in some perfumes is there more delight
Than in the breath that from my mistress reeks.
I love to hear her speak, yet well I know
That music hath a far more pleasing sound;
I grant I never saw a goddess go;
My mistress, when she walks, treads on the ground:
    And yet, by heaven, I think my love as rare
    As any she belied with false compare.

ONE HUNDRED THIRTY-ONE

THOU art as tyrannous, so as thou art,
As those whose beauties proudly make them cruel;
For well thou know'st to my dear doting heart
Thou art the fairest and most precious jewel.
Yet, in good faith, some say that thee behold
Thy face hath not the power to make love groan:
To say they err I dare not be so bold,
Although I swear it to myself alone.
And, to be sure that is not false I swear,
A thousand groans, but thinking on thy face,
One on another's neck, do witness bear
Thy black is fairest in my judgement's place.
    In nothing art thou black save in thy deeds,
    And thence this slander, as I think, proceeds.

ONE HUNDRED THIRTY-TWO

THINE eyes I love, and they, as pitying me,
Knowing thy heart torments me with disdain,
Have put on black and loving mourners be,
Looking with pretty ruth upon my pain.
And truly not the morning sun of heaven
Better becomes the grey cheeks of the east,
Nor that full star that ushers in the even
Doth half that glory to the sober west,
As those two mourning eyes become thy face:
O, let it then as well beseem thy heart
To mourn for me, since mourning doth thee grace,
And suit thy pity like in every part.
    Then will I swear beauty herself is black
    And all they foul that thy complexion lack.

ONE HUNDRED THIRTY-THREE

BESHREW that heart that makes my heart to groan
For that deep wound it gives my friend and me!
Is't not enough to torture me alone,
But slave to slavery my sweet'st friend must be!
Me from myself thy cruel eye hath taken,
And my next self thou harder hast engross'd:
Of him, myself, and thee, I am forsaken;
A torment thrice threefold thus to be cross'd.
Prison my heart in thy steel bosom's ward,
But then my friend's heart let my poor heart bail;
Whoe'er keeps me, let my heart be his guard;
Thou canst not then use rigour in my gaol:
    And yet thou wilt; for I, being pent in thee,
    Perforce am thine, and all that is in me.

ONE HUNDRED THIRTY-FOUR

SO, now I have confess'd that he is thine,
And I myself am mortgaged to thy will,
Myself I'll forfeit, so that other mine
Thou wilt restore, to be my comfort still:
But thou wilt not, nor he will not be free,
For thou art covetous and he is kind;
He learn'd but surety-like to write for me
Under that bond that him as fast doth bind.
The statute of thy beauty thou wilt take,
Thou usurer, that put'st forth all to use,
And sue a friend came debtor for my sake;
So him I lose through my unkind abuse.
    Him have I lost; thou hast both him and me:
    He pays the whole, and yet am I not free.

ONE HUNDRED THIRTY-FIVE

WHOEVER hath her wish, thou hast thy 'Will,'
And 'Will' to boot, and 'Will' in overplus;
More than enough am I that vex thee still,
To thy sweet will making addition thus.
Wilt thou, whose will is large and spacious,
Not once vouchsafe to hide my will in thine?
Shall will in others seem right gracious,
And in my will no fair acceptance shine?
The sea, all water, yet receives rain still
And in abundance addeth to his store;
So thou, being rich in 'Will' add to thy 'Will'
One will of mine, to make thy large 'Will' more.
    Let no unkind, no fair beseechers kill;
    Think all but one, and me in that one 'Will.'

ONE HUNDRED THIRTY-SIX

IF thy soul check thee that I come so near,
Swear to thy blind soul that I was thy 'Will,'
And will, thy soul knows, is admitted there;
Thus far for love my love-suit, sweet, fulfil.
'Will' will fulfil the treasure of thy love,
Ay, fill it full with wills, and my will one.
In things of great receipt with ease we prove
Among a number one is reckon'd none:
Then in the number let me pass untold,
Though in thy store's account I one must hold
That nothing me, a something sweet to thee:
    Make but my name thy love, and love that still,
    And then thou lovest me, for my name is 'Will.'

ONE HUNDRED THIRTY-SEVEN

THOU blind fool, Love, what dost thou to mine eyes,
That they behold, and see not what they see?
They know what beauty is, see where it lies,
Yet what the best is take the worst to be.
If eyes corrupt by over-partial looks
Be anchor'd in the bay where all men ride,
Why of eyes' falsehood hast thou forged hooks,
Whereto the judgement of my heart is tied?
Why should my heart think that a several plot
Which my heart knows the wide world's common place?
Or mine eyes seeing this, say this is not,
To put fair truth upon so foul a face?
    In things right true my heart and eyes have err'd,
    And to this false plague are they now transferr'd.

ONE HUNDRED THIRTY-EIGHT

WHEN my love swears that she is made of truth
I do believe her, though I know she lies,
That she might think me some untutor'd youth,
Unlearned in the world's false subtleties.
Thus vainly thinking that she thinks me young,
Although she knows my days are past the best,
Simply I credit her false-speaking tongue:
On both sides thus is simple truth suppress'd.
But wherefore says she not she is unjust?
And wherefore say not I that I am old?
O, love's best habit is in seeming trust,
And age in love loves not to have years told:
    Therefore I lie with her and she with me,
    And in our faults by lies we flatter'd be.

ONE HUNDRED THIRTY-NINE

O, call not me to justify the wrong
That thy unkindness lays upon my heart;
Wound me not with thine eye but with thy tongue;
Use power with power and slay me not by art.
Tell me thou lovest elsewhere, but in my sight,
Dear heart, forbear to glance thine eye aside:
What need'st thou wound with cunning when thy might
Is more than my o'er-press'd defence can bide?
Let me excuse thee: ah! my love well knows
Her pretty looks have been mine enemies,
And therefore from my face she turns my foes,
That they elsewhere might dart their injuries:
    Yet do not so; but since I am near slain,
    Kill me outright with looks and rid my pain.

ONE HUNDRED FORTY

BE wise as thou art cruel; do not press
My tongue-tied patience with too much disdain;
Lest sorrow lend me words and words express
The manner of my pity-wanting pain.
If I might teach thee wit, better it were,
Though not to love, yet, love, to tell me so;
As testy sick men, when their deaths be near,
No news but health from their physicians know;
For if I should despair, I should grow mad,
And in my madness might speak ill of thee:
Now this ill-wresting world is grown so bad,
Mad slanderers by mad ears believed be.
    That I may not be so, nor thou belied,
      Bear thine eyes straight, though thy proud heart go wide.

ONE HUNDRED FORTY-ONE

IN faith, I do not love thee with mine eyes,
For they in thee a thousand errors note;
But 'tis my heart that loves what they despise,
Who in despite of view is pleased to dote;
Nor are mine ears with thy tongue's tune delighted,
Nor tender feeling, to base touches prone,
Nor taste, nor smell, desire to be invited
To any sensual feast with thee alone:
But my five wits nor my five senses can
Dissuade one foolish heart from serving thee,
Who leaves unsway'd the likeness of a man,
Thy proud heart's slave and vassal wretch to be:
    Only my plague thus far I count my gain,
    That she that makes me sin awards me pain.

ONE HUNDRED FORTY-TWO

LOVE is my sin and thy dear virtue hate,
Hate of my sin, grounded on sinful loving:
O, but with mine compare thou thine own state,
And thou shalt find it merits not reproving;
Or, if it do, not from those lips of thine,
That have profaned their scarlet ornaments
And seal'd false bonds of love as oft as mine,
Robb'd others' beds' revenues of their rents.
Be it lawful I love thee, as thou lovest those
Whom thine eyes woo as mine importune thee:
Root pity in thy heart, that when it grows
Thy pity may deserve to pitied be.
  If thou dost seek to have what thou dost hide,
  By self-example mayst thou be denied!

ONE HUNDRED FORTY-THREE

LO! as a careful housewife runs to catch
One of her feather'd creatures broke away,
Sets down her babe and makes all swift dispatch
In pursuit of the thing she would have stay,
Whilst her neglected child holds her in chase,
Cries to catch her whose busy care is bent
To follow that which flies before her face,
Not prizing her poor infant's discontent;
So runn'st thou after that which flies from thee,
Whilst I thy babe chase thee afar behind;
But if thou catch thy hope, turn back to me,
And play the mother's part, kiss me, be kind:
  So will I pray that thou mayst have thy 'Will,'
  If thou turn back, and my loud crying still.

ONE HUNDRED FORTY-FOUR

TWO loves I have of comfort and despair,
Which like two spirits do suggest me still:
The better angel is a man right fair,
The worser spirit a woman colour'd ill.
To win me soon to hell, my female evil
Tempteth my better angel from my side,
And would corrupt my saint to be a devil,
Wooing his purity with her foul pride.
And whether that my angel be turn'd fiend
Suspect I may, yet not directly tell;
But being both from me, both to each friend,
I guess one angel in another's hell:
    Yet this shall I ne'er know, but live in doubt,
    Till my bad angel fire my good one out.

ONE HUNDRED FORTY-FIVE

THOSE lips that Love's own hand did make
Breathed forth the sound that said 'I hate'
To me that languish'd for her sake;
But when she saw my woeful state,
Straight in her heart did mercy come,
Chiding that tongue that ever sweet
Was used in giving gentle doom,
And taught it thus anew to greet;
'I hate' she alter'd with an end,
That follow'd it as gentle day
Doth follow night, who like a fiend
From heaven to hell is flown away;
    'I hate' from hate away she threw,
    And saved my life, saying 'not you.'

ONE HUNDRED FORTY-SIX

POOR soul, the centre of my sinful earth,
.... * these rebel powers that thee array,
Why dost thou pine within and suffer dearth,
Painting thy outward walls so costly gay?
Why so large cost, having so short a lease,
Dost thou upon thy fading mansion spend?
Shall worms, inheritors of this excess,
Eat up thy charge? is this thy body's end?
Then, soul, live thou upon thy servant's loss,
And let that pine to aggravate thy store;
Buy terms divine in selling hours of dross;
Within be fed, without be rich no more:
    So shalt thou feed on Death, that feeds on men,
    And Death once dead, there's no more dying then.

ONE HUNDRED FORTY-SEVEN

MY love is as a fever, longing still
For that which longer nurseth the disease,
Feeding on that which doth preserve the ill,
The uncertain sickly appetite to please.
My reason, the physician to my love,
Angry that his prescriptions are not kept,
Hath left me, and I desperate now approve
Desire is death, which physic did except.
Past cure I am, now reason is past care,
And frantic-mad with evermore unrest;
My thoughts and my discourse as madmen's are,
At random from the truth vainly express'd;
    For I have sworn thee fair and thought thee bright,
    Who art as black as hell, as dark as night.

---

* Original text unknown; emendations suggested by various editors include "Thrall to," "Rebuke," and "Fool'd by."

ONE HUNDRED FORTY-EIGHT

O me, what eyes hath Love put in my head,
Which have no correspondence with true sight!
Or, if they have, where is my judgement fled,
That censures falsely what they see aright?
If that be fair whereon my false eyes dote,
What means the world to say it is not so?
If it be not, then love doth well denote
Love's eye is not so true as all men's 'No.'
How can it? O, how can Love's eye be true,
That is so vex'd with watching and with tears?
No marvel then, though I mistake my view;
The sun itself sees not till heaven clears.
    O cunning Love! with tears thou keep'st me blind,
    Lest eyes well-seeing thy foul faults should find.

ONE HUNDRED FORTY-NINE

CANST thou, O cruel! say I love thee not,
When I against myself with thee partake?
Do I not think on thee, when I forgot
Am of myself, all tyrant, for thy sake?
Who hateth thee that I do call my friend?
On whom frown'st thou that I do fawn upon?
Nay, if thou lour'st on me, do I not spend
Revenge upon myself with present moan?
What merit do I in myself respect,
That is so proud thy service to despise,
When all my best doth worship thy defect,
Commanded by the motion of thine eyes?
    But, love, hate on, for now I know thy mind;
    Those that can see thou lovest, and I am blind.

ONE HUNDRED FIFTY

O, from what power hast thou this powerful might
With insufficiency my heart to sway?
To make me give the lie to my true sight,
And swear that brightness doth not grace the day?
Whence hast thou this becoming of things ill,
That in the very refuse of thy deeds
There is such strength and warrantise of skill
That, in my mind, thy worst all best exceeds?
Who taught thee how to make me love thee more
The more I hear and see just cause of hate?
O, though I love what others do abhor,
With others thou shouldst not abhor my state:
    If thy unworthiness raised love in me,
    More worthy I to be beloved of thee.

ONE HUNDRED FIFTY-ONE

LOVE is too young to know what conscience is;
Yet who knows not conscience is born of love?
Then, gentle cheater, urge not my amiss,
Lest guilty of my faults thy sweet self prove:
For, thou betraying me, I do betray
My nobler part to my gross body's treason;
My soul doth tell my body that he may
Triumph in love; flesh stays no farther reason;
But, rising at thy name, doth point out thee
As his triumphant prize. Proud of this pride,
He is contented thy poor drudge to be,
To stand in thy affairs, fall by thy side.
    No want of conscience hold it that I call
    Her 'love' for whose dear love I rise and fall.

ONE HUNDRED FIFTY-TWO

IN loving thee thou know'st I am forsworn,
But thou art twice forsworn, to me love swearing,
In act thy bed-vow broke and new faith torn
In vowing new hate after new love bearing.
But why of two oaths' breach do I accuse thee,
When I break twenty? I am perjured most;
For all my vows are oaths but to misuse thee
And all my honest faith in thee is lost,
For I have sworn deep oaths of thy deep kindness,
Oaths of thy love, thy truth, thy constancy,
And, to enlighten thee, gave eyes to blindness,
Or made them swear against the thing they see;
    For I have sworn thee fair; more perjured I,
    To swear against the truth so foul a lie!

ONE HUNDRED FIFTY-THREE

CUPID laid by his brand, and fell asleep:
A maid of Dian's this advantage found,
And his love-kindling fire did quickly steep
In a cold valley-fountain of that ground;
Which borrow'd from this holy fire of Love
A dateless lively heat, still to endure,
And grew a seething bath, which yet men prove
Against strange maladies a sovereign cure.
But at my mistress' eye Love's brand new-fired,
The boy for trial needs would touch my breast;
I, sick withal, the help of bath desired,
And thither hied, a sad distemper'd guest,
    But found no cure: the bath for my help lies
    Where Cupid got new fire—my mistress' eyes.

ONE HUNDRED FIFTY-FOUR

THE little Love-god lying once asleep
Laid by his side his heart-inflaming brand,
Whilst many nymphs that vow'd chaste life to keep
Came tripping by; but in her maiden hand
The fairest votary took up that fire
Which many legions of true hearts had warm'd;
And so the general of hot desire
Was sleeping by a virgin hand disarm'd.
This brand she quenched in a cool well by,
Which from Love's fire took heat perpetual,
Growing a bath and healthful remedy
For men diseased; but I, my mistress' thrall,
    Came there for cure, and this by that I prove,
    Love's fire heats water, water cools not love.

SUBJECT INDEX

actors, Elizabethan, 215, 219-222
Actors' Remonstrance, The, 232
Adonis, myth of, 69-70, 314; see also Venus; Venus and Adonis
adultery, courtly love and, 82-83
allegory, 26
Amanda, 232, 234
Amoretti, Spenser's, 32-33
Apology for the Believers in the Shakespeare-Papers, An, 16
Arnold, Matthew, 11, 53
art, beauty and, 212-213; vs. external world, 242; joy and, 194; sensuous elements in, 206
Astrophel and Stella, 6, 18
atheism, 77

Bacon, Sir Francis, 208
Baconian theory, 26
Barnstorff, D., 13, 175
beauty, art and, 212-213; death and, 194, 237; genius and, 229-230; love and, 80; "lovely boy" and, 101-102; lust and, 68; and marriage, 88; sexuality and, 156; time and, 237; and truth, 104, 126; youth and, 122-123
Bembo, Pietro Cardinal, 14, 33, 82
Benson, John, 7-9, 13, 28, 58-59, 84
Berowne (Biron), Love's Labour's Lost, 74, 77-78, 85, 235

Blackfriars Theatre, 200, 220
Boaden, William, 12
Booke of Sir Thomas Moore, The, 3
boy actors, 176 ff., 214, 218, 223, 239
Bray, Sir Denys, 9, 39
Brooke, Tucker, 9
Bruno, Giordano, 82, 211
Burbage, Richard, 203, 233-234, 244
Burghley (Burleigh), Lord William Cecil, 17, 215
Butler, Samuel, 7, 14, 29

Capellanus, Andrias, 83-85, 90
Castiglione, Baldassare de, 33
Catholic Church, "dark lady" as symbol of, 225
Cavalieri, Tomasso, 209
Chapman, George, 19, 26, 77, 178-179, 200, 212
Chaucer, Geoffrey, 48, 90
child, as personification of love, 139; as progeny, 120, 134, 208
Christian love, tradition of, 31-32, 48, 85
clichés, mastery of, 147
Coleridge, Samuel Taylor, 9, 28-29
conscience, love and, 157-159
courtly love, 32-37, 53, 83-85

Subject Index

criticism and scholarship, 3-21; historical, 19; Victorian, 11
Cymbeline, 76, 244

Daniel, Samuel, 18
Dante, Alighieri, 10-11, 33, 39, 48-49, 65, 83, 86-87, 137, 151, 157
"dark lady," 6, 9, 16, 38, 51-52, 63, 65, 76, 89, 97, 113, 149, 155, 225, 232, 234; identity of, 16-18, 226-227, 231-232; as spirit of corruption, 125
Dark Lady of the Sonnets, The, 17, 95
Davenant, Sir William, 17
daydreams, as poetic agent, 144
death, 53; beauty and, 80, 194; imminence of, 149; longing for, 146; love and, 49; and lust, 229; poetry and, 196-197; time and, 43-44, 90, 224-225, 237
dedication, Thorpe's, 4, 174, 191
Devereux, Robert, 2nd Earl of Essex, 77, 213, 235
Diotima, *Symposium,* 81, 84, 90, 208
Divine Comedy, The, 33, 48, 87, 138
Donne, John, 34, 61, 83, 101
Dostoevsky, Fyodor, 151, 158
double entendres, 62, 64
Drake, Nathan, 12
dreams, as poetic agent, 144, 154
Dyce, Alexander, 10, 14

Eliot, T. S., 137, 141
Elizabeth I, 7, 16, 26, 29, 221, 226
Elizabethan Love Sonnet, The, 20
Empson, William, 115, 119
ennui, self-love and, 141, 144
Erewhon Revisited, 29
Eros, hymns to, 34; incarnations of, 32, 38, 42, 49, 53, 133, 139
Essex, *see* Devereux, Robert

Faerie Queene, The, 37, 84
Faustus, Doctor, 73, 200
First Folio, 13
Fitton, Mary, 17-18, 168, 226
French models, in sonnets, 98
friendship, 20; cult of, 71; ideal, 96, 105; love and, 209, 211; progress of, 105
Friendship, Essay on, 210
Fripp, E. I., 17

Gildon, Charles, 8
Globe Theatre, 233, 235, 237, 250
God, love and, 211; love of, 31-33, 86; as reality, 133
Goethe, Johann Wolfgang von, 153, 240
good and evil, 20, 105, 108
Gossip from a Muniment Room, 18
Granville-Barker, H., 149
Griffin, Bartholomew, 67
Grillparzer, Franz, 14

Hall, William, 13, 174
Hamlet, character, 106, 112, 116, 137, 223, 241
Hamlet, 3, 76, 102, 329, 344
Harte, William, 11
Harris, Frank, 18, 97
Hathaway, Anne, 16-17
Hathaway, William, 13
hell, imagery of, 45; pun on, 63-64, 96
Henry IV, 67, 75-76, 89
Henry V, 51

Subject Index

Herbert, William, third Earl of Pembroke, 12-13, 17, 95, 99, 168, 172, 174, 187, 201, 226, 249
Hermaphroditus 69-72, 75, 232
Hero and Leander, 67, 200, 208
Herrick, Robert, 34
Hervey (Harvey), William, 13
homosexuality, 14-16, 28-29, 37, 59, 62, 65, 71-72, 77, 82, 84-85, 87
Hotson, Leslie, 7
"hues," pun on, 95, 137, 178
"Hughes, W.," 11-12, 26, 95
"Hughes, Willie," 12, 177 ff.
"H.W.," 28; *see also* "W.H., Mr."
hysteria, love and, 137, 155

"I," of sonnets, 11, 19, 26
Ignotus, 78, 80
imagery, in poems and plays, 19-20; in sonnets, 45-46
immortality, 80, 133
infatuation, poetics for, 129-161
Italian models, in sonnets, 98

Jaggard, William, 58-59, 62, 66, 69, 74
jealousy, 143-144, 146, 157, 327
Jonson, Ben, 5, 211, 216, 233, 250
Julius Caesar, 75, 89

Keats, John, 10, 104, 126-127
King Lear, 76, 87, 97, 135-136, 239
Knight, Charles, 8

Laura, Petrarch and, 33, 36, 39, 94
Lee, Sir Sidney, 17, 19
"lie," pun on, 63-64
love, 14-20; all-male, 72-82; as "child," 139; conscience and, 157-158; conventions of, 98-99; courtly, *see* courtly love; experience of, 30-31; immortality of, 41; longing and, 153; pretense of, 228-229; religious feeling and, 109-111; shame and, 89; sin and, 87; and truth, 116, 148; two kinds of, 84; wisdom and, 207
Lover's Complaint, A, 4, 36, 58, 203, 205
Love's Labour's Lost, 50, 58, 67, 79, 85, 234, 241; plot of, 73-77
lust, 20, 68, 89-90; desire and, 229; vs. love, 87, 97; "shame" and, 88-89, 128, 228-229

Macbeth, 81, 189
Malone, Edmund, 8, 14
Man Shakespeare and his Tragic Life-Story, The, 18
Mann, Thomas, 143, 157
Marlowe, Christopher, 67, 78, 99, 201, 237, 239
marriage, 46-47, 53, 88; children and, 208; exhortation to, 120, 192; love and, 80
"master-mistress of my passion," 99-100, 136-137
Measure for Measure, 65, 119
melancholy, 89
Meres, Francis, 6, 50, 57, 173, 196
Merchant of Venice, The, 65, 67, 75, 89-90
Metamorphoses, 71, 90
metaphor, 47, 49, 115
Michelangelo Buonarotti, 14, 32, 82, 209
Midsummer Night's Dream, A, 189
Milton, John, 8, 10, 42, 238

Subject Index

mistress, of sonnets, 33-35, 61, 89, 95-96, 105; as "fiction," 93; "master," 99-100; shared, 151
Montaigne, Michel de, 134, 210
Muse, dramatic, 134, 177, 179, 192-197
Mutual Flame, The, 15
Myrrha, myth of, 73

narcissism, 39, 121-123
Narcissus, myth of, 46, 138, 154, 157, 159, 215
Nashe, Thomas, 202
neo-Platonic love, 74, 82
Newdigate-Newdegate, Lady, 18

obscenity, 62, 64, 69-70, 85
Orpheus, 72, 82, 84
Ovid, 32, 35, 44, 53, 67, 70-74, 82, 90, 98

Palladis Tamia: Wits Treasury, 6
Partridge, Eric, 16
Pascal, Blaise, 131-132, 151
Passionate Pilgrim, The, 6, 50, 58, 60, 65-66, 69, 73, 77, 79
Pembroke, Earl of, *see* Herbert, William
Petrarch, 33, 38-39, 53, 87, 90
Phoenix and the Turtle, The, 46-47, 151
Plato, 33, 36, 81, 136, 207, 212
Platonic beauty, 42
Platonic love, 33-35, 48, 207, 209-210
plays, sources for, 26
Poems: Written by Wil. Shakespeare. Gent., 7, 58
poetry, conventions of, 98; Elizabethan, 5-6; literary tradition of, 29-30; as poet's experience, 25; as vainglory, 136

polite language, convention of, 99
priapic parallel, 159
Progress of the Soule, The, 101
pronouns, changing of, 7-8, 28, 59, 84; masculine and feminine, 5
Proust, Marcel, 52-53
puns, 96, 204; obscene, 62, 64, 69-70, 85
Puritans, stage and, 216
Psalms, 131-132
Psyche, 160; incarnation of, 53
Pygmalion, myth of, 133, 138, 154, 157, 159

Quarto of 1609, 36

Raleigh, Sir Walter, 77-78, 83, 233
Rape of Lucrece, The, 6, 12, 94
realism, art and, 206; dramatic, 202-203
religious feeling, poetry and, 106; in sonnets, 110
rhyme schemes, 9, 98, 137-138, 197
Rich, Lady Penelope, 18, 226
"rival poet," of sonnets, 18-19, 26, 94-95, 138-140, 151
Rollins, Hyder, 8, 14-15

Sachs, Nathan, 144
Salmacis, 69-71, 215, 232
Salmacis and Hermaphroditus, 232
self-love, 45, 123-124, 140; vs. marriage, 120
self-pity, 141, 242
self-reliance, 196
Sense of Shakespeare's Sonnets, The, 15, 20
sex, intellect and, 207-208
sexual feelings, disgust for, 97; veiled, 102

Subject Index

sexual infidelity, 62
sexual satisfaction, Christian love and, 86; vs. friendship, 156
sexual terms, Shakespeare's, 16
Shakespeare, William, "abnormal relationship" of, 97; "anonymity" of, 157; Berowne (Biron) as reflection of, 235; concept of love, 83-84; experience recreated in poetry, 94; fame by 1598, 7; feminine aspect of, 16; hasty marriage, 15; homosexual episode, 15; idea of beauty, 212-213; imagination, 97; as lyric poet, 6; as master of cliché, 147; self-reliance of, 196-197; "unwholesome" personality of, 29
Shakespeare: A Critical Biography, 16
Shakespeare and His Times, 12
Shakespeare: Man and Artist, 17
Shakespearean Moment, The, 20
Shakespeare Quarterly, 21
Shakespeare's Bawdy, 16
Shakespeare's Imagery, 19
Shakespeare's Predecessors, 217
Shake-speares Sonnets, 58
Shakespeare's Sonnets Dated, 7
Shakespeare's Sonnets Reconsidered, 14
Shaw, G. Bernard, 17-18, 94-95, 97-98, 100, 113
Shepheardes Calender, The, 36
Sidney, Philip, 6, 38, 211, 213, 226
sin, 20; awareness of, 105; lust as, 87
Socrates and Alcibiades, 123
Some Versions of Pastoral, 115
Songs and Sonnets, 34
sonnet form, disrepute of in 17th century, 8-9; literary tradition of, 29-30; rhyme scheme in, 9
sonnets, Shakespeare's: as allegorical riddles, 26; anti-feminism in, 83; autobiographical nature of, 11, 128; cycles in, 39-52; dates of composition, 7, 234; as dialogue, 118; first printing of, 4, 57-58; as generalized truth, 127-128; homosexuality in, see homosexuality; "I" of, 11, 19, 26; imagery in, 19-20, 45-46; lust and sin in, 20; lyric vs. narrative quality of, 8, 20, 93; order or sequence of, 4, 8, 39, 57-66, 132, 236-237; persons represented in, 5, 11, 95-96; pronoun changes in, 7-8, 28, 59, 84; ribaldry in, 50; as Shakespeare's earliest work, 29
Southampton, Earl of, see Wriothesley, Henry
Spenser, Edmund, 20, 32, 34, 36, 84, 233
Spurgeon, Caroline F. E., 10, 19
Stationers' Register, 4
Steevens, George, 13
Story of a Novel, The, 143
suicide, thoughts of, 144
Symposium, The, 81-82, 90, 155, 207-208

Tempest, The, 68, 224
Thorpe, Thomas, 4, 8, 11, 58-60, 63, 65, 191
time, death and, 90, 135 224-225, 237; as "enemy," 43, 74; eternity in, 135
tragedies, later, 76
truth, beauty and, 42, 104, 126; different kinds of, 93; love as, 148
Twelfth Night, 88, 244

Subject Index

Two Gentlemen of Verona, The, 51, 67, 75
"Two Loves" theme, 60-61, 66, 72, 85, 88
Tyler, Thomas, 18
Tyrwhitt, Thomas, 11

Variorum Edition, 8-9, 14-15
Venus, hymn to, 34; incarnations of, 32, 34, 42
Venus and Adonis, 6, 27, 45, 67-69, 71, 80, 94, 205, 232, 234
Vernon, Elizabeth, 17
Virgil, 29, 36
Vita Nuova, 33, 86, 155

"W. H., Mr.," 5, 115; character of, 28; speculation about, 11-14; Wilde's theory of, 167 ff.
"Will," puns on, 63, 156-157
Willobie, Henry, 174, 235
Willobie his Avisa, 28, 235
woman, attack on, 72, 82; cult of, 71; "falsity" of, 101; idealization of, 82-83; lust and, 97; puns on, 62-63; as "trap of sin," 89
Wriothesley, Henry, Third Earl of Southampton, 12, 17, 27, 77, 95, 172

"youth," of sonnets, 133-134, 203; beauty of, 122; Shakespeare's relation to, 42; *see also* "W. H., Mr."

INDEX OF FIRST LINES

A woman's face with Nature's own hand painted, 269
Accuse me thus: that I have scanted all, 317
Against my love shall be, as I am now, 290
Against that time, if ever that time come, 283
Ah, wherefore with infection should he live, 292
Alack, what poverty my Muse brings forth, 310
Alas, 'tis true I have gone here and there, 314
As a decrepit father takes delight, 277
As an imperfect actor on the stage, 270
As fast as thou shalt wane, so fast thou grow'st, 264

Be wise as thou art cruel; do not press, 329
Being your slave, what should I do but tend, 287
Beshrew that heart that makes my heart to groan, 325
Betwixt mine eye and heart a league is took, 282
But be contented: when that fell arrest, 296
But do thy worst to steal thyself away, 305
But wherefore do not you a mightier way, 267

Canst thou, O cruel! say I love thee not, 333
Cupid laid by his brand and fell asleep, 335

Devouring Time, blunt thou the lion's paws, 268

Farewell! thou art too dear for my possessing, 302
For shame! deny that thou bear'st love to any, 264
From fairest creatures we desire increase, 259
From you have I been absent in the spring, 308
Full many a glorious morning have I seen, 275

How can I then return in happy plight, 273
How can my Muse want subject to invent, 278
How careful was I, when I took my way, 283
How heavy do I journey on the way, 284
How like a winter hath my absence been, 307
How oft, when thou, my music, music play'st, 323
How sweet and lovely dost thou make the shame, 306

I grant thou wert not married to my Muse, 300
I never saw that you did painting need, 300
If my dear love were but the child of state, 321

Index of First Lines

If the dull substance of my flesh were thought, 281
If there be nothing new, but that which is, 288
If thou survive my well-contented day, 275
If thy soul check thee that I come so near, 327
In faith, I do not love thee with mine eyes, 329
In loving thee thou know'st I am forsworn, 335
In the old age black was not counted fair, 322
Is it for fear to wet a widow's eye, 263
Is it thy will thy image should keep open, 289

Let me confess that we two must be twain, 277
Let me not to the marriage of true minds, 317
Let not my love be call'd idolatry, 311
Let those who are in favour with their stars, 271
Like as the waves make toward the pebbled shore, 289
Like as, to make our appetites more keen, 318
Lo, as a careful housewife runs to catch, 330
Lo, in the orient when the gracious light, 262
Look in thy glass, and tell the face thou viewest, 260
Lord of my love, to whom in vassalage, 272
Love is my sin, and thy dear virtue hate, 330
Love is too young to know what conscience is, 334

Mine eye and heart are at a mortal war, 282
Mine eye hath played the painter and hath stell'd, 271
Music to hear, why hear'st thou music sadly? 263
My glass shall not persuade me I am old, 270
My love is as a fever, longing still, 332
My love is strengthen'd, though more weak in seeming, 310
My mistress' eyes are nothing like the sun, 324
My tongue-tied Muse in manners holds her still, 301

No longer mourn for me when I am dead, 294
No more be grieved at that which thou hast done, 276
No, Time, thou shalt not boast that I do change, 320
Not from the stars do I my judgement pluck, 266
Not marble nor the gilded monuments, 286
Not mine own fears, nor the prophetic soul, 312

O, call not me to justify the wrong, 328
O, for my sake do you with Fortune chide, 314
O, from what power hast thou this powerful might, 334
O, how I faint when I of you do write, 299

Index of First Lines

O, how much more doth beauty beauteous seem, 286
O, how thy worth with manners may I sing, 278
O, lest the world should task you to recite, 295
O me, what eyes hath Love put in my head, 333
O, never say that I was false of heart, 313
O, that you were yourself! but, love, you are, 265
O thou, my lovely boy, who in thy power, 322
O truant Muse, what shall be thy amends, 309
Or I shall live your epitaph to make, 299
Or whether doth my mind, being crown'd with you, 316

Poor soul, the centre of my sinful earth, 332

Say that thou didst forsake me for some fault, 303
Shall I compare thee to a summer's day? 268
Sin of self-love possesseth all mine eye, 290
Since brass, nor stone, nor earth, nor boundless sea, 291
Since I left you mine eye is in my mind, 315
So am I as the rich, whose blessed key, 285
So are you to my thoughts as food to life, 296
So is it not with me as with that Muse, 269
So, now I have confess'd that he is thine, 326
So oft have I invoked thee for my Muse, 298
So shall I live, supposing thou art true, 305
Some glory in their birth, some in their skill, 304
Some say thy fault is youth, some wantonness, 307
Sweet love, renew thy force; be it not said, 287

Take all my loves, my love, yea, take them all, 279
That god forbid that made me first your slave, 288
That thou art blamed shall not be thy defect, 294
That thou hast her, it is not all my grief, 280
That time of year thou mayst in me behold, 295
That you were once unkind befriends me now, 319
The expense of spirit in a waste of shame, 323
The forward violet thus did I chide, 308
The little Love-god lying once asleep, 336
Then hate me when thou wilt; if ever, now, 304
Then let not winter's ragged hand deface, 262
The other two, slight air and purging fire, 281
They that have power to hurt and will do none, 306
Thine eyes I love, and they, as pitying me, 325
Those hours that with gentle work did frame, 261

Index of First Lines

Those lines that I before have writ do lie, 316
Those lips that Love's own hand did make, 331
Those parts of thee that the world's eye doth view, 293
Those pretty wrongs that liberty commits, 279
Thou art as tyrannous, so as thou art, 324
Thou blind fool, Love, what dost thou to mine eyes, 327
Thus can my love excuse the slow offence, 284
Thus is his cheek the map of days outworn, 293
Thy bosom is endeared with all hearts, 274
Thy gift, thy tables, are within my brain, 320
Thy glass will show thee how thy beauties wear, 297
Tired with all these, for restful death I cry, 292
'Tis better to be vile than vile esteemed, 319
To me, fair friend, you never can be old, 311
Two loves I have of comfort and despair, 331

Unthrifty loveliness, why dost thou spend, 261

Was it the proud full sail of his great verse, 302
Weary with toil, I haste me to my bed, 272
Were't aught to me I bore the canopy, 321
What is your substance, whereof are you made, 285
What potions have I drunk of Siren tears, 318
What's in the brain that ink may character, 313
When forty winters shall besiege thy brow, 260
When I consider everything that grows, 266
When I do count the clock that tells the time, 265
When I have seen by Time's fell hand defaced, 291
When, in disgrace with fortune and men's eyes, 273
When in the chronicle of wasted time, 312
When most I wink, then do mine eyes best see, 280
When my love swears that she is made of truth, 328
When thou shalt be disposed to set me light, 303
When to the sessions of sweet silent thought, 274
Where art thou, Muse, that thou forget'st so long, 309
Whilst I alone did call upon thy aid, 298
Whoever hath her wish, thou hast thy 'Will,' 326
Who is it that says most? which can say more, 301
Who will believe my verse in time to come, 267
Why didst thou promise such a beauteous day, 276
Why is my verse so barren of new pride, 297

Your love and pity doth the impression fill, 315

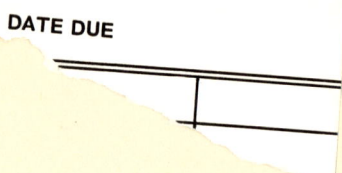